T5-BQC-901

Library of
Davidson College

Published under the auspices of
THE CENTER FOR JAPANESE AND KOREAN STUDIES
University of California, Berkeley

THE POLITICAL CULTURE OF JAPAN

BRADLEY M. RICHARDSON

The Political Culture of Japan

UNIVERSITY OF CALIFORNIA PRESS
Berkeley, Los Angeles, London

University of California Press
Berkeley and Los Angeles, California
University of California Press, Ltd.
London, England
Copyright © 1974, by
The Regents of the University of California
ISBN: 0-520-02019-7
Library of Congress Catalog Card Number: 76-153551
Printed in the United States of America

FOR MY MOTHER

CONTENTS

Preface	ix
1. Political Culture and Japanese Experience	1
2. Political Involvement	29
3. Evaluative Attitudes	65
4. Participation Attitudes	83
5. Voting Attitudes	102
6. City and Countryside	128
7. Age and Political Culture	189
8. Man and Politics in Postwar Japan	229
Appendix: Political Behavior Research in Japan	247
Selected Bibliography	257
Index	263

PREFACE

This is a study of popular political culture, or political attitudes, in postwar Japan. There are many reasons for making a study of this kind in Japan, not the least of which is the need to document the effects on popular political outlooks of the postwar occupation democratization policies. Like Germany and Italy, Japan has experienced a marked discontinuity in political leadership, formal institutions and political socialization in recent decades. Systematic study of postwar political cultures in these countries should provide interesting information on the substantive effects of these discontinuities, as well as suggesting interesting insights into the nature of mass attitudinal change.

These and other reasons for studying postwar Japanese political culture are discussed in Chapter One. At this point some simple statements about what this study attempts to accomplish are in order, as well as some caveats about major assumptions and methodological orientations. It should be made clear from the beginning that I have concerned myself only with the nature of mass political attitudes in Japan, and not with the opinions and actions of political groups or elites. From time to time I have made simple assessments of the implications of my findings for democratic government, as is the convention in political science. Still, it is clear that mass attitudes are only one component of the overall tendencies toward democracy or some other political system in a particular society. Indeed, the political role orientations and behavior of elites are of extreme importance. Even though the tendencies in mass attitudes are also critical in many cases, they do not constitute the sole indicator of political system tendencies.

Since one of the major concerns of this study was to investigate the degree and scope of attitudinal change in Japan resulting from postwar political reforms, it is obvious that some clear idea of the nature of prewar political culture should be presented as a basis for comparison. Unfortunately, I don't believe a very systematic appraisal of prewar political culture really exists. There are excellent commentaries on the state of mass democracy and voting practices in the prewar era, but they are typically based on fragmentary evidence, and in my opinion tend to highlight only parts of prewar tendencies in political attitudes. In spite of these problems, I have commented on the nature of prewar political culture at several points, and have made some general assessments even in the absence of systematic evidence from the prewar era itself. My comments are based on evidence presented in Chapter Seven, where the political attitudes of older people are compared with those of postwar political generations. Since this evidence comes late in the book, it seems appropriate to note its relationships to the more casual statements made earlier, lest the reader be unduly alarmed.

My evidence is by and large the findings of public opinion surveys conducted in Japan. While it is true that opinion surveys do not escape the problem of validity — nor do most other techniques of research — I have paid very special attention to the problem of making valid generalizations. The work I report here grew out of my doctoral dissertation, and involved the study of nearly three hundred Japanese surveys over a period of several years. At all times I was concerned with establishing general tendencies in political attitudes through discovery of converging patterns of evidence. I particularly wanted to avoid the problems of drawing conclusions about all Japanese on the basis of the results of surveys conducted at only one place or at only one point in time. I was also concerned about evaluating the validity of the measurements of political attitudes in the various studies I used. While it is true that the discovery of general trends does not guarantee validity of measurement, it at least enhances the expectation that my statements approximate reality. Obviously, this does not mean that the survey instrument is the unique way to identify attitudes, but it does mean that I have tried to use survey evidence — which permits statements about large populations — carefully.

The surveys of political attitudes I used for evidence were in most cases conducted in the decade between 1958 and 1967. The choice of this particular time frame was in part determined simply by the availability of studies with substantial numbers of replicative questions beginning in 1958, and my feeling that I had to establish some reasonable cutoff point in the research in order to reach closure. But it was reasonable to look at political attitudes from this period for some additional reasons. Japanese politics had become sufficiently institutionalized by 1955 to permit at least the beginning of an examination of the effects of postwar changes and reforms. It was also desirable to begin the study of postwar political culture while persons who grew up in the prewar era were still numerous in the sampled populations.

Even small works such as this owe their origins to a far greater number of persons than can reasonably be acknowledged. Nevertheless, at least some attempt should be made to show appreciation for the many kinds of tangible and intangible help received. Above all, I am especially indebted to those in Yokohama, Atsugi and Nita who quite generously and freely gave of their time to answer a foreigner's questions about their lives and politics. Among these, Hatsuo Koseimura of the Atsugi City Office and Eichi Koganei, headman of Nanasawa hamlet, were especially kind, and their friendship and advice helped advance the field research at critical junctures. Professors Robert Scalapino, Junnosuke Masumi, Takeshi Ishida, Tadashi Fukutake, Jōji Watanuki, Haruo Matsubara and Kyōichi Sonoda offered valued advice and intellectual sustenance at various points. So also did Akira Ikeda of the Kōmei Senkyo Remmei, and Eiichi Yamaoka, Seiji Yamada, Masao Sōma, Takeshi Shibuya, Tadao Sakuma and Kanji Naitō, all of whom participated in the research effort of the Komei Senkyo Remmei in addition to pursuing their own important scholarly research. Ingrid Lachenicht, Jean Willis, Becky Howe and Robert Bezdek gave freely of their typing and editorial skills and helped the manuscript reach completion. Akira Kubota and Haruhiro Fukui read the manuscript and made valuable criticisms.

A debt of a different kind is due other persons, particularly Shotarō Ikegai, a fictive father, and an especially good friend, the late Shōhei Nakazawa. It is hoped that by virtue of their example, as persons brought up in an earlier period of Japan's experience, the author is less naive about the value of the indigenous components of the political culture of Japan.

1

POLITICAL CULTURE AND JAPANESE EXPERIENCE

Scholars have speculated about the nature of man's relationship to the events and outcomes of public processes since self-conscious thought about political life first began. The focus of concern has naturally varied over time, but in recent times one of the main themes of enquiry has concerned the scope and effects of political involvement among ordinary members of political communities. Interest in these matters has received special stimulus in the twentieth century as a result of successful totalitarian movements, as well as the expansion of opportunities for self-government in areas of the world less familiar with the evolutionary development of Western democratic concepts.

In the past two decades the political motivations and behavior of ordinary people have also been subjected to increasingly intensive empirical scrutiny. This development has been influenced by the growing ability to collect and analyze large volumes of data and by the widespread acceptance of sociological and social psychological models of behavior and their use in political science. As a result of these encouraging circumstances, the empirical study of mass political behavior has come to be one of the main concerns of students of public life.

The formulation of man's mental attitudes toward politics in terms of political culture constructs is an outgrowth both of the concern in Western political philosophy with comprehending and facilitating the development of the democratic polity, and of the interest of scholars in the political attitudes of ordinary people. The political culture approach has thus sought, in part, to identify the particular attitude structures congenial to the existence of a democratic and participant political society.[1] It has also sought simply to characterize the cultural or attitudinal substrata underlying the behavior of both masses and elites in particular political systems.[2] The principal feature distinguishing the political culture approach from other kinds of political attitude research is a concern with developing attitude profiles for whole systems, whether these be nations, intermediate political units such as the American states, informal political entities such as tribes or perhaps even isolated small communities.[3]

The political culture approach is explicitly comparative in focus. This has led to formulations of the origins of political attitudes that are somewhat different from those found in many studies of behavior within single systems. For example, American political behavior research typically examined political attitude formation and change in terms of the variation in such factors as people's social characteristics, group memberships, political loyalties, or campaign experiences.[4] Such emphases were generally appropriate given the objectives of research, and the relationships uncovered have provided important insights into previously unspecified sectors of political behavior.

Consideration of cross-system variations among these same kinds of conditioning factors is obviously one legitimate way to undertake

---

[1] Gabriel Almond and Sydney Verba, *The Civic Culture* (Princeton: Princeton University Press, 1963, and Boston: Little, Brown, 1965) is the main example of the search for a democratic political culture.

[2] Lucian W. Pye and Sidney Verba, *Political Culture and Political Development* (Princeton: Princeton University Press, 1965 and 1969) is the main location for studies of this kind. But examples of an inductive approach are found elsewhere, notably in the country studies of the Little, Brown comparative politics series.

[3] See, for example, Samuel C. Patterson, "The Political Cultures of the American States," in Norman R. Luttbeg (ed.), *Public Opinion and Public Policy* (Homewood, Illinois: Dorsey Press, 1968), pp. 275–291.

[4] The conceptual orientations of the early voting studies which provided major impetus to the behavioral "revolution" are summarized in Peter H. Rossi, "Four Landmarks in Voting Research," in Eugene Burdick and Arthur J. Brodbeck (eds.), *American Voting Behavior* (Glencoe: Free Press, 1959), pp. 5–54. The major voting study incorporating an attitudinal model of voting choice is Angus Campbell, Philip E. Converse, Warren E. Miller and Donald E. Stokes, *The American Voter* (New York: Wiley, 1960). Wherever attitudes described here under the political culture rubric parallel phenomena identified in American and European voting and participation research, it will be made clear in the text.

comparative research. Indeed, cross-national or cross-unit differences in the distribution of these variables may be important contributions to distinctive patterns in political culture.[5] The political culture approach, however, seeks to expand understanding of attitude formation processes by taking into account some additional variables that presumably contribute specifically to cross-national or cross-unit differences in feelings about politics. In particular, persons using political culture concepts have looked to the effects of more general cultural systems on political socialization, as well as at times stressing the importance of national patterns in political experiences. Utilization of political culture concepts thus leads the researcher to expand his horizons and look for less familiar kinds of socialization influences and their effects on cross-national differences.[6]

The political culture approach seems especially suitable for studying the attitudes of ordinary people toward politics in Japan, which is the goal of this book. It is well known that Japanese society manifests some conspicuous features at the general cultural level, and it can be assumed that these are important for the nature of political attitude formation. The fact that Japanese society is community and group oriented, that it is consensualistic in its decision-making processes, and that, in a residual sense, it is paternalistic in certain social sectors in its personal relationships, can hardly be omitted from an analysis of political socialization processes and their effects. Indeed,

---

[5] For some excellent examples of cross-national research based on sociological or social psychological models of choice, involvement and participation, where conceptual frameworks are less comprehensive in focus than those of the political culture approach, see Stein Rokkan and Angus Campbell, "Norway and the United States of America," *International Social Science Journal* 12 (1960), pp. 69–99; Angus Campbell and Henry Valen, "Party Identification in Norway and the United States," in Angus Campbell, Philip E. Converse, Warren E. Miller and Donald E. Stokes, *Elections and the Political Order* (New York: Wiley, 1966), pp. 245–268; and, Philip E. Converse and Georges Dupeux, "Politicization of the Electorate in France and the United States," in *ibid.*, pp. 269–291.

[6] Actually, two aspects of the political culture approach represent at least partial departures from the typical emphases of most political behavior research at the mass level. General culture and characteristic social processes in particular units are given greater emphasis as contributants to the formation of political outlooks. The inventory of attitudes is also expanded in order to examine those dimensions of political outlook of relevance beyond the voting and participational frame of reference. Among other things, the political culture approach has examined such previously unresearched attitudes as people's pride in their governmental institutions. For examples of the attitudinal categories employed in political culture research at one point or another, see Table 1-10.

much of the scholarly comment on Japanese political experience has paid more than passing attention to these kinds of things. Utilization of the political culture model in effect sensitizes the observer to the importance of such factors and stimulates the researcher to include general cultural qualities in his inventory of relevant independent variables.

So far, I have noted that the political culture approach has emerged out of both a normative interest in the political proclivities of ordinary people and the strong enthusiasm in recent years for empirical research into political behavior. It was pointed out that by virtue of its comparative focus the political culture approach takes into account some kinds of potentially very important variables that have not been included in more parochial studies of political attitudes. It was further argued that sensitivity in the political culture approach to the influence of more general social practices and norms on political attitudes is advantageous for research in a country like Japan.

At this point, however, certain qualifying statements about the political culture approach are in order. In the first place, it should be pointed out that the political culture approach has typically sought to characterize and analyze only structures or patterns in popular political *attitudes*. Attitudes in this sense are simply orientations toward political objects or, in some cases, predispositions to do things. They are preconditions for behavior, and should not be confused with behavior itself. However, it has been assumed in some of the literature on political cultures that there exists a linear relationship between identifiable attitudes and various forms of political behavior.[7] While it is plausible that most attitudes identified in political culture research may be ultimately linked with behavior, at the same time it is necessary to appreciate the potential complexity of such links. Establishment of precise behavioral implications of the attitudes reported here is

---

[7] Exceptions to this characterization of the political culture approach can be found in reanalyses of the Almond and Verba data, and in recent work by the Verba group using findings from the second major cross-national cultural study. See Norman H. Nie, G. Bingham Powell, Jr., and Kenneth Prewitt, "Social Structure and Political Participation: Developmental Relationships," *American Political Science Review* 63 (June and September 1969), pp. 361–378 and 808–832, and Sidney Verba, Norman H. Nie and Jae-on Kim, "The Modes of Democratic Participation: A Cross-National Comparison," in Harry Eckstein and Ted Robert Gurr (eds.), *Comparative Politics Series* 2 (Beverly Hills: Sage Publications, 1971), Publication no. 01-013.

thus a matter for further empirical research — behavioral interpretations should be made only with appropriate caution. Some beginning toward establishing links between attitude patterns and behavior is found in the final chapter. However, this exercise will in part illustrate the importance of this general caveat.

Some caution is also appropriate with respect to the handling of intranational variation. In many cases it is necessary to deal with complexly stratified attitude structures within particular populations. In other words, while something identifiable as a national culture may exist in terms of majoritarian tendencies in a particular society, important internal differences may still exist within this dominant trend.

The political culture approach admits that societies are differentiated and that subcultures may exist within cultures, but it leaves certain remaining problems. For example, at some point it may become impossible to denote the line between a dominant culture and subcultures. Although this may be less of a problem in Japan than in some other places, there are still problems in this regard with the materials used in this study. If, in terms of psychological awareness, for example, three-quarters of the Japanese public is involved in politics, is the dominant cultural pattern one of awareness, or are there two subcultures here? In this study I have accepted majoritarian or pluralitarian tendencies as indicators of general patterns; it is assumed that because of individual circumstances certain kinds of persons may be less characteristic than others in regard to those patterns. In the case of the example at hand this orientation seems acceptable, but there are cases in the evidence where resolution of this problem is not so simple. While this conceptual problem has not been successfully resolved, it is important to at least note that I am aware that it remains a problem.

A second kind of problem exists where specific subgroups of the population manifest substantially different orientations toward politics. Men and women, for example, vary in their political orientations as do people of different ages, occupations and residential situations. There are, in fact, multiple axes of differentiation in modern industrial societies and the consequence is multiple dimensions within political culture patterns. Political culture studies have dealt with this problem cavalierly at best, indicating simply that subcultures of various kinds may exist, without saying whether the same individuals may be members of different subcultures, how much they may overlap or precisely how these kinds of subcultures should be defined.

I will not burden the reader further with conceptual problems of this kind and in fact have adopted certain solutions to the dilemma of subcultures. It has been assumed here that the existence of subcultural systems, like that of identifiable cultural systems, presupposes a common means of communications or cultural diffusion. This leads us to look for physical proximity, or some other kind of communications nexus, or common experience as a prerequisite for identifying a particular pattern as subcultural. This in turn leads us to assume that urban-rural variation in Japan, for example, can be seen as subcultural. The same can also be said for differences between certain age groupings in the population. We would not say, however, that political differences between men and women necessarily represent the same kind of phenomenon. Rather, we would see these patterns more as reflecting differences in social and political roles defined by the general culture.

While the political culture approach does expand the possible variables in the analysis of attitude formation, many others are still ignored. In the analysis that follows I have endeavored to expand the range of considerations beyond those normally considered in behavioral research as well as in most political culture studies. In the absence of convincing measures for the relevant variables, some of the discussion will be somewhat speculative in nature. But the possible importance of such things as political scandals and corruption, the character of the interpretation of political events by the mass media and qualitative aspects of local community life cannot be ignored, even in those cases where, at this stage of research, analysis depends especially heavily on inference. In addition to inductively expanding the range of influences to be considered at various points in the analysis, I have also recognized that there are internal variations in more general social practices or norms, as well as in a wide range of other potentially important factors. In no instance has it been assumed that some kind of cultural or social symmetry pervades Japanese life.

Japanese Political Culture and Empirical Theory. We noted earlier that the literature on political cultures encompasses two contrasting definitions of basic questions. These are associated with different theoretical perspectives, although it must be remembered that in both instances the primary goals are more descriptive than explanatory. What can best be called the *participant culture* approach simply looks for the kinds of political attitude structures believed supportive of democracy, and for their roots in typical social practices. In particular, political attitudes are seen as corresponding to general cultural emphases, as displayed for example in participatory behavior at home, school or work.[8] A second, *inductive* perspective seeks out the political culture patterns or attitudinal correlatives of actual behavior in a particular place, and endeavors in turn to link identifiable orientations with socialization processes or historical experience.

Generally speaking, the second of these two approaches has been found more suitable for the study reported here. In view of recent efforts to expand the popular dimension of Japanese political life, it is inevitable that the extent of "democratization" in popular political attitudes be evaluated at some point.[9] But it is essential that we look at these matters in terms of Japanese political culture patterns rather than from a predetermined perspective reflecting parochial American expectations about the appropriate requisites for democratic behavior. Utilization of the participant culture approach would place undesirable restraints on both the kinds of questions asked and the evidence permitted to answer them. Even though this study, in its design and question formulation, undoubtedly reflects the influence of Western definitions of democracy, there are still a substantial number of findings from surveys which directly tap native Japanese cultural dimensions. In order to arrive at an understanding of the Japanese political norms which responses to such queries afford, the inductive approach to political culture is by far the more satisfactory choice.

But the inductive approach accomplishes relatively little in de-

---

[8] Educational differences between countries are also given analytical emphasis at some points; see Almond and Verba, *The Civic Culture*, pp. 315–324. Other demographic variables are also considered, but major emphasis is placed on educational attainment as a contribution to intranational variation and cross-national uniformity.

[9] I refer here, of course, to the postwar efforts by the American occupation to reform Japanese political and social life in the period 1945–52. The best summary of the overall occupation period is Kazuo Kawai, *Japan's American Interlude* (Chicago: Chicago University Press, 1960).

fining the kinds of questions raised in the research here. In other words, it is important to have a sense of direction even though the inductive style of research is employed in the overall research plan. In order to accomplish this task we can begin by looking at some of the main tendencies in Japanese mass political behavior and asking ourselves under what conditions behavior of a particular kind might be generated. In accomplishing this we can refer to established hypotheses of earlier research on Japan, as well as the findings of the large body of political behavior literature. Thus, while proceeding by and large inductively, we will still be guided in part by hypotheses derived from extant research. Through an eclectic approach of this kind we can take advantage of the exploratory possibilities inherent in inductivism, at the same time avoiding an aimless and unstructured approach.

One of the striking aspects of Japanese mass political behavior has been its traditionally very high levels of voter participation. The importance of voter turnout in Japan has been overstressed to some degree by observers unfamiliar with the high turnout found in many European countries.[10] Still, voting rates in the contests for the Japanese House of Representatives were exceedingly high immediately after the franchise was granted. Despite a decline over time, presumably because of expansion of the franchise, they remain higher today than comparable American figures (Table 1-1). Moreover, the turnout for local Japanese elections is still among the highest in the world.

We can immediately ask what kinds of cultural attributes underlie these high turnouts. Research has shown that American electoral participation correlates highly with psychological involvement in politics,[11] so we can begin by looking at the level and content of political involvement in Japan. Further, persons who actually vote typically feel efficacious toward politics, so that the presence of widespread confidence in political processes and leadership could underwrite a high level of voting participation. Nevertheless, some observers have felt that the Japanese turnout reflects more a pervasive acceptance of the principle that voting is a duty than it reflects high levels of political

---

[10] Comparative sources are cited in Ch. 6, n. 1.

[11] See Angus Campbell, *et al.*, *The American Voter*, pp. 101–107, for evidencce on this relationship.

TABLE 1-1. THE FRANCHISE AND TURNOUT IN HOUSE OF REPRESENTATIVES ELECTIONS IN JAPAN, 1890–1967

Election	Date	Enfranchisement Rate (%)	Electorate	Turnout Rate (%)	
1	July 1, 1890	1.13	450,872	93.7	
2	February 15, 1892	1.08	434,594	91.6	
3	March 3, 1894	1.07	440,113	88.8	
4	September 1, 1894	1.12	460,483	84.9	
5	March 15, 1898	1.06	452,637	87.5	
6	August 10, 1898	1.17	502,292	79.9	
7	August 10, 1902	2.20	982,868	88.4	
8	March 1, 1903	2.12	958,322	86.2	
9	March 1, 1904	1.65	762,445	86.1	
10	May 15, 1908	3.27	1,590,045	85.3	
11	May 15, 1912	2.95	1,506,143	89.6	
12	March 25, 1915	2.88	1,546,411	92.1	
13	April 20, 1917	2.57	1,422,126	91.5	
14	May 10, 1920	5.46	3,069,148	86.7	
15	May 10, 1924	5.66	3,288,405	91.2	
16	February 20, 1928	20.12	12,408,678	80.3	
17	February 20, 1930	20.19	12,812,895	83.3	
18	February 20, 1932	20.02	13,103,679	81.7	
19	February 20, 1936	20.66	14,304,546	78.6	
20	April 30, 1937	20.54	14,402,497	73.3	
21	April 30, 1942	20.36	14,594,287	83.2	
22	April 10, 1946	51.22	36,878,417	72.1	(78.5)*
23	April 25, 1947	55.95	40,907,493	68.0	(74.9)
24	January 23, 1949	52.63	42,105,300	74.0	(80.7)
25	October 1, 1952	55.68	46,772,584	76.4	(80.5)
26	April 19, 1953	55.24	47,090,167	74.2	(78.4)
27	February 27, 1955	56.17	49,235,375	75.8	(80.0)
28	May 22, 1958	57.58	52,013,529	77.0	(80.0)
29	November 20, 1960	59.01	54,312,993	73.5	(76.0)
30	November 21, 1963	61.62	58,281,678	71.1	(72.4)
31	January 1, 1967	63.60	62,992,860	74.0	(74.8)

SOURCES: The information on the first thirty elections for the House of Representatives is from Kōmei Senkyo Remmei, *Shūgiin Giin Senkyo no Jisseki* (1967), pp. 13–52. (Prefectural turnouts and preference summaries are also available for the first 30 elections from this source.) Figures for the 1967 election are from Sōrifu Tōkeikyoku, *Nihon Tōkei Nenkan 1967*, p. 522.

*Turnout for males in the postwar period is included in parentheses for 1946 through 1967, in order that the postwar and prewar figures might better be compared.

interest and trust.[12] So it is useful to identify the kinds of attitudes that contemporary Japanese entertain toward the voting act itself, while also investigating the more general and diffuse evaluative perspectives regarding the political system as well as definitions of individual roles and involvement which may also contribute to participation. These are the topics of Chapters Two through Four.

A second central tendency in mass political behavior in Japan is the pronounced stability of aggregate partisan preferences during much of the postwar period. While it is true that there have been very important changes in the level of mass support for particular parties, as well as some major discontinuities in party identities not attributable to the character of popular support, the dominant tendency at the aggregate level in the 1950s and 1960s has been one of stability. Majorities, or more recently near majorities, of the electorate have thus supported the Liberal Democratic Party or predecessor parties from the conservative camp, while important minority groupings have received a slightly varying but somewhat similarly frozen share of the vote (Table 1-2).[13] Moreover, parallel with the general stability in partisan behavior, there has been a very high level of consistency, or stability, in support for particular candidates, as can be seen in the information on incumbents, returnees and new contestants in Table 1-3.[14]

The presence of these particular patterns suggests another series of questions appropriate in a study of Japanese political culture. Does

---

[12] See Jun'ichi Kyōgoku and Nobutaka Ike, "Urban-Rural Differences in Voting Behavior in Postwar Japan," *Economic Development and Cultural Change* 9 (October 1960), Part II, pp. 171–172. Their comments on the importance of duty in voting in Japan, and its origins in administrative practices and social setting, have been the inspiration for the analysis developed at several points in the discussion that follows.

[13] These comments on stability in partisan strengths are based on observation of the aggregate patterns, where conditions are more akin to those found in some European systems, in which "frozen" cleavages are observed, than to either the alternating patterns of the United States and Britain or the moving cleavage pattern of postwar France. This in no way denies the importance of the secular decline in support for the Liberal Democrats in at least the House of Representatives elections — House of Councillors patterns were dissimilar in the late 1950s and 1960s, a fact which is generally ignored — or the importance of individual shifts in preference which contributed to these declines.

[14] Some linkage may exist between the stabilization of partisan alternatives after 1955 and the strength of incumbents at the polls, as the two patterns clearly converge.

TABLE 1-2. Partisan Vote in House of Representatives Elections, 1952–1967

Year	Conservative (%)	Socialist (%)	Democratic Socialist (%)	Communist (%)	Other (%)	Total (%)
1952[a]	66	21	—*	3	10	100
1953	65	27	—	2	6	100
1955	63	29	—	2	6	100
1958	58	33	—	3	6	100
1960	58	28	9	3	2	100
1963	55	29	7	4	5	100
1967	49	28	10	5	8[b]	100

Sources: Data are from Jichishō Senkyokyoku, *Shūgiin Giin Sōsenkyo, Saikō Saibansho Saibankan Kokumin Shinsa* (Tōkyō 1964), p. 10 and Sōrifu Tōkeikyoku, *Nihon Tōkei Nenkan 1967*, pp. 522–523.

[a] For years prior to the 1958 election, the Conservative category includes support for the Progressive, Liberal and Democratic parties (and factions of the Democratic grouping) in the relevant periods; the Socialist grouping was also divided into left and right wing segments. For this reason, information on the pre-1958 elections is somewhat misleading where inferences about party loyalties are concerned. Nevertheless, there is a pronounced stability over time in the collective Conservative and Socialist vote in comparison with many other systems.

[b] Includes the six percent gained by the Kōmeito.

* Indicates no data available for this year. Used throughout all tables.

the apparent stability in preference reflect high levels of satisfaction with political performance? Or has the status quo been accepted by virtue of apathy and pessimism regarding the constructive potential of politics in any particular form? Moreover, do these patterns in preferences reflect the presence of strong attachments to various parties, as might be the case were the American experience translatable to Japan? Or, alternatively, are candidate preferences of underlying and dominant importance, especially given the reputed frequency of mobilization of some sectors of the electorate by individual candidates' vote-getting machines? Some answers to these kinds of questions will be provided when attitudes about political actors and voting choices are reported in Chapter Five.

In the discussion that follows, I have not tried to answer literally all of these questions, since in many cases the attitudinal profiles to be described were not easily linked to the aggregate behavior patterns noted here. (This was mainly due to shortcomings in the evidence about attitudinal effects on behavior.) Still, these are the important

TABLE 1-3. CANDIDATE TURNOVER AND SUCCESS RATIOS IN JAPAN HOUSE
OF REPRESENTATIVE ELECTIONS, 1949–1963

	1949	1952	1955	1958	1960	1963
I. Candidates						
Incumbents	51.5%	45.5%	70.6%	66.2%	72.2%	73.7%
Returnees	7.3	29.6	19.3	22.0	13.7	13.5
New Candidates	41.2	24.9	10.0	11.8	14.1	12.8
All Candidates	100.0	100.0	100.0	100.0	100.0	100.0
II. Success Ratios in Categories:						
Incumbents	56.6%	53.0%	73.1%	69.3%	75.1%	78.4%
Returnees	45.3	45.5	36.7	48.8	43.0	50.4
New Candidates	22.2	21.5	14.2	15.3	18.7	16.0

SOURCES: The data are from Jichishō Senkyokyoku, *Shūgiin Giin Sōsenkyo, Saikō Saibansho Saibankan Kokumin Chōsa* (1963), p. 13.

The figures in part I indicate the ratios of candidates in each category among *all* candidates. From these figures we can observe the degree of novelty facing the electorate as a whole. Figures show that a majority of the candidates in these elections were incumbents at a time considerably preceding the formation of the major parties in 1955.

In part II the percentages represent the ratio of successful candidates within each category.

questions that shape the direction of the research, and the reader can readily perform the inferential leaps appropriate to linking attitudes and behavior in a general sense.

The kinds of questions and hypotheses suggested here can in turn be linked at various points to postulates about the effects of well-known Japanese cultural traits on political socialization and political culture. It is plausible, for example, that feelings of group and community obligation in Japan may underwrite an especially high level of duteous feelings about the vote. Furthermore, acceptance of and dependence upon paternalistic social relationships, which can still be observed in varying degrees in different social sectors in Japan today, may have much to do with attitudes toward politicians and with the characteristic evaluations by voters of political performance.

In looking for effects of this kind we are moving toward question and hypothesis formulation on the basis of inferences about the effects of known population attributes or experiences. In other words, research in the political culture of Japan can be legitimately directed both by questions formed by our established knowledge of Japanese society as well as by hypotheses about the roots of observed political behavior. Proceeding in a similar vein, we must inevitably consider the effects of discontinuities in political experience and in social setting.

Although many continuities undoubtedly can be observed between prewar and postwar political cultures in Japan, it is equally important to appreciate the degree of change in political life and socialization patterns in these two periods. Admittedly, there are some possible contradictions in statements about popular political postures in prewar Japan. The mass political mood during the 1920s is sometimes believed to have been one of enthusiasm for new liberal ideas. To be sure, this characterization best fits the better educated and urban citizens, but it contrasts especially sharply with our image of the electorate having been organized into voting blocs, or being peculiarly deferential to the dictates of an arbitrary and unresponsive bureaucracy.[15] Perhaps it is best to assume that the prewar period did indeed have its paradoxes and important sectoral differences where popular political attitudes are concerned, but that, overall, tendencies were toward authoritarian or "subject" attitudes about the relationship of the ordinary man to political life.[16]

Whatever the precise nature of prewar sentiments, it is quite clear that the early postwar period witnessed a sharp break with known political tradition. The economic underpinnings of social and political hierarchy in the rural sector were removed by a far reaching land reform, while educational curricula, political institutions, economic organization and labor relations were all subjected to controlled change designed to favor the implementation of political democracy. The sum effect of these reforms, and the widespread and self-conscious concern for "democratic behavior," was to at least disseminate the norms of

---

[15] Bloc voting has been normally seen as mainly a rural manifestation, and especially deep cleavages between urban and rural political subcultures may have existed in prewar Japan. The best discussion of these kinds of phenomena for the prewar period are found in Richard K. Beardsley, John W. Hall and Robert E. Ward, *Village Japan* (Chicago: Chicago University Press, 1959 and 1969), pp. 422–435. Prewar traditions, where the role of the administrative bureaucracy is concerned, are cited in Nobutaka Ike, *Japanese Politics: An Introductory Survey* (New York: Alfred A. Knopf, 1957), pp. 148–149.

[16] The term "subject" refers to passive acceptance of politics accompanied by perhaps high levels of awareness of the relevance and actions of government. See Almond and Verba, *Civic Culture*, pp. 17–18.

popular government throughout Japanese society. To some degree, the reforms also undermined older social practices in specifically the rural area, and created vested interests in the new system among organizations of the trade union movement and the political left.[17]

Assuming that precise definition of prewar patterns is no longer possible, there are at least two ways in which we might go about the study of the impact of postwar social and political reforms on Japanese political culture. One way is cohort analysis. Utilization of this technique would require precise characterization of the attitudes of persons in particular age groups at various points in time, and might permit us to characterize different groupings of the population in terms of the permanent effects of their exposure, or nonexposure, to prewar political influences.[18] In other words, if we found that older persons, educated by and voting in the prewar system, were clearly distinctive in political outlooks at *different* points in time in the postwar era, we would then be able to make some highly plausible inferences about the nature of both prewar and postwar political cultures and their sources.

Unfortunately, this kind of analysis is difficult to accomplish across a broad number of attitudinal categories in the Japanese case. It is possible to conduct a very simple cohort analysis where the same

---

[17] Included in the major reforms of the early postwar occupation period were revision of the constitution, changes in provisions for the autonomy of local political units, decentralization of education and police administration, changes in the legal status of women and introduction of women's suffrage, land reform and decentralization of big business ownership and control. As the result of these and related events, leftist or "progressive" parties and labor unions became a major force in Japanese politics for the first time, and democracy became a conspicuous theme in political rhetoric and the popular consciousness.

The character of the relevant postwar political and social reforms will not be discussed extensively here, since they have been considered in sufficient detail elsewhere. The events of the immediate postwar period are summarized in especially readable fashion in Robert A. Scalapino and Junnosuke Masumi, *Parties and Politics in Contemporary Japan* (Berkeley and Los Angeles: University of California Press, 1962), especially pp. 22–44. The reader is referred to the literature cited therein for further information on the critical events of the occupation period, but special reference should be made to the study of the postwar land reform and its effects on rural society in R. P. Dore, *Land Reform in Japan* (London and Toronto: Oxford University Press, 1959), and the detailed discussion of the events of the early postwar period in Kazuo Kawai, *Japan's American Interlude*.

[18] For citations of the relevant theoretical and methodological literature on cohort analysis, see Ch. 7, n. 2.

or similar questions have been used over time, but most of the more interesting kinds of questions have not been asked repeatedly over the necessary intervals of time. A second method for researching the problem of the impact of postwar reforms on political culture is simply to examine the political cultural outlooks of persons from particular age groupings at a single point in time, then endeavor to analyze, through appropriate statistical techniques, to what degree their attitudes are reflective of true generational differences and to what degree they might result from more "normal" kinds of life cycle influences. This is what I have done in Chapter Seven, along with presenting a substantial amount of descriptive data about the tendencies among different age groupings.

The well-documented existence of important social and culture differences between urban and rural sectors in Japan, as well as the higher frequencies of political participation found in rural districts (Tables 1-4, 1-5, 1-6), leads to yet another set of questions. We know from the findings of various sociological and anthropological studies that social relationships differ markedly in rural and urban Japan; some differences in accepted social norms can also be detected. For a variety of reasons, the rural sector seems to be somewhat more traditional than the urban areas. We might assume that in rural Japan residual elements of earlier social practices may be associated with political attitudes more characteristic of earlier phases in Japan's development; this expectation is borne out in some cases by the evidence presented in Chapter Six.

But there are some important deviations from this expectation as well. There are practices and outlooks in the rural area which foster political cultural beliefs which hold out more promise for the development of popular government in Japan than is the case in the urban sector. Some of these sectoral differences in political culture are of plausible importance to urban and rural trends in voting participation which have long attracted the attention of students of Japanese politics. Since the urban districts of Japan have continued to grow in importance in the postwar period (Table 1-7), and increasing numbers of people have also turned to employment outside the traditional agricultural sector (Table 1-8), thus coming under the influence of urban life in varying degrees, these are matters of obvious importance.

TABLE 1-4. ELECTION TURNOUT AND PLACE OF RESIDENCE

	Urban (%)	Rural (%)	All (%)
Local Elections:			
1955 Mayoralty	84	92	86
1955 Assembly	85	92	—
1959 Mayoralty	86	91	88
1959 Assembly	86	93	—
1963 Mayoralty	82	90	86
1963 Assembly	82	92	—
Prefectural Elections:			
1955 Gubernatorial	70	83	75
1955 Assembly	72	83	77
1959 Gubernatorial	76	84	78
1959 Assembly	76	85	80
1963 Gubernatorial	72	82	75
1963 Assembly	74	84	77
House of Representatives Elections:			
1952	66	80	74
1955	72	81	76
1958	74	81	77
1960	70	80	74
1963	67	79	71

SOURCES: 1955 (Local and prefectural): Jichichō Senkyobu, *Chihō Senkyo Kekka Shirabe*, 1956, p. 13. National means are omitted for local assembly elections; since ward assemblies are included in the calculations their low turnout levels considerably depress the national mean. The category urban in the above entries does not include major cities; turnout in the large cities is typically much lower than is the case in the provincial cities for which figures are shown here.

1959 (Local and prefectural): Jichichō Senkyokyoku, *Chihō Senkyo Kekka Shirabe*, 1959, p. 13.

1963 (Local and prefectural): Jichishō Senkyokyoku, *Chihō Senkyo Kekka Shirabe*, 1963, p. 8.

House: _____, *Shūgiin Giin Sōsenkyo Saikō Saibansho Saibankan Kokumin Shinsa*, 1964, p. 4.

The Japanese findings are also of importance to empirical political theory, and in discussing urban-rural differences later we will look critically at the postulates of both social modernization theory and center-periphery models of political behavior. It is obvious that urban-rural differences in Japan at the time our data were collected hardly fit the conditions of contrast between traditionality and modernity anticipated in postulates of social modernization theory about

TABLE 1-5. HOUSE OF REPRESENTATIVES
ELECTION TURNOUT AND URBANIZATION

Year	Turnout vs. Level of Urbanization*
1925	−.419
1930	−.520
1935	−.535
1940	−.391
1950	−.718
1955	−.591
1960	−.643

SOURCES: With certain exceptions, electoral and census information is from the same year period; however, 1928 election turnouts are matched with 1925 census figures, 1936 election outcomes are paired with 1935 population data and 1942 election participation is compared with 1940 population information.

The source of the population information is Sōrifu Tokeikyoku, *Nihon Tōkei Nenkan 1967*, pp. 12–16. Election turnout figures are from Kōmei Senkyo Remmei, *Shūgiin Giin Senkyo no Jisseki: Dai Ikkai-Dai Sanjukai*, 1968, pp. 39–51.

* The unit of analysis is prefectures. Pearson's product-moment correlations are used to indicate the direction and intensity of the relationship between levels of urbanization, measured in terms of proportion of prefectural population living in cities, and prefectural mean turnout.

the relationships between change and political behavior. It is particularly important to note in this context the degree to which cosmopolitan and integrative forces are present in postwar Japan. It is also essential that we be aware of the scope of change particularly in rural Japan in the postwar period itself (Table 1-9), inasmuch as farms are increasingly owner-run and improvements in the economic positions of typical farm families have been remarkable. Indeed, the scale of rural affluence in recent years is a highly believable contribution to some of the patterns reported at later points in this book.

TABLE 1-6. POLITICAL PARTICIPATION AND PLACE OF RESIDENCE

	Metropolitan (%)	Urban (%)*	Rural (%)	(N)
Discussion of national affairs:[a]				
At home	59	61	61	
With neighbors	24	24	44	
At workplace	42	43	35	
At meetings	27	38	43	(5,000)
Discussion of local affairs:[a]				
At home	56	61	64	
With neighbors	26	38	48	
At workplace	40	43	36	
At meetings	27	38	44	(5,000)
Articulation of interest:[b]				
Often/sometimes	15	—	26	(354)
Solicitation of somebody else's vote:[b]				
National election	5	—	16	
Local election	4	—	14	(354)

SOURCES: All figures represent percentages of total relevant sub-samples.

[a] Kōmei Senkyo Remmei, "Kōmei Senkyo on Jittai", 1958, p. 83. This is the only national study where frequencies for discussions outside the family are reported. Many local studies including my own have presented findings on frequencies of discussions in general or discussions in some special context; in a few cases findings diverged from the above. However, it is assumed in this case that the national figures are more representative, since sample selections are believed to have been carried out more carefully and local context effects are less likely to have biased the results.

[b] These data are from my 1964 survey of political attitudes and voting choice behavior in Yokohama and two rural communities. The findings on interest articulation are supported by the results reported in Miyagi ken Senkyo Kanri Iinkai, "Kōmei Senkyo Jittai Chōsa", 1962, appendix, p. 8. Similar patterns in urban-rural vote solicitation were mentioned in Hiroshima ken Senkyo Kanri Iinkai, "Senkyo Ishiki ni kan suru Yūkensha no Jittai", 1965, p. 78. In this instance, 28% of the respondents in a farm community reported having "helped out" in a local election campaign in contrast with 13 percent of those who lived in a small industrial suburb of Hiroshima City. However, only 3% of those interviewed in the same study on an island in the Inland Sea reported having been engaged in these kinds of activities.

* The category of urban in this table refers to provincial cities, where both social and political characteristics are more like those in rural districts than in the large metropolitan centers.

TABLE 1-7. URBANIZATION IN JAPAN, 1920–65

	% Population in Cities	% Population in Large Cities	% Population in Middle Cities	% Population Elsewhere
1920	18	8	4	88
1925	22	10	4	86
1930	24	12	6	82
1935	33	18	7	75
1940	38	20	9	71
1945	—	8	7	85
1950	38	13	12	75
1955	56	16	18	66
1960	64	20	21	59
1965	68	23	23	54

SOURCES: These data are calculated from information in Sōrifu Tōkeikyoku, *Nihon Tōkei Nenkan 1967*, pp. 12–19. Figures in all cases represent percentages of the *total* population.

The information in column one pertains to the ratio of the population living in all administratively defined cities (*shi*) in the respective years. That in the other columns pertains to population distributions in respectively cities of over 500,000 persons, those between 100,000 and 499,000 and places outside of the large and middle-sized urban districts. Relevant to this latter category, 41% of the entire population lived on farms in 1955, 37% in 1960, and 31% in 1965. See, *ibid.*, p. 92.

TABLE 1-8. AGRICULTURE AS AN OCCUPATION, 1940–65

	Agriculture as % of Labor Force	% Farm Units Where Farming Is Full-time Activity
1940	—	74
1950	47	50
1955	40	35
1960	32	34
1965	24	22

SOURCES: Sōrifu Tōkeikyoku, *Nihon Tōkei Nenkan 1967*, pp. 67 and 87.

TABLE 1-9. FARM TENANCY AND AGRICULTURAL INCOME, 1940-65

	% Units Owner Run	% Units Owner-Tenant	% Units Tenant Run
1940	31	42	27
1950	62	33	5
1955	70	26	4
1960	75	22	3
1965	80	18	2

	Receipts	Disposable Income**	Expenses	Surplus	Price Index
1950	268.5*	193.9	174.1	19.8	—
1955	505.4	347.6	312.8	34.9	95
1960	609.4	419.1	368.4	50.7	100
1965	1,156.3	775.1	654.5	120.6	125

SOURCES: Sōrifu Tōkeikyoku, *Nihon Tōkei Nenkan 1967*, on ownership and tenancy p. 87, for farm incomes p. 126; the price index is that for commodities purchased in rural districts and is from p. 379.
* All farm income information except the price index is in thousands of yen and represents national averages for household units.
** Disposable income is that which remains after disbursements for taxes are made, and includes grants and subsidies.

Yet urban-rural differences in community life and social practices *are* still important to political culture, and produce patterns in attitudes and behavior which do not accord with the predictions about individual behavior in modernization theory. As a consequence, some possible modifications in the relevant theories are proposed. Finally, a review of the findings reported here, and the multivariate analysis of relationships between place of residence and the confounding influence of urban-rural differences in educational attainment, will help to clarify the current ambiguity of the status of urban-rural differences as a relevant variable in political behavior analysis.

In looking at theories about urban-rural differences from the perspective of Japanese evidence I am of course deviating from a pure inductive approach. Still, examination of social modernization concepts and the center-periphery approach in terms of the Japanese findings is set within a larger inductively defined perspective. In other words, rather than letting theoretical perspectives define our research plan in an inflexible way, I have sought to integrate established hypotheses with the Japanese evidence where examination of the findings suggested that this was a worthwhile enterprise. Adoption of a highly pragmatic and exploratory posture of this kind raises questions appropriate to philosophy of science that obviously cannot be treated here. But I trust that a clear statement of perspective will enhance reader understanding of the nature of the effort I have engaged in, even if I seem to deal with questions of social science method rather cavalierly in the process.

Methodology and Organization. The political culture approach has generated a fairly wide range of conceptual categories for attitudinal research. Without slighting earlier behavioral investigations, it is fair to say that the literature on political cultures concerns itself with a substantially wider range of political outlooks than that typically found in research with a less self-conscious concern for cross-national comparison — indeed, this is one of the distinct advantages of the political culture approach. In Table 1-10 I have endeavored to identify the kinds of attitudes considered at various points in discussions of

TABLE 1-10. THE POLITICAL CULTURE APPROACH

Focus	Concept
Political System	Salience/relevance of "politics"
	System affect
	Political instrumentalism:
	levels and specific system goals
	Preferred institutional format
	Preferred procedural format
Political Actors	Preferred elite qualities
	Partisan loyalties
	Evaluations of performance
	Evaluations of responsiveness
	Trust-distrust
	Deference
Popular Roles	Awareness and understanding
	Interest/election outcome concern
	Personal competence/efficacy
	Activist participation
	Obligational participation

SOURCES: The concepts are selected from various writings in Lucian W. Pye and Sidney Verba, *Political Culture and Political Development* (Princeton: Princeton University Press, 1965), and from Gabriel Almond and Sidney Verba, *The Civic Culture* (Princeton: Princeton University Press, 1963).

political culture, in order to better demonstrate the value of the political culture perspective.

In this investigation there was some restraint on focus, in addition to that provided by the basic questions just outlined. The data reported here is derived from a large number of unpublished Japanese research materials — the advantages of this approach will be discussed shortly. In effect, the focus of my research was influenced to a considerable degree by the kinds of information available.

Accordingly, I have classified the responses to hundreds of survey questions into four basic categories of attitudes. Feelings that politics is relevant, self-assessments of interest in politics and concern about election outcomes, manifestations of awareness or knowledge about politics, and feelings that politics can do something for people were all classified as *involvement attitudes* (Chapter Two). Responses in this category in every case indicated some felt connection between individuals and politics or some popular awareness of the content of public affairs.

Assessments of the quality of political performance or satisfaction with how politics is conducted, feelings about the political efficacy of ordinary people and appraisals of the responsiveness of politicians have been termed *evaluative attitudes* (Chapter Three). Attitudes in this category were more clearly reflective of self-conscious measurement of potentialities or performance against some implicit standards than was the case elsewhere, although it could certainly be said that some suggested that this was a worthwhile enterprise. Adoption of a highly kind of evaluation is implicit in replies to most kinds of survey questions about politics.

Japanese voters' assessments of their reasons for voting, indications of willingness to actively engage in community leadership, and preferences for collective political action or independent postures toward political leadership were termed *participation attitudes* (Chapter Four), since all of these replies had some kind of connection with feelings about appropriate kinds and intensity of political action. Finally, attitudes toward different campaign objects and responses reflecting different kinds of emphases in electoral decisions were designated as *voting attitudes* (Chapter Five).

Since the term "attitude" has had various meanings in social science research, the use of it here requires some clarification. I have been quite pragmatic in using the generic expression even where various sentiments appropriate to concepts of belief, value, and affect have been discernible in varying degrees.[19] This was done simply because it is obvious that no single concept fits the complex of sentiments assumed present in answers to some questions used in this study. Generally speaking, however, two kinds of phenomena can be seen as subsumable under the concept (attitude) in our research. In some places the term "attitude" denotes states of mind or orientations toward political objects and situations, rather than predispositions to engage in a specified kind of behavior. Even though some actions can be assumed to be consequent to these states of mind, the precise connections will have to be established by further research.[20] Elsewhere, questions had been formulated in such a way that the content of responses was more closely akin to the concept of attitude as specifically a predisposition to behave in certain ways. Both of these conceptions of the content of attitudes accord with precedents in social science research; as we proceed it will be indicated where each interpretation (of attitude) fits most closely.

Formulation of the research reported here was stimulated in large part by the availability of several hundred unpublished replicative studies of political attitudes and political behavior in Japan. The Japanese Fair Election League, a private organization concerned with

---

[19] The meanings used in the research reported here do conform to the various content given the concept of attitude in social psychology at different places. What I have not done is take a strong position in favor of one or another strict definition from among the alternatives espoused by different social psychologists. See William J. McGuire, "The Nature of Attitudes and Attitude Change," in Gardner Lindzey (ed.), *Handbook in Social Psychology* (Reading, Massachusetts: Addison-Wesley, 1968), Vol. III, pp. 136–272.

Speculations later in the book about the processes of attitudinal change in postwar Japan also fit to a certain degree the social psychological models. It should be noted, however, that most social psychological theories of change in attitude structures focus upon small group situations rather than societies as a whole.

[20] This interpretation of the meaning of attitude is consequent with some concepts in social psychology where a "given attitude is a quasi-open structure functioning as part of a wider context." See Solomon E. Asch, *Social Psychology* (Englewood Cliffs, New Jersey: Prentice-Hall, 1952), p. 580 ff.

In other words, individual attitudes are parts of a larger complex of orientations, the interaction of which determines the course of behavior. The value of looking at attitudes in this way becomes clearer when we see that, in Japan, among some subgroups in the population political interest is closely associated with inclinations to go out to vote, while among other subgroups feelings of duty are most important.

study of electoral practices, has been engaged in a massive national and regional survey research effort since the 1950s that is unique in the world. The League has conducted at least one nationwide survey annually in recent years and, with the help of local affiliates, has also originated annual studies in most of the country's forty-six prefectures.[21] Since the League's research efforts have been coordinated at the national level, many of the same questions have been asked in studies conducted at different points in time and in different parts of the country. The results of the League's surveys thus form a body of findings that is particularly suitable for use in identifying political attitude patterns in Japan. Special emphasis here has been put on aggregation of the findings of nearly two hundred of the League's studies from the early and middle 1960s. While data from the League thus forms the core of the evidence in most cases here, it has been supplemented in some instances by results of other surveys conducted during roughly the same period.[22]

Aggregation of the findings of a large group of replicative studies

---

[21] The Fair Election League is especially interested in the question of corrupt election practices and seeks to improve standards in this area through various kinds of popular education projects. It works closely in these pursuits with election administration authorities at various levels of government. Surveys are conducted in order to examine the effects of its educational programs, and to investigate the public's perceptions of electoral practices. But a great deal of work has also been done on popular attitudes, participation and communications behavior as a by-product of these interests. Only a small number of the League's hundreds of unpublished reports have been used in scholarly research thus far.

[22] Included in the evidence are the findings from my own 1964 survey of voter attitudes in Yokohama and two rural areas, Atsugi and Nita. Sample strata were selected for the explicit purpose in this case of comparing the effects of different types of urban and rural settings on political attitudes and behavior. Included in the sample were persons from the "new" middle class, or white-collar category, residents of an older urban district, labor union members and their families, and people living in both a modernizing rural district and in a remote and isolated farm area. The results of this study are reported in Bradley Richardson, "Political Behavior and Attitudes in Contemporary Japan," unpublished Ph.D. dissertation, University of California, Berkeley, 1966. However, reanalysis of my own study data was the source for the information used here; accordingly, the citation "Richardson 1964" used hereafter refers to the study itself rather than to a particular publication or document.

My interest in using the League's research reports stemmed from concerns developed in my dissertation research, coupled with a desire to identify representative patterns in popular attitudes that would apply to the general Japanese population. As the work progressed, I placed increasing emphasis on the findings of the League's studies, for the simple reason that I discovered a rich body of data that I felt should be brought to light in aggregate form.

affords some definite advantages. In the first place, we can be certain that many of the tendencies reported here are indeed representative of patterns in Japanese voters' political attitudes in the general time period in question. Even though deviatory findings were found in a few cases, in most instances there were clear patterns of convergence. This fact lends special confidence to the observations made here. Moreover, in some cases it is possible to develop special insights into the effects of local context where the results of local studies deviate from clearly established national patterns.

Secondly, it is important to note that the League's research has not been confined to examination of attitudes toward solely national politics and elections. The League and its affiliates have also conducted studies on attitudes at the time of local and prefectural elections, and have shown a special interest in questions of differences in political orientations among various political levels. The results of the League's surveys thus afford special multidimensional insights into the nature of political attitudes in contemporary Japan, a fact that is of special importance in the Japanese setting, as we will see later. Indeed, the combined data on attitudes toward both local and national politics contributes to pathbreaking insights into the multidimensionality of political culture in Japan.

There are other special benefits accruing from use of the League's research reports. For one, the fact that the studies were conducted by Japanese scholars and research groups is important. Many of the survey questions tapped dimensions of the Japanese public's political attitudes that might have been ignored in research by foreign scholars. This is true not only of questions repeatedly asked in the League's coordinated surveys but of some items as well used by creative scholars in individual studies conducted under the League's sponsorship.

There were some problems inherent in the special kind of secondary analysis used in this study. In a few instances there were deviations in the findings of different surveys that could not be attributed to visible effects of time, context or sample design. I have assumed in such situations that the results of a majority of the relevant surveys indicated representative tendencies, but on such occasions have noted the tentative nature of my observations as well as the presence of deviating evidence. Moreover, few of the League's surveys had been analyzed using combined indices of attitudinal tendencies. This made it inevitable that much more detailed description of attitudinal patterns be presented here than would have been the case otherwise. However, this proved to be an advantage in some instances, since replies to individual questions in many cases diverged in most interesting ways, a fact which encouraged profitable speculation on several occasions.[23]

Research employing evidence of the kind I have just described obviously contributes directly to making descriptive statements about the nature of political culture in Japan. For a variety of reasons, however, it is less suitable for analyzing the relevant political socialization processes with any degree of sophistication. In order to overcome this deficiency, various kinds of multivariate statistical operations were conducted, using the findings from my own 1964 survey. As is well known, it is possible through multivariate analysis to make statements with some precision about the kinds of influences among a variety of possible factors that account for the greatest effect in various dependent variables or consequences. In effect, tests of propositions about the causes of particular attitudinal tendencies are more conclusive using multivariate techniques than is usually possible with contingency tables (even though contingency table analysis was obviously suitable for the presentation of the descriptive findings).

In choosing a multivariate statistical model that would be most suitable for this study, several considerations had to be met. Since these led to a technique that is not very widely known, it is important to acknowledge clearly what these considerations were. In the first place, my data were usually ordinal in nature, as is not infrequent with survey findings. In other words, responses to questions about political attitudes often reflected the candidates' self-ranking on some implicit scale, in which different orders of, for example, interest in politics were reflected. Moreover, answers to questions in some cases did not meet even the requirements of an ordinal scale, simply implying the presence or absence of certain attributes. Thus, the data clearly did not fit the

---

[23] For example, the frequency of optimistic feelings about ordinary people's political efficacy contrasted substantially with those of perceptions about the quality of political life, and the differences in response patterns led me to feel that reported feelings of efficacy might be interpreted most appropriately as formally learned attitudes about politics.

requirements of interval assumptions, and the more familiar correlation or regression analyses could not be legitimately employed.

Also, some of the better known statistical models are typically based on assumptions about the linearity of relationships between variables. My data clearly did not meet these assumptions, particularly where the effects of age differences were concerned. In some cases age did have a linear effect — as people grew older, for example, they were sometimes less knowledgeable about certain aspects of politics, the decreases occurring systematically with each advance in age. But in many cases the effects of age were curvilinear, with middle-aged persons manifesting more links with politics than other kinds of persons.

Given these characteristics in the data, what was needed was a multivariate statistical technique that would work legitimately with nonlinear, ordinal or attribute kinds of information. A technique suitable for my purposes was found in *effect parameter analysis*, a statistical model developed by James Coleman. The Coleman method provides easily interpretable indexes of the effect, for example, of being an urban rather than rural resident. In simple bivariate analyses the effect index, or parameter, is the same as the difference between the two sides of the familiar contingency table. Thus, where 80 percent of urban residents are inclined to support a political party in contrast with 60 percent of rural residents, the effect index of residence would simply be 20 percent. In multivariate operations, the indexes have the same kind of meaning although the underlying statistical calculations are obviously more elaborate.[24]

The Coleman model will be used specifically in the analysis of the effects of place of residence in Chapter Six and of age in Chapter Seven. Chapters Two through Four, which deal with tendencies in the Japanese population as a whole, are largely descriptive in nature, and simpler statistical analysis suffices for that purpose.

---

[24] The Coleman approach is discussed in James S. Coleman, *Introduction to Mathematical Sociology* (New York: Free Press, 1964), Ch. 6. For an application in comparative analysis see Kenneth Thompson, "Cross-National Voting Behavior Research: An Example of Computer Assisted Multivariate Analysis of Attribute Data," in Harry Eckstein and Ted Robert Gurr (eds.), *Comparative Politics Series* 1 (Beverly Hills: Sage Publications, 1970), Publication no. 01-003.

Before turning to the substance of this book, I wish to make clear my feeling that exploratory research is highly desirable at this stage in our understanding of popular political behavior in Japan. Although in a few instances in this research I have tested hypotheses formulated in studies of other cultures, I have placed major emphasis on describing the Japanese tendencies in political attitudes and on developing tentative hypotheses from my examination of the observed trends and understanding of the Japanese setting. In generating new hypotheses that are believed to be especially suitable in the Japanese frame of reference, I am making a contribution to future research in that country as well as suggesting some possibilities for new research in other places. Wherever possible, these hypotheses are tested in the multivariate models introduced in Chapters Six and Seven, in order that some preliminary sense of their applicability may be gained.[25]

---

[25] Since citations from the Kōmei Senkyo Remmei materials were especially numerous, I have used an abbreviated form of reference in most cases. Citations generally take the form of a single name and year. For example, "Aomori 1962" refers to "Aomori Ken Senkyo Kanri Iinkai, "Kenmin no Seiji Ishiki" (Aomori: 1962)." The full titles of all research reports and abbreviated references can be found in the bibliography.

In most instances abbreviated citations have been placed paranthetically within the text, thus avoiding the cumbersome process of having footnotes for each reference. However, in a few cases where there were especially numerous references for a particular finding, footnotes have been used.

I have also distinguished in the citations between results that are included in the tables and those that have not been reported in this form. Thus an abbreviated citation without a page reference, e.g., "Kōmei 1958," refers to data that are reported in a subsequent table. Citations with page numbers refer to data not included in tables, e.g., "Kōmei 1958, p. 124." Since it is important to distinguish studies based on nationwide samples and those based on regional or local samples, wherever data is taken from a national survey it is so indicated in the table source citation.

A final note of caution about statistical techniques is appropriate. Statistical significance testing is a common feature in survey research studies of political behavior. It serves as a means of evaluating the probability with which a particular set of consequences in the findings can be assumed to duplicate reality. These tests have generally been omitted here. In the first place, they were not normally available in the findings of the Kōmei Senkyo Remmei studies. While they could have been computed on the basis of the data at hand, this did not seem necessary where converging patterns showing representative trends were typical. In other words, the additional computations seemed superfluous in the kind of research conducted here. Where this was not the case, as in the multivariate calculations of data from my own 1964 study alone, the results of significance tests are included. But this usage is mainly suggestive. Since the sample was stratified by districts, significance tests are not literally appropriate in manipulations of observations from the whole sample. This is a commonly violated limitation, however, and the results of the tests are used here in accordance with the growing tendency to ignore this problem.

2

POLITICAL INVOLVEMENT

Characterization of the quality and level of mass involvement in politics is a subject of perennial concern for both philosophers and empirical social scientists. In general, the normative theory of democracy anticipates the presence of an alert and concerned citizenry. Clearly, the precise amounts and qualities of involvement functional to the preservation of popular government have yet to be defined, although empirical research has shown that extant democratic systems have large numbers of uninvolved members. It is not yet evident whether the presence of substantial numbers of semiapathetic voters is in some way functional to maintaining a stable democratic system, or whether popular government truly requires pervasive commitments by a citizenry with vital interests at stake, regardless of the cost to stability.[1]

Nevertheless, it is not the intention of this study to evaluate what levels of psychological involvement are requisite for the functioning of democracy in postwar Japan. It is important, however, to determine empirically what kinds of involvement are present in Japan. The mere presence of some degree of authoritarian influences in recent political styles, followed by reforms designed to directly or indirectly stimulate democratic feelings make these questions worthy of investigation. Moreover, contemporary Japan is a transitional political system — because of the scope of ongoing social change — and this makes a characterization of popular involvement in the postwar era all the more essential.

---

[1] For a few citations from the voluminous literature where topics of this kind are considered, see Ch. 4, n. 19.

Much research on political involvement has taken a comparatively undifferentiated view of the character of individual attitude structures. Partly as a result of concern over the potential inaccuracy of individual items as measures of attitudes, quite a few studies have dealt with involvement as measured by scales based upon multiple question items.[2] This has seemingly contributed to the assumption in some places that political involvement is largely a unidimensional orientation, although in a few cases multidimensional models have been postulated consciously or otherwise. Despite the methodological advantage of scalar techniques, involvement attitudes are dealt with here in multidimensional terms. This is due in part simply to the nature of the evidence used, but there are other reasons that make this approach desirable. Political attitude structures are clearly not unidimensional in the Japanese case; different levels and patterns of response can be seen where attitudinal content varies. There are also significant fluctuations depending on whether local or national politics is concerned, and whether objects of attitudes are more distant or proximate to everyday concerns and direct experience. The presence of these differences, which might be submerged in indexes or scales, suggests that political culture is substantially more complex than some earlier research has indicated. Moreover, attention to these complexities of attitude structure is especially fruitful in a transitional frame of reference, and encourages speculation about the possibility of different rates of change where various kinds of attitudes are concerned.

Involvement attitudes are essentially mental states or orientations

---

[2] For an example of this practice the reader is referred to Angus Campbell, Gerald Gurin and Warren E. Miller, *The Voter Decides* (Evanston: Row, Peterson, 1954), and Angus Campbell, Philip E. Converse, Warren E. Miller and Donald E. Stokes, *The American Voter* (New York: John Wiley, 1960), p. 107. Actually, the authors in this case also looked at some items separately. But they also found a sufficiently high degree of correlation between items to facilitate use of the scalar technique in some places, and one does get the impression of a coherent syndrome of psychological involvement.

There are also examples in various places where a differentiated view of attitude structures has been taken. In a recent study indexes were used extensively to measure multiple dimensions of media attentiveness and other attitudinal clusters, and in this case the economies inherent in scale or index construction were employed to supplement a clearly multiple approach to attitude structures. See Norman H. Nie, G. Bingham Powell, Jr. and Kenneth Prewitt, "Social Structure and Political Participation: Developmental Relationships, Part I," *American Political Science Review* 63 (June 1969), pp. 375–378.

reflecting the importance of politics to the individual or the individual's relationship to politics as a general object. Included within this category are voters' feelings about the relevance of politics, their manifest knowledge of public affairs, and their self-assessments of the degree to which politics is an object of personal interest or concern. Involvement attitudes also encompass feelings about the degree to which politics is a relevant instrumental activity, or a process whereby representation of the needs and wants of individual voters, communities and groups is sought. The content or frame of reference of involvement attitudes is typically more generalized or abstract than is the case in attitude categories discussed later, and it is important that this be kept in mind. Thus, the presence of certain kinds of involvement attitudes may or may not lead to particular levels and kinds of political participation, but their distribution does indicate how people think about politics as a general object and what kinds of perceptions voters have of their own generalized relationships to public life.[3]

Political Relevance. Voters' beliefs about the relevance of politics to their ordinary lives and interests provide a direct measure of the salience of public affairs at the mass level within a particular political unit. Although feelings about political relevance may not have immediate consequences in all concrete instances of individual behavior — measures of a more personal kind of saliency such as are provided in expressions of interest in politics may prove to be more reliable predictors of participation levels — nevertheless, self-conscious feelings about the importance of politics in an abstract frame of reference are important data for the student of comparative politics. Feelings about political relevance indicate the character of popular beliefs about the degree to which politics should be taken seriously and the extent to which public affairs is seen as meaningful for ordinary persons, re-

---

[3] For a general statement about the links between involvement attitudes and participation see Robert E. Lane, *Political Life: Why People Get Involved in Politics* (Glencoe, Illinois: Free Press, 1959), pp. 143–146. A more recent empirical study on these matters, which includes data on Japan, is Sidney Verba, Kenneth Prewitt and Jae-on Kim, "The Modes of Democratic Participation: A Cross-National Comparison," in Harry Eckstein and Ted Robert Gurr (eds.), *Comparative Politics Series* 2 (Beverly Hills, California: Sage Publications), Publication no. 01-013. Jōji Watanuki has also dealt with these matters in "Social Structure and Political Participation in Japan," Report 32 from The Laboratory for Political Research, University of Iowa, May 1970. Finally, the impact on participation of some of the attitudes reported here will be shown in Ch. 8.

gardless of whether perceptions are structured in positive and constructive terms, or as negative or threatening.

The findings of several surveys show that many Japanese voters feel that politics is important in the sense we have been discussing. Between one-half and three-quarters of the electorate are of the opinion that politics is relevant, the incidence of such beliefs being in some cases greater than for other kinds of involvement attitudes (Table 2-1).

TABLE 2-1. RELEVANCE OF POLITICS

	Yes (%)	Very* (%)	Somewhat* (%)	No (%)	Don't Know (%)	Total (%)	(N)
National politics is closely related to our daily problems[a]	74	(47)	(27)	15	12	101	(354)
Local politics is closely related to our daily problems[a]	78	(46)	(32)	11	11	100	(354)
The difficulties of the people will be improved if national politics get better[b]	51	—	—	30	19	100	(433)
Our lives will obviously improve if a good Diet member is sent out[c]	66	—	—	14	20	100	(500)
The results of elections have an effect on many aspects of our lives[d]	58	(20)	(38)	35	7	100	(295)

SOURCES:
[a] Richardson 1964 post-election survey. [b] Fukuoka 1964B, p. 55. [c] Fukuoka 1961, p. 28. [d] Saga 1963, p. 21.
* Figures in parentheses are marginals for subgroups within the overall "yes" group. The statements used to identify particular attitudes here and in subsequent tables are paraphrases of the original questions. Totals are slightly more or less than 100 percent in some instances as the result of rounding.

According to the findings of one recent survey, three-quarters of the electorate believed that politics was "important to their lives," and many of these persons — nearly half of all voters — felt that politics was "very relevant" (Richardson 1964). Elsewhere, nearly 60 percent of those interviewed were of the opinion that "election outcomes directly affect our lives" (Saga 1963).

Although the literature on political culture has so far assumed that relevance has mainly positive connotations, it is important to realize that this is not necessarily true. Indeed, Japanese voters' appreciation of the importance of politics had both positive and negative connotations, as the results of other studies show.[4] Two-thirds of the voters in one region felt that their conditions would improve "if a good Diet member were elected" (Fukuoka 1961), while just over half of those interviewed at a later date in the same district felt that the difficulties of people's lives could be ameliorated through improvements in the conduct of national affairs (Fukuoka 1964B). The "way in which politics is conducted" was also cited most frequently, in a negative frame of reference, as a specific cause for difficulties experienced in people's daily lives, according to a study conducted in one of Japan's major cities (Nagoya 1959, p. 85). Similarly, 74 percent of the voters in one of Japan's western prefectures felt that price increases were attributable to the national government's "mode of conduct" (Hiroshima 1965, p. 82). Obviously, where tendencies of this kind occur, the analyst must contend with ambiguities introduced by differences in measurements. Still, the ambiguity suggested by these findings from different districts may also occur in real life.

Levels of popular appreciation in Japan of the importance of politics are probably quite high comparatively. Cross-national analysis indicates that the frequency of feeling in Japan that politics is relevant is most similar to that found in West Germany and Great Britain and greater than that found in Italy. On the other hand, slightly fewer Japanese than Americans said they found politics relevant.[5] But the incidence of attitudes that politics was "very relevant" was higher in Japan than in any of the other countries for which data were available.

A substantially abstract appreciation of the importance of politics to persons' lives does not necessarily mean, however, that political action is seen as the sole or most desirable way of resolving normal

---

[4] Almond and Verba found that relevance was generally associated with positive evaluations of governmental impact, but a different question was used. See Gabriel Almond and Sydney Verba, *The Civic Culture* (Boston: Little, Brown, 1965), p. 48.

[5] Almond and Verba, *ibid.*, pp. 46–47. Question content in my own survey items and those of Almond and Verba was sufficiently equivalent to permit comparison.

living problems. Where question alternatives offered a choice between different methods for improvement of people's "living conditions," only about one-third of the respondents to a national survey felt that their lives could best be improved by "changing politics and society." Although this option was chosen over others, one-quarter of the sampled population felt the goal in question could best be accomplished "by exerting one's own efforts," and a comparable ratio of those interviewed advocated "depending on the trends of the national economy" (Kōmei 1967, p. 137).[6]

Nevertheless, feelings that politics is relevant are still seemingly important to the maintenance of other types of political involvement attitudes. In numerous studies conducted throughout the country at different times voters replied that their interest in public affairs was the result of "the fact that politics has an effect on our lives" (Gumma 1963, p. 15; Tochigi 1963, p. 4; Ōita 1962, p. 8). While the mass public in Japan might look to activities other than politics for solutions of some kinds of problems, in many instances feelings about the salience of political matters is obviously the attitude upon which other dimensions of involvement are based.

The feeling that politics is relevant is quite common then in Japan, and the frequency of voters' appreciation of the importance of politics compares favorably with that found in other highly urban and industrial societies. But both "positive" and "negative" experiences could plausibly contribute to such "high" levels in Japan. This is shown literally in voters' replies to some questions, as we have seen, but a review of broader patterns in recent Japanese political history suggests a similar line of interpretation. Exposure to the frequently authoritarian styles of prewar and wartime politics was obviously an important socializing experience for some Japanese, and their contemporary experience is very possibly affected by such reminiscences. To a large number of older voters the effect of wartime deprivation itself may underline their feelings about the relevance of politics, while the special role of government administrators in earlier periods may

---

[6] Relevance measured in this fashion approximates the meaning of political salience — and its mode of measurement — urged by Moshe M. Czudnowski in "A Salience Dimension of Politics for the Study of Political Culture," *American Political Science Review* 62 (September 1968), pp. 882 ff.

also have been instrumental in shaping attitudes about relevance.[7] Among persons who have grown up since the war an awareness of democratic values, coupled with the effects of postwar reforms, has certainly stimulated an abstract appreciation of the value of politics. Many other voters find politics relevant because of expectations regarding the instrumentality of the political process.[8] Finally, the feelings of many Japanese voters may derive from their exposure to socialization processes in which the voting right was itself considered an obligation to exercise the franchise.[9] Obviously, political attitudes can have multiple meanings; an individual can entertain quite different or even weakly integrated perspectives at both single and various points in time. Studies conducted in the United States have shown that, although political involvement is fairly stable during election campaigns, there are important lapses between elections.[10] Moreover, other research has indicated that belief systems in the mass public are very weakly integrated. Considerable variation in attitude toward such a generally peripheral area as politics is thus highly plausible.[11]

---

[7] Although there are difficulties in expressing their effects quantitatively, the prevalence of feelings that administrative officials were harsh in dealing with ordinary people could have been a factor in the widespread feelings that politics is relevant as well as in giving "politics" a negative connotation. For a discussion of popular sentiments about officials in earlier periods see Nobutaka Ike, *Japanese Politics: An Introductory Survey* (New York: Alfred A. Knopf, 1957), p. 148.

[8] Instrumental expectations, as we shall see later, are widespread components of voting choices, and many voters see politics instrumentally in a more general frame of reference. Instrumental considerations are also seen as a frequent basis for supportive ties between local influentials and politicians and national election candidates. For comments on this phenomenon, see R. P. Dore, *Land Reform in Japan*, pp. 416–18.

[9] In open interviews with Japanese voters I found substantial evidence that people felt that it was a mark of the good citizen to take politics seriously, to be informed and participate in elections. Attitudes of this kind could readily contribute to affirmative replies about the relevance of politics in survey interviews. Of course, association of obligations of these kinds with idealized citizen roles is not uniquely Japanese, and feelings that the vote is a duty are widespread in other cultures. For references on this point see Ch. 4.

[10] Also, there are changes within the American electorate during campaigns in the form of increases and decreases among different kinds of persons, with the result that the stability may be more apparent than real. See Robert E. Lane, *Political Life*, pp. 141–143.

[11] See the supportive discussion on this point in Philip E. Converse, "The Nature of Belief Systems in Mass Publics," in Norman R. Luttbeg (ed.), *Public Opinion and Public Policy: Models of Political Linkage* (Homewood, Illinois: Dorsey, 1968), pp. 246–275.

Political Understanding and Awareness. Beliefs about the relevance of politics and political processes are only one measure of political commitment. To be considered involved in politics, individuals must manifest more than an abstract appreciation of the meaning of public affairs. Among other things, it is axiomatic that they should know something about the institutions, events and issues of politics, and feel that politics is something they can understand.

Comprehension of politics and political processes can be measured in several ways. Public opinion surveys frequently contain questions designed to identify voters' feelings about particular issues. Frequencies of "don't know" responses to questions of this kind provide one source of information about popular levels of political comprehension and awareness. Questions aimed directly at the voter's assessment of his knowledge about politics are also common. In this case voters are asked whether or not they know anything about an issue, event or institution; questions about the content of constitutions are a typical example of this kind of query. Finally, respondents may be asked to evaluate their confidence in their own comprehension of political affairs or processes. Surveys using each of these techniques are reported here.[12]

It is instructive to begin by looking at evidence on voters' confidence in their understanding of public affairs. Feelings of this kind encompass individual reactions to the very real difficulty of following political events, as well as the more subjective dimension of assessing personal abilities to understand. As such, they represent an overlap between measures of self-assessed awareness and efficacy attitudes, and tap underlying sentiments about the complexities of political life markedly different in content from typical information and awareness measures. In order to identify this dimension of popular reaction to political life, respondents to my 1964 survey were asked simply to indicate the degree to which they found national and local politics difficult to comprehend.[13] It is evident from the replies that remarkably few

---

[12] One survey which included a factual question required the interviewer to evaluate the accuracy of the answers; the results of this question are also included here.

[13] The fact that the question was expressed in the negative may have introduced some bias into responses. But the frequency of unsolicited comments to the effect that "politics is difficult" lends credence to the assumption that a general sentiment in fact is tapped by this question.

Japanese citizens feel a sense of confidence in understanding what goes on in politics and elections. Less than one-fourth of the sample felt themselves capable of readily understanding national affairs, while only a few in this group — just 3 percent of all the persons interviewed — felt that national politics was "very easy" to understand.

When these frequencies are compared with levels of feelings that politics is relevant, it can immediately be seen that only about one-third as many voters felt they could understand politics as compared to the number expressing appreciation of the general importance of politics. A discrepancy between the level of voters' feelings of relevance and their assessment of their ability to understand is observable in other nations, so this is not a phenomenon unique to Japan.[14] But the range of difference is comparatively larger in Japan, so some consideration of the possible causes of this condition is called for.

It must be remembered that Japan's postwar political system is fundamentally one of transition. The scope of institutional change after the war was itself considerable, but changes in more diffuse social and political norms are even more important here. Both a comparison of public opinion trends over time and the results of national character studies show the extent of transformation in these areas.[15] While there is little systematic knowledge about the actual process of adaptation, where the content of attitudes varies, the existence of differential rates of change is entirely plausible. The gap between feelings about the saliency of public affairs and self-evaluations of comprehension ability may be an example of differential adaptation at work. While some voters possibly feel they have a low level of cognitive competence simply because they are unfamiliar with postwar institutions and processes where national politics is concerned, it is doubtful if this alone could account for the very high incidence of feelings that politics is difficult to understand. Politics receives extensive attention in the daily media, and at least 90 percent of the electorate report some kind of exposure to political news and commentary on a regular basis

---

[14] Differences were observed in the countries studied by Almond and Verba (*The Civic Culture*, pp. 46–47). See also the marginals from the revised codebook for the five-nation study (Inter-University Consortium for Political Research), variable 0030.

[15] See, for example, findings on changes in feelings that one should leave management of public affairs to "good leaders" in Tōkei Sūri Kenkyūjo, *Kokuminsei no Kenkyū: Dai Niji Chōsa* (Tōkyō: 1959), p. 95.

(Kōmei 1962A, pp. 13–14). It is more satisfactory to infer that while many voters have become abstractly aware of contemporary affairs and norms regarding enhanced popular opportunities, their feelings about their own competence have yet to catch up with their more general appreciation of politics. Or expressed generically, some abstract appreciation of public affairs may be readily learned and accepted — perhaps even quite casually — while feelings of self-confidence depend on actual or vicariously perceived experiences and are thus developed more slowly.[16]

The credibility of this interpretation is enhanced by a look at Japanese voters' feelings about their understanding of local politics. Where only 23 percent of the electorate felt competent to understand national politics, 37 percent indicated that local affairs were easy to comprehend (Richardson 1964). Since local affairs are close at hand and therefore more familiar, at least among voters living in small cities and rural districts, it is possible for voters to adjust more rapidly to changed opportunities for political involvement in this sector than in the more distant sphere of national politics. Of course, there are other influences at work which contribute to higher frequencies of a "positive" response to local politics. It must be remembered that political changes in Japan are conditioned by factors including, among others, the very special character in some sectors of the country of the immediate social environment.

Examination of voters' self-assessment of their ability to understand politics is one way of looking at the question of political knowledge or awareness. It is also important to examine the results of surveys asking voters about factual aspects of politics or for their opinions on issues. Responses to such questions tell us something about the actual levels of voters' knowledge of politics, even though in most cases response levels still depend on self-assessment of their own knowledge levels.

---

[16] Similar forces may have been factoral in the differences observed between levels of feelings of political relevance and those of self-evaluated comprehension competence in Germany and Italy. Like Japan, both countries were governed by authoritarian political leadership within the time span of the memories of many of today's voters. (Of course, feelings of relevance may in many cases be negatively construed in all three countries.) But the differences in Japan were still greater than those elsewhere (although in Italy feelings of relevance and comprehension competence were *both* low).

More Japanese voters were able to answer direct questions about their political knowledge or opinions (Table 2-2) than felt confident in their comprehension of either national or local political affairs. Between 48 and 89 percent of the sampled groups claimed to know something about national institutions and processes, issues, or elections and election trends, in contrast with the smaller ratio of voters who felt that they really understood politics.

Perhaps this difference is attributable simply to variations in question content. The questions on knowledge and opinions were quite simple; answers required little thought or self-examination. Questions on the self-assessed difficulty of political comprehension, on the other hand, probably required a more considered reply. But it is still plausible that voters depreciate their understanding of politics because of a more general lack of confidence in politics, particularly since the potentialities for meaningful mass democratic participation have only received widespread popular emphasis for a comparatively short period of time.

It is equally important to observe that knowledge of political affairs, measured by simple factual questions, varied substantially depending upon the nature of the object of individual questions. Respondents were generally most knowledgeable about events or issues that affected them directly either because of self-interest or participation in elections.[17] Such a pattern of awareness is not necessarily unusual, but these differences do tell us something about the scope and quality of popular political involvement in Japan.

These general observations can be illustrated extensively by the evidence at hand. For one thing, Japanese voters knew more about the scheduling of elections, candidates' partisan affiliations and certain

---

[17] Here, and subsequently, I am assuming that some events or processes are of greater relevance to voters because they are personally involved (such as participation in elections), or because the events or processes pertain to certain issues which have a tangible effect on voters' lives (such as policies about income and education). This assumption is supported by concrete evidence from respondent assessments of the importance of economic and other issues related to their daily lives, in replies about "wants" from politics in my own and other surveys. Questions of constitutional revision and other issues of national and international politics, with the exception of the broad question of war and peace, meet with rather little concern. See, for example, Ibaragi 1962, pp. 44–45, and Chiba 1962, p. 280.

This assumption also conforms, albeit somewhat crudely, to the analysis of issue familiarity and intensity of issue opinion in Angus Campbell, *et al.*, *The American Voter*, pp. 171–79.

TABLE 2-2. POLITICAL AWARENESS

	Yes (%)	No* (%)	Total (%)	(N)
Formal Institutions and Processes:				
Knew all or part of Constitution[a]	78	22	100	(953)
Knew how Prime Ministers are selected[b]	71	29	100	(1,000)
Knew that Election Law revision was an issue in Diet[c]	55	45	100	(402)
Issues:				
Had opinion on income doubling policy[d]	79	22	101	(660)
Had opinion on education costs increases[e]	89	11	100	(916)
Had opinion on Constitution revision[e]	56	44	100	(916)
Election Trends:				
Knew tendencies in voter turnout in General Elections[f]	48	51	99	(2,505)
Knew that ratio of partisan candidacies in local elections was increasing[g]	49	52	101	(2,426)
Election Dates and Candidates:				
Knew that House of Councillors election was scheduled[h]	76	23	99	(4,306)
Knew that local elections were scheduled[i]	84	16	100	(2,484)
Could identify all or some candidates' party affiliations in House of Councillors election[j]	77	23	100	(660)

SOURCES:
[a] Miyazaki 1962B, p. 93. 16% felt they knew it all, and 62% felt they knew parts.
[b] Mie 1964, p. 93. 34% felt they knew this "well," and 37% felt they "knew it."
[c] Miyagi 1962, appendix p. 41. [d] Fukushima 1962, p. 179. [e] Miyazaki 1964, pp. 122 and 126.
[f] Kōmei 1964B, p. 67 (national). [g] Kōmei 1964A, p. 126 (national). [h] Kōmei 1962A, p. 14 (national).
[i] Kōmei 1967BB, p. 83 (national). [j] Fukushima 1962, p. 185. Percentages of respondents who knew different candidates' partisan affiliations were as follows:

Number of Candidates Identified	Percentage
1	20%
2	17
3	13
4	9
5	7
6	12

* "No" included "don't know," "unclear," "can't say" or "no answer." In most instances, respondents were asked to assess their own level of knowledge.

issues of general interest than other aspects of politics. Seventy-six and 84 percent of the national electorate knew that national and local elections, respectively, were scheduled in the near future (Kōmei 1962A; Kōmei 1967BB). Elsewhere, 77 percent of those interviewed in a largely rural prefecture of northern Japan could identify one or more of the candidates' party ties before a national election, and roughly two-thirds of this group were able to correctly identify the affiliations of at least half of the candidates (Fukushima 1962).[18]

Similarly, 89 percent of those interviewed in another region had opinions on the question of education cost increases, while 79 percent of a different group of respondents were able to express views on Prime Minister Ikeda's income doubling plan (Fukushima 1962; Miyazaki 1964). But only 56 percent could offer comments on the constitution revision issue — a subject that can be readily assumed to have less direct impact than issues of income or education costs (Miyazaki 1964).

A slightly smaller ratio of those interviewed on at least one occasion claimed knowledge about formal institutions and processes than said they knew about salient issues and elections; elsewhere this kind of knowledge was reported with frequencies comparable to those just reported. Seventy-eight percent felt that they knew a part or all of the postwar constitution (Miyazaki 1962B), while 71 percent saw themselves as aware of the way in which the prime minister is currently selected (Mie 1964).

Still fewer voters felt they had information about election system reform policies and other less personally immediate aspects of electoral politics.[19] Only 48 percent of the respondents in a recent national survey knew that at the time the Election System Deliberation Council was engaged in a study of possible voting reforms (Kōmei 1967BB, p. 53), and only 55 percent of those interviewed in one district were aware that election reform was then a topic in Diet debates (Miyagi 1962).[20] Similarly, only 48 percent of the electorate surveyed in one nationwide

---

[18] It is interesting to note at this point, that only in the vicinity of one-quarter of the respondents to a national sample could indicate some knowledge of the party platforms of the two major parties at the time of a General Election; see Jichi 1958, p. 20. This information is also relevant to the analysis in Ch. 5.

[19] These questions were asked because of the interest of the Fair Election League (Kōmei Senkyo Remmei) in election practices and voter knowledge thereof.

[20] Sixty-two percent of those in another prefecture were aware of the fact that the debate was going on. Saga 1963, p. 47.

study knew the trends in voter turnout in national elections (Kōmei 1964B), and a similarly small ratio of those interviewed throughout the country in the same year were knowledgeable about trends in party affiliations in local elections (Kōmei 1964A). Finally, only 29 percent of the national electorate reported knowledge of a malapportionment in the ratio between population size and number of allotted seats between urban and rural constituencies in House of Representative elections (Kōmei 1961, p. 87).[21]

Comparative analysis of levels of cognitive competence and political awareness in Japan with other countries could help identify some of the effects of Japan's special political experiences. Unfortunately, comparative research in this area is extremely difficult to carry out, because of the problem of question equivalence and the necessity of controlling some of the unique cultural factors in different systems affecting awareness. Despite such obstacles some comparative assessments will be made, though the results are necessarily tentative.

Comparison of Japanese, American and Western European voters' feelings about their ability to understand politics indicates some important cross-national variations. Clearly, fewer Japanese believe themselves competent than is the case elsewhere. Between 28 and 41 percent in different years of American voters *disagreed* with the proposition that "politics and government seem so complicated that a person like me can't really understand what's going on," in contrast with the 23 percent of Japanese citizens who felt that national politics was not difficult to comprehend.[22] Moreover, nearly half of the persons interviewed in the United States and Great Britain in the Almond and Verba five-nation study felt they understood national politics, with even more persons manifesting competence of this kind in Germany.[23] Only in Italy could a frequency approximating the Japanese levels be seen.

---

[21] A similar proportion of another national sample, 27 percent, knew about this problem, but in Tōkyō 43 percent of those interviewed were informed about the malapportionment question. Kōmei 1964B, p. 9, and Tōkyō 1965, p. 19.

[22] American data is from John P. Robinson, Jerrold G. Rusk and Kendra B. Head, *Measures of Political Attitudes* (Ann Arbor: Institute for Social Research, 1968), p. 635. Even though the question formats were different, the cross-national differences are sufficiently great to warrant emphasis here.

[23] Comparative figures were calculated from the five-nation study codebook. The findings on Germany in this study are supported by more recent results from DIVO surveys. See *Polls* (summer 1965), p. 25.

If comparisons do not suffer too severely from slight differences in question content, then fewer Japanese feel that they can really understand politics than do voters in some other highly urban and industrial countries. Since there is a very high level of attention to politics in the Japanese media, possible cross-national variations in mass communication exposure must be discounted as a factor of importance. Media content, on the other hand, may be a critical influence. Accounts of national affairs in the Japanese media tend to stress the seemingly inexhaustible maneuverings of factions within the major party groupings, along with rather formal accounts of position-taking and decision-making. Although this aspect of politics is not a contrivance of the media, the average person can hardly avoid a sense of dismay when confronted by the intricacy of politics at this level.[24] Perhaps his responses to this phenomenon are even more acute than would be our own, given the characteristically Japanese appreciation of the importance of contacts and "connections."

But differences in the length of exposure to democratic norms and institutions — especially at the popular level discussed earlier — may also be relevant at this point, albeit in a slightly different focus. Although both Japanese and Germans have experienced recent discontinuities in political style, the German political tradition has a somewhat deeper experience with democratic thought and practices than is the case in Japan. It goes without saying that the British and American experience with democratic ideas and processes is longer than is the case in Japan, however pessimistic we may be about the realities of democracy in Western experience.

The character of social structure and related sentiments could also be relevant here. Japan and Italy, where feelings of cognitive competence are comparatively low, have highly parochial societies.[25] Although community structure varies substantially between these two

---

[24] Of course, comprehension confidence in the United States may be affected by the proliferation of decision-making centers produced by federalism and a comparatively meaningful separation of powers.

[25] For comments on localism and rural social structure and norms in Italy see Joseph LaPalombara, "Italy: Fragmentation, Isolation and Alienation," in Lucian W. Pye and Sidney Verba (eds.), *Political Culture and Political Development* (Princeton: Princeton University Press, 1969), pp. 282–329, and Edward Banfield, *The Moral Basis of a Backward Society* (Glencoe: Free Press, 1958). Rural communities in Italy may vary substantially, however, from the Banfield conception. See Robert C. Fried, "Urbanization and Italian Politics," *Journal of Politics* 29 (August 1967), p. 512.

countries, localism is a prominent aspect of popular sentiments and public life in both systems. This might have some bearing on popular feelings about more remote political affairs.

Still, however relevant it may seem at first glance, localism does not necessarily preclude following or understanding national affairs. Moreover, compared to Great Britain, the Federal Republic of Germany and the United States, respondents in Japan and Italy were relatively as deficient in their confidence to understand local affairs as they were in regard to national politics. This being the case, localism must remain ambiguous for the present as a factor influencing cross-national patterns in popular confidence to understand national affairs.

By contrast, Japanese voters appear to be as well informed as their American counterparts about formal political institutions, recurring political processes and important issues.[26] It would appear, then, that postwar political reforms in Japan, as well as changes in social structure and levels of affluence, have been accompanied by comparatively high rates of diffusion of political knowledge.[27] This

---

[26] Comparisons were made between responses to questions about knowledge of the respective constitutions, knowledge about election practices and terms of office, knowledge of impending elections, knowledge about candidate identities and party labels and, finally, knowledge (or expression of opinions) on general belief items about approved or disapproved governmental roles and general postures toward broadly defined policy areas.

For Japan, in addition to the information in Table 2-2, sources included Miyazaki 1962B, the annual summaries of public opinion poll findings of the Information Office, Secretariat to the Prime Minister (Naikaku Sōridaijin Kanbō Kōhōshitsu), 1955–61, and Allan B. Cole and Naomichi Nakanishi, *Japanese Opinion Polls with Socio-Political Significance 1947–57* (Medford, Massachusetts: Fletcher School of Law and Diplomacy, Tufts University, and Williamstown, Massachusetts, Roper Opinion Poll Research Center, Williams College, n.d.).

For the United States, findings were examined from Hadley Cantril and Mildred Strunk, *Public Opinion, 1936–45* (Princeton: Princeton University Press, 1951) and John P. Robinson, et al., *Measures of Political Attitudes*, especially pp. 519–33 and 622–23.

The analysis was limited to questions of domestic politics, policies and events. I sought to identify representative patterns in both countries, but this was made difficult by the complexities of issue histories in both cases. Furthermore, the fact that there were no cases where identical questions could be compared remains a major drawback to analysis of this kind. These considerations were instrumental in the restriction of this analysis to a comparison of only American and Japanese voter information levels.

[27] But, high levels of knowledge of formal institutions, and perhaps even of some issues, may have been present in the "subject" oriented political culture of prewar Japan. This possibility cannot be ruled out, even though most accounts stress the prevalence of political apathy, particularly among residents of the sizable rural sector.

might encourage a sanguine attitude in the student of Japanese political affairs, even if he laments the number of uninformed voters as sizable in Japan as elsewhere.[28]

Nevertheless, some differences between the Japanese and American electorates should not be overlooked. Although Japanese citizens seem to be as well informed as Americans about political processes and institutions, and probably some kinds of issues as well, they are still less knowledgeable in the more general area of beliefs about governmental roles.[29] This does not necessarily represent some "deficiency" measured against the abstract requirements of democratic theory — the cues and stimuli for the formation of such beliefs are probably less common in political communication in Japan — but it does serve to highlight important differences in the attitudes of Japanese towards politics when these attitudes are compared with those of voters in at least the American political system.[30]

These tendencies in patterns of political information are part of a more general tendency among Japanese voters toward both formalism and pragmatism in their overall attitudes toward politics. Japanese voters are formalistic in at least two senses. Voters not only know less about general political beliefs than they do about formal processes and institutions, but in many cases they also combine a high level of abstract appreciation of politics with a markedly lower inclination to actively participate in politics. In other words, many voters — and this

---

[28] For a statement of idealized democratic requirements and relevant levels of awareness among the American electorate, the reader is referred to Bernard Berelson, "Democratic Theory and Public Opinion," *Public Opinion Quarterly* 16 (fall 1952), pp. 313–30. See also the discussion of the American electorate's issue awareness and ideological structure in Angus Campbell, *et al.*, *The American Voter*, Ch. 10.

[29] I see no reason to believe that this reflects a disinclination to express views, especially in light of my impression that many Japanese are sensitive to the responsibility for being informed.

[30] The importance of cross-national variations in communications is often overlooked. Conservative candidates for office in Japan were especially noncommunicative about issue positions, according to a study by Dore in the mid-1950s. Basic conservative party programs have contained commitments to ideas about general policies and the proper role of government, but these have not been really widely communicated. It is probably safe to say that few public cues about general governmental roles have been given by the majority conservative grouping(s) in postwar Japanese politics, comparable to those associated with the major political parties in the United States. For the leftist parties in Japan the story is quite different and ideologies are clearly articulated; but these groups or their candidates have only influenced a minority of voters so far. See Ronald P. Dore, "Japanese Election Candidates in 1955," *Pacific Affairs* 29 (June 1956), p. 180.

is especially true for some urban dwellers — are informed about "textbook" or issue aspects of politics, and report concern about political affairs, while at the same time they are comparatively disinclined to undertake any kind of political action outside of voting.[31]

Trends of this kind might be expected among electorates in political systems such as Japan, where an earlier authoritarian style probably plays some residual role in attitude formation. They may also be a correlative of especially high levels of self-consciousness about an ideal citizen role defined largely in terms of "subject" content. As will be observed later, there are various grounds for believing that many Japanese voters can be characterized in just this way. Finally, formalistic political awareness among some people may be a consequence of campaign styles which themselves reflect the influence of earlier political-cultural traits. Even though there are high levels of ideological content in leftist party positions, conservative candidate appeals appear to be largely devoid of consistent policy content.[32]

Paralleling these tendencies toward formalism are equally important inclinations toward pragmatism or instrumentalism in political attitudes. Japanese take a strong interest in what politics can do for them, their community or their occupation. Many Japanese are able to answer direct questions regarding their political demands,

---

[31] A gap between the levels of "abstract" political commitment (or concern) and an inclination toward active participation in politics does exist elsewhere. Interestingly, however, differences comparable to those in Japan are found only in the Federal Republic of Germany and Italy, among the industrialized nations studied by Almond and Verba. See *The Civic Culture*, pp. 46–47 and 129.

[32] In other words, the seeming conservative indifference to a need for more concrete programmatic appeals could reflect an authoritarian lack of concern for this kind of "popular" activity. But if we were to leave things at this level of understanding, we would be doing an injustice to the subject.

In the first place, it would appear that many conservative candidates "campaign" on the basis of appeals to essentially local interests, regardless of whether these campaigns are conducted openly or, as appears to be especially common, by private contacts with local influentials and politicians. And it would appear that this kind of support seeking is quite effective.

Secondly, it is important to appreciate the fact that conservative leaders have been and are active in the formulation of policy and do take stands on issues of importance to various groups or the electorate in general, even though they may not always campaign on the basis of programmatic appeals.

Finally, the relative lack of a communicated conservative program holds more for the 1950s than for the early 1960s, when income doubling received unprecedented emphasis in public statements. But a conservative "ideology" would seem comparatively lacking, except in very diffuse terms.

and the desire for representation of interests plays a substantial role in voting choices.[33] The fact that more voters are knowledgeable on issues directly affecting their interests, at the same time lacking opinions on more general belief questions, is a corollary of this more general tendency toward pragmatism. Whatever the standards of "democratic" behavior may be — and these may not be the same in different political systems — it is important to observe that a large part of the Japanese electorate is informed on those matters which most directly affect their self-interests.

Interest in Politics. It would seem axiomatic that interest in political affairs be treated as a central dimension of political involvement, whether of individuals or the aggregate citizenry of a particular country. However, when we say that voters are interested in politics we are in effect saying something rather different from reporting that they see politics as salient or that they are knowledgeable about what goes on in politics. Notwithstanding the importance of other dimensions of involvement, interest in politics may be the quotient that turns a passive observer of political affairs into an active participant, and it may be the factor that is crucial to the development of truly popular politics.[34]

However, it is essential to recognize that there may be different kinds of political interest and that variation in the content of people's concern for politics is potentially important to individual behavior as well as to the political styles of a particular system. Interest might consist simply of fervent response to the public appeals of a demagogue or dictator. Or it might imply an alert concern for the opportunities inherent in popular politics for the representation of individual or group interests. Recognition that the content of interest may vary inevitably leads to a concern for the meaning of popular involvement in Japanese politics. The extent to which postwar changes in the political climate of Japan have stimulated widespread citizen interest in

---

[33] See the discussions in this and following chapters for a fuller elaboration of this point.

[34] In other words, "subject" motivated appreciation of politics and knowledge about political affairs could certainly prevail without substantial popular interest and participation. Moreover, empirical research has repeatedly shown the importance of interest in motivating participation. Its importance in the Japanese case will be shown in Ch. 8.

TABLE 2-3. INTEREST IN POLITICS AND ELECTIONS

	Yes (%)	Strong* (%)	Some* (%)	No (%)	Don't Know (%)	Total (%)	(N)
General Political Interest:							
Interested in politics[a]	53	(8)	(45)	47	—	100	(20,000)
Daily interest in politics[b]	60	(18)	(42)	38	2	100	(206)
Same question[c]	64	(23)	(41)	34	3	101	(389)
Same question[d]	69	(25)	(44)	30	2	101	(—)
Same question[e]	52	(17)	(35)	45	3	100	(517)
Thinking seriously about national affairs[f]	50	(12)	(38)	31	18	99	(541)
Interested in national politics[g]	67	(19)	(48)	33		100	(354)
Interested in local politics[g]	67	(21)	(46)	33		100	(354)
Interest in Elections:							
Interest in elections[b]	71	(32)	(39)	29		100	(206)
Same question[c]	80	(39)	(41)	18	2	100	(389)
Interest in elections and politics[h]	75	—	—	16	9	100	(280)
Concern about national election outcome[g]	71	(30)	(41)	28	1	100	(354)
Concern about local election outcome[g]	66	(29)	(37)	32	2	100	(354)
Thinking about and comparing the candidates in the coming election[i]	17	—	—	77	7	101	(402)
Interest in Specialized Aspects of Politics:							
Interest in political articles in press[j]	29	—	—	71	—	100	(—)
Same question[k]	28	—	—	58	14	100	(459)
Interest in Diet debates[k]	18	—	—	82	—	100	(459)

SOURCES:

[a] *Nihon no Seijiteki Mukanshin* (Tōkyō, 1961), p. 35.
[b] Kōmei 1966/1, pp. 83 and 85.   [c] Kōmei 1966/4, pp. 51 and 57.
[d] Kōmei 1966/2, p. 65.   [e] Kumamoto 1960, p. 23.   [f] Iwate 1963, appendix p. 4.
[g] Richardson 1964 post-election survey.   [h] Saga 1964, p. 1.
[i] Miyagi 1962, appendix p. 35.   [j] Tokushima 1962, p. 105.
[k] Tokushima 1958, pp. 52 and 68.
* Figures in parentheses are for subgroups within the "yes" category.

public affairs is obviously important to note, but defining Japanese voters' political concerns is equally significant.

Looking first at the question of levels of political concern, we can see that somewhere between one-half and two-thirds of the Japanese public report that they are interested in politics or concerned about public affairs (Table 2-3). Because of the variation in levels of self-assessed interest among respondents in different surveys, it is impossible to say what figure is most representative of tendencies for all Japanese voters during this period. Some of the differences undoubtedly resulted from location. Where subsamples were drawn from large cities, somewhat higher frequencies of political interest were reported, in contrast with those conducted largely in rural areas or small cities.[35] Subcultural differences may have played a part in some cases as well.[36]

But it is also plausible to infer from the data that interest in politics increased during this period. When the findings from studies conducted in 1964–66 are compared with those conducted in 1960–63, a clear increase is noted. Two political events of major importance in Japan's postwar political history occurred during this period: the struggle over the United States-Japan Security Treaty ratification and the Liberal Democratic Party's widespread commitment to an income doubling economic program. In this same period there was a substantial rise in popular incomes.[37] It is entirely plausible to believe

---

[35] For evidence in greater detail on this kind of variation, see my "Political Behavior and Attitudes in Contemporary Japan," unpublished Ph.D. dissertation, University of California, Berkeley, 1966, p. 12. The results of seven surveys in different kinds of places are shown, and important differences are noted between isolated mountain communities and hamlets in lowland areas, as well as between cities and rural districts.

[36] This appears to be the case for largely rural Fukushima prefecture, where political interest is consistently much higher than in neighboring prefectures, including comparatively more urbanized Miyagi. See Kōmei 1966 (4), p. 6. Because of this tendency in Fukushima, which apparently reflects local political history, Fukushima findings were omitted from this table. Comparable, albeit less conspicuous, "subcultural" patterns undoubtedly exist elsewhere.

[37] There is some direct evidence that voters in at least one district saw themselves as more interested than usual in the political events of 1960, and this kind of reaction could have had some effect on overall patterns in later years. Thus, 76 percent of the persons interviewed in the autumn of 1960 felt that they had been "very" or "somewhat interested" in the political events of the preceding year, in contrast with the substantially lower 52 percent who reported that they were "ordinarily interested" in politics. See Kumamoto 1960, pp. 22 and 44.

Income doubling commitments as a *political* object could have stimulated increased popular interest in politics, or the effect of prosperity by itself could have

that these events or the prosperity of the period resulted in an increase between 1960–1966 in the public concern for politics.

Although overall interest in politics may be on the increase in Japan, this is not to say that "strong interest" in public affairs is characteristic of the Japanese electorate. In all of the cases examined the ratio of those respondents answering that they were "somewhat interested" in politics was greater than those who said they were "very interested" (the latter varying between 8 and 25 percent of the electorate, see Table 2-3). Weak interest and apathy still characterize the attitude of the majority of voters in Japan.[38]

So far we have discussed only undifferentiated political interest. Closer scrutiny shows that levels of interest in politics among voters vary in accordance with the question. For example, more voters were customarily interested in elections, or were specifically concerned about election outcomes, than found politics in general interesting (Table 2-3).[39] "Strong interest" or concern was also a more common response regarding elections than to politics in general.

This could be attributed simply to the fact that ordinary citizens are more directly involved in going out to vote than they are in the distant events of "politics." But it is also plausible that party or candi-

---

had this kind of impact. Average monthly cash earnings of employees nearly doubled between 1960 and 1966, although some of this increase was meaningless due to inflation. See Sōrifu Tōkeikyoku, *Nihon Tōkei Nenkan 1967*, p. 390. Unfortunately I see no practical way of pursuing this interpretation at present. There is little point in analyzing national election turnouts and relating these to trends in popular incomes in this period, for the simple reason that there was no systematic increase in voting participation in the same period. Survey findings, whose use would obviate the ecological fallacy problem, are limited in different ways, mainly by the general absence of information on income levels.

If we look further back in time in Japan, the tendencies over time are even less clear. Earlier studies utilizing nationwide samples reported levels of popular political interest ranging between 50 and 70 percent. However, it must be emphasized that question content was different from that in the studies reported above. Earlier queries focused generally on interest in *specific* elections, which could have resulted in higher proportions of "yes" answers. See Allan B. Cole and Naomichi Nakanishi, *Japanese Opinion Polls*, pp. 390, 396, 400, 413 and 420.

[38] Nevertheless, proportions of "strong" interest in politics and elections also increased between the earlier and later periods.

[39] Similar tendencies can be seen outside Japan. More American voters were interested in the 1960 and 1964 elections than reported that they followed politics customarily, according to the SRC findings. See John P. Robinson, *et al.*, *Measures of Political Attitudes*, pp. 624–25. See also Robert E. Lane, *Political Life*, p. 141.

date loyalties motivated some voters to claim stronger concern for elections than for general public affairs.

Popular concern for politics can be further differentiated: a comparatively smaller ratio reported interest in *specific* aspects of political processes than indicated concern for elections or politics in general. Less than 20 percent of the respondents in one prefecture said they were "thinking about the candidates" in a forthcoming national election (Miyagi 1962). And few voters — less than 30 percent of those interviewed — claimed interest in newspaper reports about politics, according to two studies conducted in one largely rural prefecture (Tokushima 1958 and 1962).[40] Interest in debates in the Diet was even less common, with only 18 percent of the public indicating concern for these matters (Tokushima 1958).[41]

Reasons for the differential between interest in general aspects of politics and interest in elections are easy to suggest. Explanations of the sizable differential between general interest levels, on the one hand, and concern for both the activities of the Diet and news coverage of political affairs on the other, are less readily apparent. One may well ask what aspects of politics are of concern to Japanese voters if not the daily activities of national officials or the parliament. In order to find some answer to this question, it is necessary to look at the reasons Japanese voters give for their interest in politics, or the things which they feel are the objects of their concerns.

Before doing this, it is instructive to review some kinds of responses to politics that might be subsumed under the general rubric of "interest." [42] Some voters, for example, might best be characterized

---

[40] Even though one of the districts examined was in a small provincial city, it is safe to anticipate somewhat higher levels of interest in these matters among large city residents.

[41] This study was conducted prior to the dramatic confrontations over the Police Duties Bill in 1958 and the Mutual Security Treaty in 1960.

[42] These categories are inspired in part by the Japanese findings and also by the discussion of party identification and political involvement in Campbell, *et al., The American Voter*, pp. 142–145. Attention to somewhat analogous conceptual problems, where behavior as well as attitudes are concerned, can be found in various writings by Verba, Almond and Milbrath; the reader is referred to the works by these authors cited earlier.

It is important that the reader appreciate that throughout this discussion we are speaking of "ideal" types, where in reality the incidence of overlap and admixture is extensive.

as *spectators* where politics are concerned. These are persons whose interest in political affairs consists largely of observation of political processes and elections. This may result from an enthusiasm for the human element in politics, whereby no small satisfaction can be gained from observing the comings and goings, personal lives and idiosyncracies of leading political figures. Others, who find the game of politics exciting, may be primarily concerned with the day to day activity of legislative bodies or cabinets. Thus, spectator interest in public affairs is characterized by a posture of observation of the events or personalities of politics.

For other voters, loyalties to particular individuals or groups may be the primary motivation for political interest. These may be candidates or parties, but ties to communities or private associations which are concerned with politics may be sufficiently strong to activate interest in the individual. A voter whose interest is motivated by such bonds might be termed a *loyalist*.

A quite different kind of interest in politics characterizes the *instrumentalist*.[43] Here concern is motivated by a preoccupation with what politicians and officials can do for one, or for some group or community. Or an instrumentalist might be primarily interested in the defense of his interests against official action or lawmakers.

Interest in politics may take other forms. It was suggested earlier that interest could result from exposure to strong leadership or from an abstract appreciation of norms of citizenship. In this case voters might be expected to claim concern for political affairs simply because they perceive that it is expected of them. Motivations of this kind could underlie spectator interest in politics. Of course, combinations of different kinds of interest is completely plausible. Nevertheless, it is desirable to know what kinds of interest best characterize the attitudes of the Japanese voter. Knowledge of this kind should help clarify the circumstances underlying greatly varied levels of interest in different

---

[43] Loyalist partisan (or group) attachments may have instrumental origins, or they may be influenced indirectly by regional, class or other group preferences that antedate the loyalist's life span. Loyalist attachments that either conform to or are contrary to instrumentalist considerations may also exist. Where strong attachments to a particular group or party are paralleled by strong instrumentalist feelings of a "rational" kind, problems of conceptual overlap do occur.

For some comments on the preconditions of instrumentalist concern, see Robert E. Lane, *Political Life*, pp. 169–75.

situations, and also provide some clues about the overall characteristics of political involvement in Japan.

Two types of evidence are available concerning the content or focus of Japanese voters' interest in public affairs. Surveys have often posed closed questions with prescribed alternatives about the reasons for or sources of the respondents' interest. In addition, my 1964 study probed respondents with an open question about the objects and focus of their interests. Although the response patterns to these two kinds of questions are not strictly comparable, the data are roughly complementary and indicate some common central tendencies.

Where alternatives were prescribed, most voters emphasized the "relevance of politics" to their lives as a reason for maintaining interest in public affairs. On separate occasions over two-thirds of the electorate attributed their interest to the relevance of politics (Kumamoto 1960, p. 27; Kumamoto 1962, p. 2). At the same time, between 12 and 15 percent of the same groups felt that "politics changes one's environment," while only five percent felt that "politicians' character and work are interesting"; between two and three percent found "politicians' maneuvers and factional struggles entertaining." Elsewhere, in a study in a city on the fringe of metropolitan Tōkyō over half of those interviewed replied in a similar vein, saying they were interested in elections because of their relationship with one's life," while an additional 36 percent were of the opinion only that "elections are an important and necessary part of politics" (Chiba 1963, p. 19). While such replies are limited by the character of the questions used, nevertheless they allow us partial understanding of the nature of Japanese voters' feelings on this subject.

On the basis of these findings alone, it can be inferred that two kinds of voter interest in politics prevail in Japan. Although the alternatives were restrictive as well as quite formal, instrumentalist orientations can be inferred from the heavy emphasis in all three studies on the fact that "politics is related to one's lives." But the frequency of concern for elections only as "an important and necessary aspect of politics" suggests that, for a significant number of Japanese, feelings of interest in elections or politics may stem from learned attitudes about citizenship. The "relevance of politics" may, in fact, have similar connotations. Spectator and loyalist interest would appear to be rather rare, given the lack of concern for "politicians' character and work" or "politicians' maneuvers and factional struggles," although survey response alternatives clearly limit any inferences about loyalist interest.

These themes were borne out to no small degree by tendencies in the replies to my own queries about the focus of voter interest in politics. Instrumentalism was particularly emphasized there, especially when the question focused on sources of interest in local affairs. Thirty-three percent of the respondents felt that, where national politics was concerned, their interests lay in issues directly related to their self-interest, but a substantially higher ratio of 55 percent emphasized concerns of this kind in the local political arena. Included among objects of interest were occupational problems, commodity price issues, questions related to welfare, housing and educational problems, concern for the pace of local development and the adequacy of local public services.

In addition to these explicit references to self-interest, one-quarter of the voters were also interested in general domestic issues at the national level — the state of economic programs, defense problems and even the issue of constitutional revision — or in foreign policy questions. The presence of both instrumentalist and spectator orientations could be inferred here, although from the tone of individual replies the former would appear to be most prevalent. Finally, only 11 percent were interested in political processes devoid of issue or self-interest content, such as "politics in general," political parties, elections and Diet debates. Although direct questions probably do not capture the full range of voter concerns about politics, it is clear that an instrumentalist interest is greater than spectator interest, while in most cases loyalist feelings are not clearly visible except where a concern for local development reflects ties to hamlet, neighborhood or some larger community.[44]

These patterns in the content of political interest could be linked with some of the attitudinal patterns discussed earlier. The comparatively low frequency of voter interest in Diet debates and news accounts of politics reported earlier, as well as some deficiencies in knowledge about the events of national political processes, are plausible

---

[44] But individual or family interests could underly a concern for local development, unless plans for luring industries and building industrial parks and roads threatened individual landholdings. For development could also mean more jobs and prospects for increased income.

correlatives of the low incidence of observed spectator concern regarding politics. The day-to-day activities of public officials and the struggles between powerful figures and factions seem to attract little enthusiasm from the average Japanese. To some degree this is the result of the presence of a widespread pessimism and distrust regarding the behavior and responsibility of politicians, about which more will be said in the following chapter. Negative evaluations of politicians and politics are in fact the norm in Japan, a fact which is apparently related to a sensitivity to the gap between the conduct of politics and desirable levels of honesty, as well as to a distaste for the open competition characteristic particularly of national and partisan politics.[45]

These tendencies in voter interest content do not on the surface, however, explain the discrepancy between the greater frequency of concern for elections and levels of interest in politics in general. But perhaps the low level of spectator interest provides some clue to this difference too, particularly when we associate this fact with a great deal of pessimism about politics and politicians. Many instrumentally and pragmatically oriented voters may see elections as a more controllable dimension of political affairs, especially since they frequently involve contacts with known politicians or local influentials who are more trusted than the more remote national political leaders and party factions. And for some, elections may be seen as the place where instrumental interests focus most clearly. But, as we observed before, loyalties to candidates and parties may also at times contribute to the higher levels of interest in elections, even though such motivations were not generally detectable in survey responses.[46]

Even though many voters are clearly still apathetic or weakly con-

---

[45] The often-mentioned idea that the Japanese distrust the motivations of parties, and feel uncomfortable about open political competition between political parties, was borne out in my interviews. Enough respondents and informants showed a concern for "balance" and harmony in interparty relationships to attract my attention to the prevalence of this theme. In fact, concern for "balance" would appear to underly some voter support for the leftist minority parties.

[46] Among other things, these loyalties may be of a second order when compared with more pragmatic concerns, or they may be felt less consciously. Or, perhaps, they are not seen as an appropriate matter for open discussion.

Party support or identification is in fact, a correlative of interest in political affairs in Japan, and the impact is comparable in scale to that among American voters. See Fukushima 1963, p. 133 and Campbell, et al., *The American Voter*, p. 144.

cerned about politics, the expansion of political opportunities in postwar Japan has been accompanied by a substantial increase in the incidence of feelings of interest in public affairs among the electorate, and this interest focuses more on instrumental or pragmatic concerns than on the activities of politicians or legislatures. Cross-national comparison, moreover, shows that levels of citizen interest in politics in contemporary Japan compare favorably with levels in other industrial democracies. The incidence of self-assessed interest among voters in Japan in the mid-1960s was similar to or only slightly less than that of Americans in the same period in regard to both general political affairs and elections.[47] Levels were also a little higher than was the case in the Federal Republic of Germany during the same period, and substantially higher than in Great Britain in the early 1950s.[48]

But one important difference could be observed, at least between the American and Japanese patterns. More Americans were highly interested in "politics" than were Japanese, even while ratios of "strong" and "ordinary interest" in elections were about the same in both countries. Thus, although postwar democracy seems to have had a salutary effect on the Japanese electorate, where some dimensions of interest are concerned, "strong interest" in public affairs would appear to lag slightly behind certain other countries. Such discontinuities are not surprising in an essentially transitional political situation. Although we will report more on this general theme later, this lag should not be allowed to overshadow the importance of apparent successes.

Japanese voter interest in politics would appear to differ from that of citizens elsewhere in at least one additional respect. Respondents to surveys on political attitudes in Japan have been asked on many occasions whether their primary interest was in national or local politics. Self-assessments of levels of interest in specific elections at the local, prefectural and national level have also been included in certain surveys, such that the results can be compared. The results of these investigations reveal a stable tendency toward interest in local affairs

---

[47] John P. Robinson, et al., Measures of Political Attitudes, pp. 624–25.
[48] See Polls 3 (autumn 1967), p. 22, and Mark Benny, A. P. Gray and R. H. Pear, How People Vote: A Study of Electoral Behavior in Greenwich (London: Routledge and Kegan Paul, 1965), p. 125. There are always problems in comparisons of this kind, some of which are noted in our discussion. But that should not lead us to ignore the obvious point, namely that the Japanese patterns are not dissimilar to those observed elsewhere.

and elections at the expense of national politics.[49] In a nationwide survey conducted after the 1967 local and prefectural elections, 53 percent of those interviewed in Japan indicated that their interest was primarily in local contests while only 15 percent said that national elections were of greater concern (Kōmei 1967A, p. 2). In another survey, 60 percent of the electorate found city, town and village elections to be of greatest interest, 25 percent favored House of Representatives elections, nine percent were interested in prefectural contests, and only two percent thought the House of Councillors elections were primary to their concerns (Kōmei 1964A, p. 39).[50] Although there has been no research employing precisely comparable questions elsewhere, these trends contrast markedly with what are asserted to be the interest patterns in the American electorate.[51]

This localism in Japanese voter concern for politics stems from the features of community structure and certain tendencies in interpersonal relationships peculiar to important sectors of Japanese society. Although social patterns are undergoing rapid change in Japan, it is clear that a sizable proportion of the electorate still lives in situations where community relationships are intimate, where community inter-

---

[49] With but one exception, this was the tendency in all of the findings of this type I have seen. The exception, where national politics was seen as holding more interest, was reported from an Asahi newspaper poll of 1955 in Allan B. Cole and Naomichi Nakanishi, *Japanese Opinion Polls*, p. 415.

In the two cases where respondents were asked *separate* questions about their interest in national and local politics respectively, the results were congruent with the findings of the preferential questions in one case and different in another. Thus, 84 percent of the electorate said they were interested in local politics in contrast with 78 percent who were concerned about national affairs, according to Fukushima 1963, p. 133. But the respondents to my own 1964 survey were as interested in national politics as they were in local affairs. These differences reflected more than anything else the fact that my own study was conducted in a large city and a nearby rural area for the most part, whereas the Fukushima investigation concentrated on more rural districts.

[50] Interest in House of Councillors elections is consistently very low, where answers to preferential questions are the source of evidence. Perhaps this reflects the electorate's appreciation of the constitutional superiority of the House of Representatives, but the fact that the lower house receives a larger share of media attention may also be relevant. Lower house elections are also "closer" to the electorate in the sense that districts are smaller and support is more often mobilized through intensive connections between candidates and local influentials. House of Councillors candidates depend comparatively more on endorsements by secondary groups. See Bradley Richardson, "A Japanese House of Councillors Election: Support Mobilization and Political Recruitment," *Modern Asian Studies* 1 (fall 1967), pp. 390–91.

[51] See Robert E. Lane, *Political Life*, p. 137.

action is at a very high level and where group memberships are concentrated more or less within community boundaries. This is obviously more true for residents of rural districts than it is for city dwellers, but these characterizations are valid in a qualified sense for many residents of neighborhoods in provincial cities and some large city dwellers as well.[52] The social world of the small community is indeed the most relevant one for a substantial sector of the Japanese population even today.[53]

Within the contours of these intimate and highly organized little communities or neighborhoods, Japanese citizens are personally familiar with local influentials and sometimes with politicians themselves. On the other hand, they tend to be less intimately familiar with politicians at the national level, although there are local variations here depending on whether or not a "native son" Diet member lives in the area or maintains close contacts with his constituency through local influentials or personal visits.[54] At the same time, individual

---

[52] As is well known to students of Japanese politics and society, most people in the rural districts live in hamlets — small clusters of residences, generally isolated by fields and forests from other similar communities. Their social structure, and the intimacy and redundant nature of personal relationships have been discussed extensively in both Japanese and English studies. The most comprehensive study in English is Beardsley, *et al.*, *Village Japan*, but R. P. Dore adds extensively to our sophistication in *Land Reform in Japan* (London, New York and Toronto: Oxford University Press, 1959), particularly in Chs. 13–15.

Neighborhoods in provincial cities and in the older sections of large cities have more differentiated patterns of social structure and less redundancy of personal relationships. But community sentiments of a diluted rural nature still existed among long-time residents in the parts of Yokohama's *shitamachi* I studied in 1964–65, and in former Atsugi Town. However, population movements are rapidly changing the character of the old districts.

[53] Since in recent years the size and relative importance of the rural sector has been shrinking because of emigration to the cities, rural residence alone can hardly account for the patterns in local-national preferences reported here. The attitudes of the sizable portion of the population living in small provincial cities and old urban neighborhoods as well as, possibly, some residual effects of earlier population patterns must be factors. Moreover, even in the newer suburban sectors of large cities there are pockets of small tradesmen and landowners whose primary commitments presumably lie in local politics. See Bakuji Ari, *Daitoshi ni okeru Chiiki Seiji no Kōzō* (Tōkyō: Tōsei Chōsakai, 1960), p. 27.

[54] Thus, residents of Atsugi, the home town of a member of the national Diet, said they "liked" the candidate of their choice — in this case the incumbent native son — more often than did residents of Nita. In Nita, the Diet representative was from another district and had spent his life in the higher levels of the civil service, with the consequence that fewer people knew him or his reputation personally or intimately. In contrast, Atsugi residents enjoyed telling stories of their own personal contact with the Diet member, and were obviously flattered to be included among his local circle of acquaintances.

Japanese also depend to a marked degree on personal relationships to get ahead or to arrange their personal and business affairs, and probably more commonly than is the case in some Western societies.[55] A corollary of this dependence on personal ties is a tendency to feel less comfortable and less familiar in situations without intimate connections. These characteristics are reflected in political attitudes at several points. We shall see later, for example, that voters feel less effective and more pessimistic about national affairs than local politics. Here it will suffice to observe that interest in local affairs at the expense of national politics is part of a broader set of more intense and "positive" responses to local affairs, whose origins in part lie in the very impersonality of national affairs for many of the electorate.

Instrumental Attitudes. Earlier we discovered that many people in Japan were typically more concerned about issues and problems relating to their own self-interest than about other aspects of politics. Instrumental attitudes, or feelings that something is wanted from politics, have been directly investigated in several Japanese surveys. It is useful to look at the results of these studies, even though it is impossible to compare this specific dimension of Japanese voter sentiments with those of citizens of other countries.

Evidence from studies in which questions about instrumental interest were asked indicates in most cases that a majority of Japanese voters is aware of the potential for representation in democratic government. On different occasions up to 90 percent of the respondents reported they were consciously aware of wanting something done for them at the national or local political level (Table 2-4). There were sizable variations in the findings of different studies, however, which reflect differences in question formation — more people replied that they had pragmatic concerns in response to *closed* questions — and possibly the influence of local contextual differences. Thus, the fact that instrumental interest was higher in studies conducted in rural

---

[55] See R. P. Dore, *City Life in Japan* (Berkeley and Los Angeles: University of California Press, 1958), pp. 207–08.

Of course, dependence on close personal ties for "getting on" and manipulation of these relationships is not an exclusively Japanese trait, although this feature of Japanese social life receives great emphasis. For an example of such behavior in a Western milieu within at least the political sphere, see Joseph LaPalombara, "Italy: Fragmentation, Isolation and Alienation," in Lucian W. Pye and Sidney Verba (eds.), *Political Culture and Political Development,* pp. 303–04.

TABLE 2-4. INSTRUMENTAL ATTITUDES

	Yes (%)	No (%)	Don't Know (%)	Total (%)	(N)
Want our Diet member to do something for us[a]	45	35	20	100	(354)
Want something done for this area by national government[b]	75	—	25	100	(—)
Something wanted from national politics[c]	89	—	11	100	(813)
Want mayor or assemblyman to do something for development of the community or to improve your life[d]	49	38	13	100	(419)
Want our local assemblyman to do something for us[a]	51	31	18	100	(354)
Something wanted or dissatisfaction regarding local affairs[e]	63	37	—	100	(300)
Want new mayor or assemblyman to do something[b]	65	—	35	100	(—)
Something wanted from local politics[f]	90	—	10	100	(475)

SOURCES:
[a] Richardson 1964 post-election study. [b] Fukuoka 1964B, pp. 58–59.
[c] Chiba 1962, p. 280. [d] Ibaragi 1962, pp. 44–45.
[e] Tokushima 1962, p. 80. 22% of the respondents reported a "strong" sense of needs while 41% said there were simply "some" wants. [f] Fukushima 1963, p. 175.

districts than among urban voters contributed to this variation. It is difficult to say whether instrumental attitudes are especially high in Japan, given the lack of literally comparable data from other places. But a seemingly high level is still notable, and can be interpreted in part as a consequence of widespread changes in the postwar political and social life of Japan.[56] Indeed, marked increases in instrumentalist expectations seem to be characteristic of the transition from more au-

---

[56] Nevertheless, there was an awareness of such matters among at least local elites in the rural districts in prewar Japan. See John K. Fairbank, Edwin O. Reischauer and Albert M. Craig, *East Asia: The Modern Transformation* (Boston: Houghton Mifflin, 1965), p. 520.

thoritarian and parochial to more popular and cosmopolitan political styles. This is the broad implication both of American nineteenth century experience and, more recently, of political life in some postcolonial nations in Africa and Asia. A rising instrumental interest is, moreover, one of the main patterns anticipated in Karl Deutsch's model of the linkage between social change and political development. In moving toward the somewhat ambiguous state of political modernization, the direct and indirect effects of postwar reforms in Japan as well as subsequent economic growth may be merely catalysts in a process begun several decades ago and only thwarted in part during the 1930s and 1940s.

Political Involvement in Contemporary Japan: Summary and Qualifications. One of the striking characteristics of Japan's contemporary political culture is the degree of stratification and differentiation in attitude structures. This is manifest in the pattern of involvement attitudes, where there are quite different tendencies both in attitude content and in the levels of different kinds of popular feelings about politics. The highest levels of involvement were found in attitudes about the relevance of politics. Interest levels for "politics" as a general topic were comparatively lower, although interest levels for elections compared favorably with levels of feeling that politics was relevant. Finally, there was a dramatic gap in levels between involvement measured in these terms and voters' self-assessed confidence in understanding politics; actual knowledge of political processes and issues was somewhat analogously stratified.

Two general themes could be discerned among these various dimensions. On the one hand, there was a fairly widespread involvement in politics in very vague and abstract terms; knowledge about politics of a textbook variety was also common. Elsewhere, there was typically a distinct gradation in response patterns, which could be seen as reflecting a variety of causal influences that included, among others, differences in individual experience with different levels and aspects of political processes as well as real variations in the importance of particular issues.

The interpretations of the various tendencies we have observed were necessarily tentative. This was especially true where changes in attitude were concerned. It is a well-known fact that the nature of change cannot be determined by cross-sectional analysis alone. It must also be remembered that political cultures are presumably complexly differentiated elsewhere, even though little has been done to explore population or subgroup characteristics specifically in these terms, or to relate attitudinal complexity systematically to socialization or adaptation theories at either the individual or system level. Thus, our own observations on Japan, including inferences drawn from data obtained in a period of transition, should be further examined against cross-national evidence.

One further qualification should be made at this point. Reporting population tendencies inescapably creates problems where we are dealing ultimately in individual psychologies. Although this weakness has been present in research elsewhere it has not always been explicitly admitted. In noting the differentiated and hierarchical nature of attitude structures in Japan it must be emphasized that so far these tendencies have been demonstrated only by comparing population tendencies gathered from reports from a large number of surveys. In other words, individual attitude structures have been inferred from data on whole populations. Clearly, without some individual conformity to general patterns such patterns would not exist; but we still do not know just what the typical individual attitude structure is.

It is also important to reiterate that while the data was selected with great care, there is a problem, at least at this point, in the fact that Japanese attitude structures were characterized here on the basis of results from a large number of studies. The differentiated nature of attitude structures notwithstanding, there is still the possibility that some of the apparent differences are the unrealistic result of dependence on surveys of different population samples.

Fortunately there is additional evidence relevant to both of these problems. Through factor analysis, a technique by which response structures can be fairly accurately identified, it is possible to directly investigate the character and degree of attitude differentiation. This kind of analysis was carried out using my own survey data, and the results are reported in Chapter Three. As will clearly be seen, the factor analysis reveals structures parallel to the differentiated patterns reported thus far. As a result of this analysis, it seems safe to conclude that these patterns of differentiation are truly present in the population.

One of the best ways to come to grips with the problem of evaluating the significant tendencies in a particular political culture is with cross-national comparison. Even though there appeared to be many apathetic voters among the Japanese surveys, the levels of involved and aware voters in Japan generally compared favorably with those in the United States, Great Britain, and the Federal Republic of Germany.[57] Experience with democratic ideas and processes, specifically at the mass level, is obviously shorter in Japan than in at least the United States and Britain. Although we cannot say just how visceral the feeling of involvement among the Japanese electorate (or of any national public) might prove under future events in which a more authoritarian style of political leadership emerged, it would appear that considerable progress has thus far been made in the diffusion of the norms and expectations of popular government. Certainly the fact that Japan was a highly integrated political system before World War II, along with comparatively high levels of popular educational attainment and development of the mass media, have been important factors in the rapid adaptation to new political concepts. Moreover, the receptivity among some sectors of the population to popular government in earlier periods certainly helped prepare the way for the kind of postwar transition that has been observed.

Nevertheless, certain tendencies are the result of the comparative youth of democracy in postwar Japan. Feelings that politics is relevant were more common than most other kinds of involvement attitudes, and this could reflect the effects of earlier political experiences as well as more recent events. It is also apparent that there has been a more rapid adjustment in some attitudes than others, and that this is a special effect of the recentness of certain political changes. The fact that in some cases quite a few more voters found politics relevant than said they were interested in public affairs is a case in point, and may reflect the relative ease of learning abstract kinds of attitudes.

The somewhat lower frequencies in Japan of "strong" interest in politics, compared with tendencies in the United States, could be interpreted along similar lines. Moreover, the fact that more interest was shown in instrumental questions than in the entertaining aspects of politics could also reflect the newness of democratic ideas in Japan. Although high levels of spectator interest in politics may not necessarily indicate a more advanced democracy, we may say they are more

---

[57] Exceptions to this statement have already been noted.

frequent where popular government has a longer history. Nevertheless, unique cultural factors are also present. The localizing effect of social patterns in Japan, for example, plays some limiting role in the development of spectator interest in national politics or political figures.

It would appear that experience with democratic processes and ideas in postwar Japan has had effects on the political involvement attitudes of much of the public. As we shall see later, even among voters who grew up before the war there were significant levels of involvement in politics as well as fairly strong concern about representation of individual and collective political wants. But outside the category of involvement attitudes, the character of Japanese political attitudes does not always permit such optimism. Despite widespread psychological involvement in politics, the orientation of the Japanese electorate of the early 1960s could be characterized as ambivalent, as will be shown in subsequent chapters.

3

EVALUATIVE ATTITUDES

The study of popular evaluations of political life derives from two concerns. On the one hand, political philosophers have sought to define the sources and character of political legitimacy and allegiance. Parallel with this focus, some empirical researchers have sought through surveys of popular attitudes to identify the scope and quality of political system support in different places.[1] In so doing, they have solicited people's appraisals of the performance of public processes and institutions. Another kind of research has focused simply on identifying and measuring ordinary people's own personal sense of efficacy, primarily in connection with studies of the roots of popular participation in politics.[2] Scholars interested in the range of popular support for specific political systems as well as persons endeavoring to discover the quality of citizens' feelings of efficacy have concerned

---
[1] See, for example, David Easton and Jack Dennis, "The Child's Acquisition of Regime Norms: Political Efficacy, "*American Political Science Review* 62 (March 1967), pp. 25–38; Jack Dennis, "Support for the Party System by the Mass Public," *American Political Science Review* 60 (September 1966), pp. 600–615 and "Support for the Institution of Elections by the Mass Public," *American Political Science Review* 64 (September 1970), pp. 819–835.

[2] Examples of this kind of emphasis include Ada W. Finifter, "Dimensions of Political Alienation," *American Political Science Review* 64 (June 1970), pp. 389–410, and various works emanating from the Survey Research Center, University of Michigan. These include Angus Campbell, Philip E. Converse, Warren E. Miller and Donald E. Stokes, *The American Voter* (New York: Wiley, 1960), pp. 103–105. See also, Alex Inkeles, "Participant Citizenship in Six Developing Countries," *American Political Science Review* 63 (December 1969), pp. 1120–1141.

themselves with identifying people's evaluations of their political setting.

In the study of Japanese political culture research on evaluative dimensions can legitimately be based on both of these perspectives. In other words, the implications of the findings on evaluative attitudes are of interest both as indicators of system support and in relation to understanding individual participation and involvement. There are many examples of antigovernment extremist violence in both prewar and postwar Japan. Since behavior of this kind obviously seems to reflect dissatisfaction with the political system, it is desirable to identify as precisely as possible the content of popular assessment of political life. To be sure, it is difficult to specifically relate the findings of mass surveys to acts of violence or participation in protest demonstrations without considering important intervening variables such as the character of ideological commitment, leadership or individual personality differences. Nevertheless, identification of popular evaluations of politics should provide a datum for at least beginning the study of behavior of this kind.[3]

Alternatively, it is reasonable to ask whether the record of high electoral participation in Japan reflects the presence of widespread feelings of personal political efficacy. Of course the connection between feelings of efficacy and satisfaction and participation also may be very complicated. But certainly the legitimacy of asking questions about evaluative feelings as possible determinants of participation should be clear.

Investigation into the character of evaluative attitudes is all the more important when we recognize that historical experience in Japan may actually have ambiguous consequences. Although it may be assumed that democracy brings with it a belief that government is accountable to popular needs, acceptance of democratic norms might also contribute to raising popular expectations beyond the level of possible fulfillment. This is all the more possible where experience with authoritarian political precepts is closely followed by a diffusion of demo-

---

[3] Frustration has clearly emerged as one of the main variables critical to violence levels, according to a growing body of cross-national studies. For example, see Ted Gurr, "Psychological Factors in Civil Violence," *World Politics* 20 (January 1968), pp. 245–278.

cratic concepts; an abrupt departure from earlier political formulas might actually be associated with sharp declines in satisfaction with political performance.

Evaluative attitudes as presented here constitute a subcategory of political culture, and include feelings about politics with a large normative component. They may include appraisals of reality, such as statements about the efficacy of elections as an instrument of improving political life, or they may include expression of satisfaction or dissatisfaction with some aspect of public affairs.[4] Whatever the specific frame of reference, evaluative attitudes are distinguished from other kinds of political attitudes simply by the fact that public performance or personal capability is measured against some implicit or explicit norm. Like feelings of political involvement, they are states of mind or mental postures regarding politics, rather than prescriptions for political behavior (even though certain evaluations can be plausibly linked with participation).

Ambivalence is a central theme in Japanese voters' evaluation of public life and their own political efficacy. Depending on question content and the specific frame of reference, majorities or pluralities of respondents expressed either optimism and satisfaction, on the one hand, or cynicism and disenchantment. The exact meaning of these patterns is not easy to determine. Some variation may have been the result of volatility in feeling throughout different survey locations or points in time. But there are some definite patterns in the data, and it is clear that the kinds of discrepancies observed elsewhere between "textbook" attitudes and orientations to real life are also found in Japan. Just as Americans who believe in liberty as a general principle would deny freedom to various political minorities, many Japanese seem to accept the ideals of democracy to some degree while rejecting

---

[4] In a secondary analysis of this kind the scholar must deal pragmatically with the surface content of questions, and attempt to establish categories accordingly. This inevitably leads to some rather arbitrary decisions, and use of "impure" or overlapping categories cannot be avoided.

I have identified the categories of "satisfaction," "efficacy," and "politician responsiveness" on the basis of surface content, while evaluative feelings about elections are grouped on the basis of the "object" of the question. (Feelings about elections may certainly involve nuances of satisfaction or efficacy.)

the possibility that real life conforms to these ideals.[5] Indeed, it is not at all unlikely that acceptance of democratic norms may actually contribute to cynicism and thus ambivalence in some cases. Whatever the underlying contributants, evaluative attitudes in Japan are markedly differentiated, and no simple profiles of contemporary reality should be drawn.

Satisfaction with Politics and Evaluations of Elections. One of the basic indicators of the degree of support for a political system could be the level of popular satisfaction with the output from public processes or the quality of public life. Measured in these terms, system support is comparatively weak in Japan today. Generally few Japanese were strongly satisfied with politicians and politics, and weak satisfaction or dissatisfaction was common (Table 3-1). Levels of satisfaction and dissatisfaction varied, however, depending on the nature and object of specific questions. Majorities or near majorities of voters in two different parts of Japan reported they were dissatisfied with the way politics in general was conducted or how "national government was going about its work" (Kumamoto 1960; Kumamoto 1962; Ibaragi 1962).[6] Elsewhere, when respondents were asked to evaluate the conduct of local politics, levels of reported satisfaction were somewhat higher, though far more voters said they were "somewhat satisfied" than indicated "strong" feelings of contentment (Aichi 1964). Also, favorable personal assessment of specific political figures was greater than favorable evaluation of national and general politics. Voters throughout Japan were inclined to report satisfaction where *both* national and local candidates were concerned (Kōmei 1962B; Kōmei 1967A). But here, too, where the category of "somewhat satisfied" was an option, a marked plurality chose this over "strong" feelings of approval (Kōmei 1962B).

Ambivalent patterns were seen in Japanese voter attitudes toward

---

[5] See, for example, the discussions in Herbert H. Hyman and Paul B. Sheatsley, "The Current Status of American Public Opinion," in Daniel Katz, et al., *Public Opinion and Propaganda* (New York: Holt, Rinehart and Winston, 1954), pp. 41-42. The discrepancies reported there are different from those discussed here, but important contradictions in popular attitudes are demonstrated.

[6] It should be pointed out that these studies were all conducted in largely rural districts, although the locations were in widely separated parts of the country. It is possible that voters in these areas were more negative than is the case elsewhere, but rural residents are normally more optimistic than city dwellers in Japan. See Chapter 6.

TABLE 3-1. SATISFACTION WITH POLITICS AND POLITICIANS

	Yes (%)	Very (%)*	Some-what (%)*	No (%)	Other (%)	Don't Know (%)	Total (%)	(N)
Satisfied with the way today's politics are carried out[a]	10	—	—	65	—	25	100	(517)
Same question[b]	17	—	—	60	4	19	100	(901)
Feeling that national government is doing a good job[c]	13	—	—	48	—	39	100	(419)
Satisfaction with methods of one's city or town politics[d]	41	(6)	(35)	34	1	24	100	(—)
Satisfaction with winning candidates in the House of Councillors election[e]	54	(10)	(44)	17	—	29	100	(2,466)
Belief that quality of local assemblymen had not worsened recently[f]	29	—	—	27	—	43	99	(2,456)

SOURCES:
[a] Kumamoto 1960, p. 33. [b] Kumamoto 1962, p. 4. [c] Ibaragi 1962, p. 48.
[d] Aichi 1964, p. 141. Results are reported for the small-city sector of the sample only. Response patterns in a rural district were similar. (Findings for the total sample could not be recalculated, as numbers were not given.) [e] Kōmei 1962B, p. 88 (national). [f] Kōmei 1967A, p. 133 (national).
* Figures in parentheses indicate sub-group within the "yes" category.

electoral processes (Table 3-2). Elections are obviously one of the central processes of a functioning democracy, and in formal frames of reference many Japanese endorsed their importance. Most people were pessimistic and critical, however, when more concrete questions were asked.

Most voters showed a strong appreciation of the value of the franchise considered alone. Nearly 80 percent of the electorate in one of Japan's major cities — in response to a "textbook" question — felt that the vote was "an important basic right," and a majority of the same group opposed the idea that "elections are meaningless" (Ōsaka

TABLE 3-2. ATTITUDES TOWARDS ELECTIONS AND ELECTION PRACTICES

	Yes (%)	No (%)	Don't Know (%)	Total (%)	(N)
Politics improve by holding elections from time to time[a]	31	32	38	101	(4,306)
Same question[b]	36	39	25	100	(5,000)
All of the candidates in this constituency obeyed the laws in the last House of Representatives election[c]	20	40	40	100	(2,535)
Same question (1960 election)[d]	11	58	29	98	(2,644)
Only a few of the candidates violated the laws in the recent local elections[e]	23	34	43	100	(2,426)

SOURCES: All studies were based on national samples. The interests of the Fair Election League dictated question focus.
[a] Kōmei 1962A, p. 43.   [b] Kōmei 1958, p. 71.   [c] Jichi 1958, pp. 15–16.
[d] Kōmei 1961, p. 58.   [e] Kōmei 1964A, p. 127. Negative answers in this instance represented expressions of opinions that "many" or "all" of the candidates had violated the election laws.

1960, pp. 72–73). But without the formal frame of reference, people were more pessimistic in evaluating the actual effects of holding elections. In numerous studies conducted nationally and in separate regions, a proportion of the electorate ranging from small pluralities to majorities expressed the opinion that by holding elections politics "stays the same" or "worsens" rather than "improving."[7] To some degree this is undoubtedly a correlative of the similarly widespread belief among Japanese voters that politicians often break the law in their election campaigns (Jichi 1958; Kōmei 1961; Kōmei 1964A).[8]

---

[7] Findings concurring with those in Table 3-2 can be found in Ibaragi 1962, p. 49; Toyama 1961, p. 19; Kumamoto 1960, p. 97; Kumamoto 1962, p. 22; Miyagi 1962, appendix p. 39; Tōkyō 1958, p. 61. In only a few instances, were pluralities more optimistic about the effects of elections; see Aomori 1961, p. 41; Aomori 1962, p. 42; and Yamaguchi 1964, p. 20.

[8] I could not find evidence of direct correlations between the two kinds of attitudes, but among population subgroups the tendency in responses to these two questions did match, so the presence of some relationship can be safely inferred.

On this scale, pessimism about elections is certainly a notable feature of Japanese political life.

Political Efficacy and Responsiveness of Politicians. Beliefs regarding the connection between opinions of ordinary citizens and the actions of their representatives were also characterized by contradictions and ambivalence. In response to questions with a formal frame of reference a positive attitude toward such connections was the rule. But, as in other areas of assessment, less theoretical questions typically elicited substantially higher levels of pessimistic replies (Tables 3-3 and 3-4). Nearly three-quarters of the voters interviewed in my 1964

TABLE 3-3. CITIZEN EFFICACY

	Yes (%)	No (%)	Don't Know (%)	Total (%)	(N)
Citizens' interest and vote has an impact on national politicians and officials[a]	73	11	16	100	(354)
Citizens' interest and vote has an impact on local politicians and officials[a]	80	8	12	100	(354)
The people's vote decides the operation of the nation's affairs[b]	62	10	28	100	(1,057)
Politics is moved by our general power[c]	71	25	5	101	(475)
The people have some effect on the machinations of politics[d]	39	27	34	100	(541)

SOURCES: [a] Richardson 1964 post-election survey. [b] Ōsaka 1961, p. 71. [c] Fukushima 1963, p. 177. "Yes" includes alternative answers that indicated feelings of efficacy toward either national or local politics, or toward *both* national and local levels. [d] Iwate 1963, appendix, p. 8.

survey felt that their interest and vote had some impact on national politics; slightly more believed this was true with local politics. Comparable frequencies were found in other studies. Sixty-two percent of the voters in metropolitan Ōsaka agreed with the proposition that "people's votes decide the way national politics is run" (Ōsaka 1960). Similarly, nearly three-quarters of the respondents in a largely rural district felt that "politics is moved by our power" (Fukushima 1963).

TABLE 3-4. RESPONSIVENESS OF GOVERNMENT AND POLITICIANS

	Yes (%)	No (%)	Don't Know (%)	Total (%)	(N)
National politicians and officials are concerned about our needs[a]	53	28	19	100	(354)
Local politicians and officials are concerned about our needs[a]	66	20	14	100	(354)
Believe prefectural government is paying attention to the voice of its residents[b]	29	24	47	100	(419)
Central government is thinking of the problems of this area[c]	36	34	31	101	(—)
City or town politics is adequately implementing our hopes and demands[d]	45	35	20	100	(402)
Believe many candidates honor their election promises[e]	5	54	41	100	(517)
Same question[f]	12	66	22	100	(500)
Same question[g]	5	36	59	100	(—)

SOURCES:
[a] Richardson 1964 postelection survey. [b] Kumamoto 1962, p. 8.
[c] Fukuoka 1964B, p. 56. [d] Miyagi 1962, appendix, p. 6. [e] Kumamoto 1960, p. 99.
[f] Fukuoka 1960B, p. 48. [g] Saga 1964, p. 45.

These findings witness to the fact that the formal precepts of popular government are clearly perceived. But the importance of the formal dimension of these questions is made clear when contrasted with responses to other kinds of questions. For example, markedly fewer voters were of the opinion that the electorate has some influence on the "machinations" of politics (Iwate 1963).[9]

Moreover, fewer people (although a majority) in one survey felt that national and local officials respectively were concerned about their needs than supported the postulate that voter interests affected politics (Richardson 1964). Elsewhere, even more modest proportions

[9] As the question was expressed in the negative, some bias may have occurred.

of the electorate had favorable attitudes toward the responsibility of their government. Only small pluralities in different parts of the country affirmed the view that national and prefectural governments were attentive to local problems (Fukuoka 1964B; Kumamoto 1962), or agreed with the proposition that local politics is "adequately implementing our hopes and demands" (Miyagi 1962). Finally, an extremely pessimistic view of political representation was evident in three separate districts when majorities or pluralities of respondents expressed the opinion that many election candidates do not honor their campaign commitments (Kumamoto 1960; Fukuoka 1960B; Saga 1964).

In the last chapter I pointed out that involvement attitudes of Japanese citizens were markedly differentiated. In particular, I noted that findings from many surveys favored the interpretation of distinct formalistic tendencies within the Japanese population. This term refers to a discrete dimension of Japanese political culture, according to which many people who found politics relevant where the frame of reference was abstract or formal still cared little about being personally involved.

Something of this nature can also be seen where evaluative attitudes are concerned, since the level of feeling of personal efficacy was higher in response to normative questions than to questions with a frame of reference in actuality. In other words, more people believed in the importance of the vote than believed politicians to be responsive. Such discontinuities in attitude structures are especially interesting. In view of the qualifications mentioned earlier about using only aggregate findings, I subjected the data from my own study to a factor analysis in order to see just what kind of structure might be found. Since factor analysis does not work very well with small numbers of variables—and, anyhow, I was interested in attitude structures that might cross categorical boundaries — information on involvement and participation attitudes as well as evaluative attitudes was included.[10]

The results of the analysis are shown in Table 3-5. They are especially interesting in view of the fact that certain dimensions that cross-cut attitudinal categories are clearly visible. Factor one in the

---

[10] For mathematical limitations in working with small numbers of variables, see Harry H. Harman, *Modern Factor Analysis* (Chicago: University of Chicago Press, 1967), p. 70.

TABLE 3-5. STRUCTURE OF POLITICAL ATTITUDES

	Factors*				
	(1)	(2)	(3)	(4)	(5)
Responsiveness — National	.56	.05	.13	.27	−.42
Responsiveness — Local	.48	.22	.33	.19	−.38
Efficacy — N	.75	−.05	.08	.26	.11
Efficacy — L	.75	.01	.09	.18	.08
Relevance — N	.77	.00	.18	.02	.03
Relevance — L	.75	−.05	.26	.10	.08
Comprehension — N	−.03	.93	.00	−.05	.02
Comprehension — L	.01	.93	−.03	.02	−.03
Interest — N	.30	−.10	.55	.14	−.09
Interest — L	.21	−.13	.64	.16	−.06
Attention — N**	.17	.03	.76	.11	−.08
Attention — L	.08	.11	.80	−.07	.05
Wants	.00	.03	.51	.21	.35
Concern — N	.19	−.04	.12	.82	−.03
Concern — L	.10	.00	.17	.80	.10
Civic Duty	.08	.11	.01	.10	.82

* Factor analysis is a statistical technique utilizable for discerning the underlying organization in attitude systems or other kinds of phenomena. The figures here represent loadings for each factor, or the degree to which a particular attitude is an important associate of some underlying dimension of the attitude system. Higher loadings reflect higher levels of association. The factor solution was obtained by orthogonal rotation.

** "Attention" was introduced into the analysis to indicate the strong electoral focus of interest in politics; this did not greatly affect the solutions, although it can be seen that concern about electoral outcomes remains an independent dimension from interest according to this analysis.

table includes appraisal of the relevance of politics and evaluation of people's political efficacy in highly idealistic or theoretical terms. Evaluation of politician responsiveness did load on this factor, and there is obviously some relationship at times between idealistic and realistic appraisals. But the loadings for assessment of responsiveness were much lower than those for efficacy, so that it is obvious that somewhat different dimensions were operative within this one factor alone.

Factor two included simply appraisals of competence in understanding national and local politics. As we have already pointed out, these are much more realistically or experientially determined perspectives. Factors three and four in the table also represent more tangible kinds of perspectives; factor three includes political interest, instrumental awareness and attention to media accounts of politics and political speeches, and factor four represents concern about election outcomes. Since the implications of the individual components have already been discussed, the meaning of these factors should be self-evident. Finally, factor five contained only one measure, that of feelings of civic duty. The factor solutions demonstrate the presence of the kinds of differences already described on the basis of other kinds of analysis, as well as evidence of some additional kinds of differences that are more relevant to following chapters.

A second axis of differentiation can be seen from the aggregate findings alone. In addition to the distinction between ideal and experiential dimensions, Japanese political attitudes are characteristically more favorable to *experientially proximate* political phenomena than to relatively remote facets of public affairs. For example, positive evaluation of the conduct of local affairs was more frequent than favorable assessment of conduct in national politics. Similarly, election candidates (whose reputations are often assiduously cultivated in their home constituencies) were viewed more favorably than such generalized and personally distant phenomena as electoral processes in themselves or the behavior of politicians in general.

Evaluative Attitudes and the Japanese Political System. As was pointed out earlier, the only sensible way to make satisfactory statements about the implications of attitude patterns among a whole national population is to look at whatever comparative evidence is available. This is especially urgent in the case at hand, given the fact that some people would link the character of evaluative attitudes to the viability of governments. If assessments of public life are in fact more ambivalent or negative in Japan than elsewhere, the prognosis for stable democratic government in Japan could be very dire.[11]

In light of this, it was very interesting to discover, through a review of survey results from Great Britain, the Federal Republic of Germany, Italy and the United States, that voters in highly industrial democracies outside Japan are also generally ambivalent in their as-

---

[11] It should be noted that comparisons across time are also valuable in this kind of context. The data reported here for the early 1960s will thus be of special value for future comparative research on evaluative tendencies in Japan.

TABLE 3-6. EVALUATIVE ATTITUDES IN WESTERN DEMOCRACIES

	United States (%)	Great Britain (%)	Federal Republic of Germany (%)	Italy (%)
The "way people vote" determines how government is run	71	83	78	61
Passage of unjust national laws can be stopped by one's efforts[a]	17	12	7	8
Passage of unjust local laws can be stopped by one's efforts[a]	27	19	24	19
People "like me" have some say in regard to government decisions[b]	61	40	25	13
Candidates keep their election promises[b]	17	13	6	9
Majority interests are not ignored in the face of the influence of some groups[b]	20	30	24	15

SOURCE: The Inter-University Consortium for Political Research codebook for the Almond and Verba five-nations survey.

* Percentages represent the proportion of all respondents in each country who expressed agreement with the stated proposition (or disagreement with a negatively worded statement). Comparatively high ratios of "don't know" answers among Italian respondents must be taken into account when drawing conclusions from these figures.

[a] Somewhat higher ratios of American voters agreed with this proposition according to the results of a 1966 SRC study. See John P. Robinson, Jerrold G. Rusk and Kendra B. Head, *Measures of Political Attitudes* (Ann Arbor: Institute for Social Research, The University of Michigan, 1968), pp. 609–10.

[b] The question was worded in the negative and percentages here were taken from the "disagree" column.

sessment of the quality of public life (Table 3-6). On the one hand, the feeling that "the way people vote" determines how governments are run was very common among voters in the four Western democracies, although Italian respondents were somewhat less hopeful in this regard. In contrast, citizens in three of the four countries were pessimistic about the degree to which "people like me" could influence the behavior of government. Only in the United States could one see a majority show of confidence in this particular sentiment. Moreover, electorates in all four countries were moderately to extremely pessimistic about the degree to which politicians would keep their election promises, the scope of sacrifice of majority interests in the face of minority pressures, and the possibilities for ordinary people to have some effect on changing unjust legislation.

Even though some differences exist between Japanese and American voters, these findings show that the Japanese patterns in evaluative attitudes are indeed far from unique.[12] Since this is the case, it would be imprudent to overemphasize the potential threats seemingly implicit in the Japanese patterns. Since antiregime movements of a scale reflecting the surveyed levels of pessimism or cynicism have not occurred in recent years in the above four countries, except Italy, it is obvious that considerable discrepancies can exist between evaluational content in attitudes and behavior threatening to political systems.

On the other hand, it could be that the real dimensions of popular support are simply not adequately tapped by many survey questions, and that some of the pessimism prevalent in various countries represents no more than a folkloric or casual rejection of politics.[13] The information on Japan presented here is derived from a much greater variety of measures than is the information from the other countries, and for this reason it is possible that comparatively more fundamental strains in Japanese attitudes are being measured. Whatever the case, the data at hand are obviously inadequate for predicting propensities to support antiregime movements, even though the cynicism prevailing in Japan and elsewhere could obviously, under favorable circumstances, be a correlative of behavior of this kind.

Comparable tendencies in evaluative attitudes in several nations require that analysis of Japan not proceed on the assumption that the Japanese patterns are necessarily the product of a unique pattern of

---

[12] Comparative information on feelings of efficacy and evaluations of governmental responsiveness was more readily available than it was for feelings of satisfaction or evaluations of the impact of elections. For this reason, I have attempted to make comparative statements only about feelings of efficacy and governmental responsiveness. But, even here, individual items were not sufficiently comparable to permit statements other than about tendencies toward ambivalence.

[13] It is interesting to note at this point that University of Michigan Survey Research Center findings indicate the presence of higher levels of efficacy feelings among American voters than did the results of the Almond and Verba study. See John P. Robinson, et al., *Measures of Political Attitudes*, pp. 635-38 and 643-46. Presumably these differences are the result in part of using different questions.

experiences or circumstances. Nevertheless, speculation about particular influences on the patterns we have reported is useful. There has been little attention to these matters elsewhere, and analysis of the Japanese experiences can suggest hypotheses for future investigation. It is also possible that to some degree the Japanese patterns may still have unique origins, and to the extent that this may prove to be the case, analysis of origins can contribute to an understanding of the actual importance of these attitudes. In other words, by looking for contributants to the patterns we have observed in Japan, it will be possible to delineate certain aspects of the Japanese experience in such a way as to develop more refined assessments of the meaning of ambivalence in political cultures. Ambivalence may have quite different consequences in different countries as the result of different backgrounds and varying intensities in both idealism and cynicism that may not be reflected in our measures.

The character of mass media coverage of public life in Japan is one of the things that could account for the widespread incidence of pessimistic evaluations of political life, and consequently ambivalence. Reports of political corruption, and violations of laws and parliamentary norms by persons in public life, receive considerable attention in the Japanese mass media and popular magazines.[14] The frequency of concern for these matters is not constant, but accounts of electoral law violations, vote-buying in Liberal Democrat conventions, corruption among party elites in all camps, and violations of parliamentary etiquette are certainly recurring themes.[15] Clearly a less than salubrious picture of the quality of political performance is provided in these sporadic outbursts of attention to the seamy side of politics. Unfortunately, no one has yet made a comparative study of these matters, but it is quite possible that the frequency of these themes in the Japanese mass media substantially exceeds that in the other major democracies.

---

[14] Comparable themes are also found at many points in recent Japanese fiction, which highlights the ease with which informed Japanese accept the belief that politics is pervasively corrupt. See, for example, the works of Mimpei Sugiura, Yukio Mishima's *After the Banquet* (New York: Alfred Knopf, 1963), and Seichō Matsumoto's *Points and Lines* (Tōkyō: Kōdansha International, 1970).

[15] It is important to realize that these accounts are not the result of distortions in media coverage. Various kinds of questionable behavior are a fact of political life in Japan.

If true, then the possibility would be fairly strong that media exposure is one of the unique factors contributing to political cynicism in Japan. Whatever the cross-national differences may be, it is quite clear that mass media content is important to the formation of negative political views in Japan, since negative attitudes are comparatively more common among persons who report greater than average attention to media accounts of public affairs.[16]

But the character of political ideals among the public in Japan is also important. Traditional and modern expectations about proper political leadership have merged in an especially interesting manner in that country. On the one hand, older values stressed that leaders should show self-denial and self-sacrifice on behalf of the community or an ideal. More recently, at least among the better-informed members of the electorate, democratic norms have been sufficiently internalized to create expectations that political leaders be honest and not engage in corruption and violations of the law. Thus, politicians who engage in corrupt activities fall short of public expectations whether they are judged by older ideas about purity of motivation or by more recently internalized expectations about the kinds of leadership appropriate to political democracy.

Notwithstanding the importance of mass media treatment of political life and expectations among media "consumers" about politicians' behavior, there are other aspects of Japanese experience which may contribute to ambivalence in special ways. Contemporary attitude patterns probably reflect to some degree reactions of various kinds to prewar political styles. Despite democratic tendencies following World War I, prewar political life in Japan has been seen as largely authoritarian in character. The central authoritarian strain in Japanese politics was underwritten by the importance of hierarchical distinctions in personal relationships in many sectors of society. Although it is possible to overestimate the importance of the authoritarian aspects of prewar life, it would be unwise to underestimate the importance of perceptions of prewar patterns in contemporary attitudes among at least some sectors of the Japanese public. In other words, it seems quite evident that political pessimism in Japan is in many cases a reflection of an

---

[16] Evidence supporting this observation will be provided in Ch. 6.

extreme sensitivity and frustration resulting from anticipation of authoritarian behavior among contemporary leaders. These sensitivities are more common to the political left and to well-educated persons, and are frequently expressed in the writings of Japan's professional political critics.

Attitudes of this kind are typically found within a larger set of responses among some classes in societies undergoing rapid change. To be sure, Japan has experienced change over a much longer period of time than is the case in many countries in the world, and it is probable that major adjustments to new political styles among at least better-informed kinds of persons occurred several decades back. Still, the effects of transitions in political styles begun at earlier points in time and deep social changes are important for present attitudes. As is well-known, many persons among the more articulate sectors of the population felt that the growth of open political competition among individuals and groups in the prewar period was motivated more by self-interest than legitimate position-taking. While responses of this kind were possibly more congruent with reality in the prewar period than at present, one can still see in contemporary attitudes a distaste for the elements of maneuver and competition regarding political office. The substantial degree of intellectualization among the urban middle class is probably associated with a particularly acute awareness of these matters, and persons in this category are typically more cynical than people in other social groupings.[17]

It is also important to appreciate the fact that, in Japan, residence itself may contribute to feelings of vulnerability or inefficacy, and in ways that are not always anticipated by empirical theory. This matter will be taken up at a later point, but the fact that political pessimism is more common in the increasingly important urban sector than rural districts reflects the effects of both social structure characteristics and the overlap between urban residence as a factor and certain other specific correlatives of political pessimism (such as frequent media ex-

---

[17] The term "intellectualized" is used for definite reasons. The urban middle class in Japan is exposed to mass media and literary content more closely accruing to the popular meaning of the term "intellectual" than is the case in some other industrial democracies. Accordingly, their attitudes toward politics are symmetrical with those of a less numerous *intellectual class,* which in turn is substantially alienated from access and control over the political process.

posure and leftist party support).[18] Urban residence has meant substantial social isolation for many persons, at least from the kinds of relationships that are most conducive to personal ties with local influentials and politicians. At the same time, "connections," or the dependence on personal ties are important features of Japanese behavior even where the intimacy and social redundancy of rural community life are absent. Isolation in these terms is a contributant to feelings of both apathy and cynicism, as was clearly shown in the replies to open questions in my own survey. While sectoral differences of this kind are not sufficiently great (nor is population distribution sufficiently skewed for this to account for the prevailing pessimism), still, urbanization is one of the conditions that must be considered in any analysis of the Japanese patterns.[19]

It is possible that the ambivalence we have observed is simply a result of contrasts between the effects of formal political socialization (found in the postwar social studies curricula, for example), and more meaningful evaluations of political life. This was made clear in earlier comments about the differences between response patterns to different kinds of questions. To the extent this is the case—and later subgroup analysis will show that there is indeed considerable merit in this interpretation—the mainstream of evaluative attitudes in Japan is essentially negative in character. Future research in Japan, as well as elsewhere, should take into consideration this possibility, and endeavor to measure whether favorable assessments basically reflect true expectations about popular opportunities or are merely the products of formal socialization experiences. Clearly, there can be close relationships between the two kinds of attitudes, but it is also possible that reality will deviate markedly from expectations in some places or at some points in time. Of course, measurement in these areas is rather difficult to carry out; nevertheless, it is important that these matters be

---

[18] Leftist party support is clearly one correlative of negativism and cynicism in Japan, as we will see later. Consequently, it is possible that the kinds of evaluative attitudes found in Japan are the direct result in part of political polarization. Evidence favoring such an interpretation is found in the results of the Almond and Verba study, where levels of pessimism in Germany and Italy were higher than in the more consensualistic American and British systems.

[19] Evidence in support of this assertion, in the form of observations on community life and group membership in urban and rural areas, will be presented in Chapter 6.

investigated thoroughly, since the ambivalence we have observed has substantially different theoretical and actual significances, depending on the nature of the connotations and intensities of the component cynicism. Among other things, it might be expected that meaningful negativism would produce antiregime sentiments at some point, more than if the main sentiments were a more casually entertained pessimism.[20] It is difficult at this point to distinguish folkloric pessimism of the kind that may be found in many developed societies from deeper and more intense strains of negativism, even though the differences in the possible behavorial implications are quite clear.

---

[20] Before leaving this discussion of evaluative attitudes, it should be noted that I have stressed only cultural or contextual effects and certain kinds of subgroup experiences as determinants of political pessimism and dissatisfaction. This does not mean that I am ignoring the importance of psychological factors. Rather, my choice of method has depended upon both the availability of certain kinds of data as well as an appreciation of the independent role played by political context or culture. For other examples of this kind of approach see Edgar Litt, "Political Cynicism and Political Futility," *Journal of Politics* 25 (May 1963), pp. 312–23, and Gabriel Almond and Sidney Verba, *The Civic Culture.*

4

PARTICIPATION ATTITUDES

Japanese political attitudes have been discussed so far in terms of general involvement in politics and voter evaluation of the quality and potential of public affairs. Here we will take up Japanese attitudes about their own roles as active participants in political processes. The postwar efforts at democratization of Japanese political culture were designed to encourage popular political participation. An examination of participation attitudes assumes a special importance when such efforts have been present, in addition to the fact that the very centrality of concepts of political participation to democratic theory assures their inclusion in an appraisal of contemporary political culture. Finally, participation attitudes are empirically close to actual behavior as far as can be determined, and merit attention for this reason as well as on the basis of other considerations.[1]

Despite much philosophical concern about the desirable scope of popular participation, important dimensions of the *motivation* to engage in political action have been generally ignored by empirical scholars until very recently. Students of political behavior have quite appropriately sought links between popular participation, on the one hand, and both psychological involvement and feelings of political efficacy, on the other. The potential importance of feelings of obliga-

---

[1] Only fragmentary evidence on the relationship between participation attitudes and participation can be found at present. But where evidence is available the link is clear. See Aichi 1963, p. 62; Aichi 1964, p. 51; and Richardson 1964. See also Ch. 8 for some specific findings on this relationship.

tion about the vote has been somewhat less appreciated, although there have been notable exceptions in the work of the University of Michigan Survey Research Center.[2] Almond and Verba's *Civic Culture* makes it apparent, however, that feelings of civic duty may underwrite high voter turnout in a number of cases outside of the United States, as well as being one of the cluster of motivations associated with the vote in the American political culture.[3]

In their path-breaking study of political culture Almond and Verba also paid particular attention to popular attitudes about the desirability and feasibility of engaging in more active kinds of political participation. They assumed, in effect, that attitudes toward participation were a component of political culture and so looked for cross-national differences in them. This concern was in line with the main objective of their study, which was the investigation of the motivational roots of a participant political culture. Although many would argue that their questions and interests reflect highly parochial normative biases, their investigation of cultural norms for participation remains a major advance. In particular, their study makes it possible to characterize nations or individuals in terms of levels of coherence between more diffuse feelings of political involvement and specific predispositions to participation. This in turn holds great promise for a more precise evaluation of the real meanings of popular attitudes about politics, a matter which is of special importance in comparative research.

The category of participation attitudes thus includes two different *types* of attitudes. The first is both motivational and normative in content, and consists of voter attitudes about both abstention from and participation in voting. The second type consists of predispositions to active participation and preferences for participation roles in political affairs. Included among the latter type are attitudes about appropriate levels of activity, preferences for collective modes of political action and predispositions toward either active or passive roles in the resolution of local community problems.

---

[2] See Angus Campbell, Gerald Gurin and Warren E. Miller, *The Voter Decides* (Evanston, Illinois: Row, Peterson, 1954), pp. 194–199, and Angus Campbell, Philip E. Converse, Warren E. Miller and Donald E. Stokes, *The American Voter* (New York: John Wiley, 1960), pp. 105–107.

[3] See especially Ch. 5, *The Civic Culture* (Boston: Little, Brown, 1965).

Attitudes Toward Turnout and Abstention. Voting is the most common form of political participation for Japanese citizens.[4] As is the case in other nations, more Japanese participate in elections than in other kinds of overt political activity. And, as was pointed out earlier, election turnout is rather high in Japan, despite a long-term decline in participation and the fact that voters in the urban districts turn out less often than those in the country or small towns.

Students of Japanese political behavior tend to explain high turnout levels by the nature of community structure and social relationships. The fact that persons will turn out to support community endorsed candidates and the vulnerability of ordinary citizens to direct appeals for voting support, backed up by social pressure and personal influence, have been most often cited as causes of high turnouts, with special emphasis placed on the role of these forces in rural sectors.[5]

Social patterns and community structure are certainly an important consideration in high turnout in many places in Japan. But the evidence from studies of voting behavior and political attitudes so far suggests that feelings of duty and obligation are also a primary motivation to vote in Japan, exceeding in importance responses to appeals to vote (at least insofar as the frequency of such appeals is reported by survey respondents).[6] For example, in response to a simple open question about their motives for actually voting, more persons in my 1964 survey cited feelings of duty or social custom than any other single motivation (Table 4-1). Forty-seven percent of those who had voted in the 1963 general election said that they had done so on the basis of feelings of duty or because everybody else was voting; the ratio among

---

[4] By "participation" I mean either going out to vote, discussion of political topics, articulation of interests or activity in election campaigns. A large body of evidence clearly shows voting to be the most common form of participation. Even if attention to either campaigns or mass media coverage of politics were seen as a form of participation, voting would still be more common according to survey results (Kōmei 1962A, pp. 12–13 and 19). But reported media attention is more common than *actual* voting in *national* elections; but as many people turn out in local elections as watch television or listen to the radio.

[5] See Robert E. Ward, "Urban-Rural Differences and the Process of Political Modernization in Japan," *Economic Development and Cultural Change* 9 (October 1960), Part II, pp. 148–49, for a concise summary of this kind of interpretation.

[6] The importance of duteous feelings and their origins are discussed in some detail in at least one commentary on urban-rural differences. See Jun'ichi Kyōguku and Nobutaka Ike, "Urban-Rural Differences in Voting Behavior in Postwar Japan," in *ibid.*, pp. 171–72.

TABLE 4-1. Attitudes toward the Vote

	National Election[a] (%)	Local Election[a] (%)
It's a question of duty; everybody was going out to vote	47	40
Because it's a right; in order to improve things	26	23
Support a particular candidate or party; want our interests represented	12	17
Response to social obligation or pressure	7	11
Other; don't know	8	9
Total:	100	100
(N)	(355)	(355)

	Small City[b] (%)	Rural Community[b] (%)
Sense of duty	45	51
It's a chance to express our opinions	26	28
It's an important right	21	15
Other; don't know	8	6
Total:	100	100

Sources:
[a] Richardson 1964. An open question was asked.
[b] Aichi 1964, p. 46. Since numbers were not indicated, tendencies in the total sample could not be recalculated. Figures reported in the text are thus rough estimates of the sample marginals. For similar results see also Aichi 1963, p. 59.

those voting in local elections that year was 40 percent. Interestingly, alternative motivations such as support for a particular candidate were slightly more important at the local level. Nevertheless, "duty" was cited by pluralities among voters in both local and national elections.[7]

This finding is supported by two other studies conducted in Japan recently, where "duty" was present as an alternative in closed questions about voting motivations. About 48 percent of those who voted in a local election in one district said they did this because of feelings of duty, while in another survey roughly 53 percent gave this same reason for voting in a House of Councillors election (Aichi 1964; Aichi 1963, p.

---

[7] Also, 45 percent of the persons I interviewed, in response to a direct closed question, agreed with the proposition "it's a citizen's duty to vote."

59). In these same studies, minorities stressed the fact that "the vote is an opportunity for expressing one's opinion," "the vote is a right" and "I was asked to vote," in decreasing order of importance. Elsewhere, however, where "duty" was not an alternative in closed questions, "possession of the franchise" was cited more than other kinds of motivations (Iwate 1965, p. 17; Tochigi 1962, p. 6). This would seem to indicate that perceptions of the value of the vote are widespread in Japan, but that they are also overshadowed by feelings of duty. (This is, of course, one of many examples of the actual complexity of popular political feelings.)

Evidence of feelings of duty among Japanese voters can also be found in answers to survey questions about the legitimacy of abstention. Ninety-five percent of the respondents to my 1964 survey disagreed with the proposition that "it doesn't matter if one abstains when the candidate for whom one intends to vote probably won't win," and 58 percent were opposed to the idea that "since many people are voting it doesn't matter if one person doesn't go out to vote" (Table 4-2). But, interestingly, most respondents felt that "one shouldn't vote if he is not really interested in the election." [8]

Findings from other surveys also sustained the theme that abstention is generally disfavored in Japan. In two separate surveys 55 and 67 percent, respectively, of the voters in one prefecture answered that abstention was bad except in cases of poor health, old age or absence from one's constituency (Gumma 1962; Gumma 1963). According to other studies, up to 60 percent of those interviewed disagreed with the proposition that "it's all right to abstain if there is no proper candidate" (Aichi 1964; Fukuoka 1964B, p. 51; Yamaguchi 1964, p. 30). In another area more voters felt it was better to vote than abstain when "there was no strongly preferred candidate" (Gifu 1963). And, according to the results of still another study, 49 percent disagreed with the idea that "one feels like abstaining when a candidate who thinks differently than you will probably get a lot of votes and win" (Yamaguchi 1964, p. 27).

---

[8] It can be inferred from this finding that taking an interest in elections and politics is seen as a civic obligation in Japan. This is especially clear when it is remembered that substantially fewer American voters agree with this proposition. See John P. Robinson, Jerrold G. Rusk and Kendra B. Head, *Measures of Political Attitudes* (Ann Arbor: Institute for Social Research, University of Michigan, 1968), p. 640.

TABLE 4-2. ATTITUDES TOWARD TURNOUT AND ABSTENTION*

	Yes (%)	No (%)	Don't Know (%)	Total (%)	(N)
Disagree with idea that it's all right to abstain when the candidate you support won't win[a]	95	5	—	100	(354)
Disagree with idea that it's all right for one person to abstain since so many others are voting[a]	58	29	12	99	(354)
Disagree with idea that one shouldn't vote when he's not really interested[a]	11	85	4	100	(354)
It's bad to abstain from voting, except under special circumstances, such as being sick, advanced in age or out of town[b]	67	28	6	101	(716)
Same question[c]	55	35	10	100	(967)
It's better to vote for the best candidate rather than abstain, when a person you prefer isn't running[d]	55	26	19	100	(573)
Disagree with the idea that it's all right to abstain when there is no appropriate candidate[e]	61	24	15	100	(195)

SOURCES:
[a] Richardson 1964 postelection study. [b] Gumma 1962, p. 36. Coded here as "no" were the responses "It can't be helped" and "Don't think it's bad." [c] Gumma 1963, p. 63. [d] Gifu 1963, p. 67. Coded as "no" responses were "Abstention can't be avoided" and "Of course, one must abstain." [e] Aichi 1964, p. 50.

* "Yes" answers in this and subsequent tables using these data refer to "duteous" replies, and "no" answers refer to non-duteous replies. Unless otherwixe indicated questions were of the dichotomized "agree-disagree" type.

As can readily be seen, the attitude that voting is desirable and that abstention is generally not a very good thing is a common one among replies to surveys conducted throughout the country. Responses to questions about personal reasons for abstention provide some indirect evidence on the importance of obligation: few voters reported

PARTICIPATION ATTITUDES 89

not voting because of feelings of apathy, indifference or dissatisfaction with politics, even when alternatives appropriate to such attitudes were included in closed questions. Most voters replied that they had not voted because of sickness, old age or absence on business.[9] Answers of this kind seem more "legitimate" in the context of prevailing attitudes toward civic duty, whereas admission of apathy would be less appropriate.

Residual effects of prewar political socialization can be seen as one of the factors favoring the rather widespread feeling in Japan today that the vote is a duty.[10] In the prewar period voters were not only told that the franchise was a political right, they were also taught that it was important for good citizens to take this right seriously and exercise it. Moreover, while voting was not generally included among the array of responsibilities to nation or emperor, it still took on the character of an obligation in a frame of reference where obligations received heavy stress in political socialization processes.

It is quite clear that other events and practices in Japan have fostered the feeling that the vote is an obligation. It is a well known fact that election administration authorities throughout the country arduously encourage voter turnout. Campaigns to get out the vote are, in fact, a feature of most Japanese elections.[11] Moreover, local communi-

---

[9] See, for example, Kōmei 1958, p. 48; Kōmei 1962B, p. 12; and Kōmei 1967B, p. 32.

[10] As far as I have been able to ascertain, this attitude was more prevalent in the prewar period than now. For this reason I have chosen the term "residual" in order to signify the continuing influence of prewar norms in the postwar period.

Subsequent observations and interpretations are based on informal interviews with informants who came to maturity in the prewar period. They also conform to the patterns among age groupings reported in Ch. 7. It should be remembered that whatever may be the differences between prewar and postwar cultures, the vote is seen as *both* a right and a duty in postwar school books.

[11] Evidence of such campaigns, in the form of banners and signs, is readily visible at election time. These activities are also reported in the election administration authorities' own documentation of their work in various elections.

Turnout campaigns were also common in the prewar period. See Kyoguku and Ike, *op. cit.* The authors also report that the franchise was probably seen as a mark of prestige in the years prior to the establishment of universal male suffrage in 1925.

Evidence of the effects of local "get out the vote" campaigns and traditions can be found in a particularly interesting set of charts of local turnout variations in postwar elections in Iwate 1963, pp. 14–15, 17, 19 and 21–25.

Still, comparatively few of the voters I interviewed were aware of having been "asked" to vote in the 1963 elections. (Two direct questions on this topic were used, in addition to the open queries about reasons for going out to vote.)

ties often compete for the prestige of having the highest turnout. These practices help create and sustain the popular impression that the vote is a normative imperative, although it is usually assumed that they are substantially more effective in the rural sector than in the cities.

The feeling that the vote is a civic duty is not unique to Japanese voters. It is quite common, in fact, among most of the industrially advanced countries where surveys of political attitudes have been systematically conducted. According to the results of a study by Almond and Verba in 1959, majorities or near majorities of voters in all of the countries investigated, with the exception of the United States, reported that they voted "*only* because it was a duty." Only in the United States were there proportionately more voters who felt that voting was a source of satisfaction and not just a duty.[12] Still, this feeling of satisfaction may entail feelings of fulfillment of an obligation in view of the findings of scholars of the Michigan Survey Research Center that feelings of civic duty are fairly widespread in the United States.[13]

We should not therefore *over*emphasize the uniqueness of feelings of civic duty in Japan even though the backgrounds of such feelings are quite clear in the Japanese case. Widespread diffusion of such sentiments may indeed reflect levels of politicization common to only highly developed countries, even though underlying political cultural content may be somewhat different in individual systems.[14] Nevertheless, since voting is often viewed by Japanese as an obligation, this fact is an important dimension of Japanese political culture, and the high frequency of such feelings cannot be ignored by persons seeking to under-

---

[12] Marginals for the Almond and Verba study were calculated from the Inter-University Consortium for Political Research codebook. The feeling that voting was a source of satisfaction was more common in Great Britain than in Italy or the Federal Republic of Germany, although less frequent than in the United States.

[13] See Robinson, Rusk and Head, *op. cit.*, pp. 639–40.

[14] It would be highly desirable to have greater knowledge of the origin of feelings of duty in a variety of cultures. Such feelings could conceivably prevail in systems that have had "subject" political cultures as well as in places where predominant values have stressed "positive" political participation. "Subject" orientations could, in turn, be the result of the effects of political tradition, social hierarchy or the special emphases accompanying periods of rapid development or political crisis.

The notion that feelings of duty may be more common in countries with a high literacy rate, and where the media have a widespread influence, is suggested by differences in the Almond and Verba findings between Great Britain and the Federal Republic of Germany, on the one hand, and Italy and Mexico, on the other.

stand high turnouts in Japan. Direct connections between this attitude and behavior will be shown in Chapter Eight.

Attitudes about Active Political Participation. As we have seen, recent studies of attitudes regarding turnout in Japan have focused primarily on motivations for voting and attitudes toward abstention. Researchers have, in effect, identified the psychological dimension of past voting acts, or the incidence of people's conceptualization of the vote as an explicit obligation. On the other hand, studies in Japan of voter attitudes toward political participation, beyond simple voting, have focused primarily on ideal solutions or preferences in hypothetical situations. They have sought to identify generalized attitudes regarding the desirability of participation in politics, views about what kind of participation is preferable or effective in order to express opinions and wants, and specific predispositions to take an active personal part in local political decisions. The findings of these studies typically indicate a general tendency toward political passivism; activist sentiments were present in comparatively low ratios (Table 4-3).[15]

Still, there were deviations from this general trend, where the results of surveys on the desirability of simply "paying attention to politics" were concerned. According to the findings of a recent series of studies conducted in different parts of the country, majorities of respondents felt that it was more desirable to "pay attention to public affairs" than simply to "follow national leaders" (Kōmei 1966/4; Kōmei 1966/2, p. 143). In a similar vein, voters in one western district most often replied that "it's better to express one's opinion," and were less inclined simply to "depend on a distinguished politician" (Kumamoto 1962).[16] As the data in Table 4-4 shows, there has also

---

[15] In the discussion that follows inclinations simply to vote or "depend" on others are considered evidence of "passive" orientations. A preference for working through groups, making petitions, adopting leadership roles or "making efforts" to resolve problems is considered an indication of an activist posture.

[16] The fact that dependence on others or "following national leaders" were alternatives in various surveys reflects an appreciation among Japanese researchers of the importance of these themes, particularly the former, in popular attitudes. For a discussion of the contemporary importance of these sentiments about paternalistic leadership in a more general (not specifically political) frame of reference, see R. P. Dore, *Land Reform in Japan* (London, New York and Toronto: Oxford University Press, 1959), especially pp. 400–04.

See also the discussion of voting choice attitudes in Ch. 5 here.

TABLE 4-3. ATTITUDES TOWARD PARTICIPATION IN POLITICS AND COMMUNITY AFFAIRS*

	Yes (%)	No (%)	Don't Know (%)	Total (%)	(N)
Better for people to pay attention to politics than to simply follow the leadership of government ministers and Diet members[a]	74	15	11	100	(389)
Opposed to the idea that it's better to depend on a fine politician than to express individual opinions (which may be difficult to reconcile)[b]	38	31	31	100	(900)
Think the best way to improve our lives is through the power of a popular group or by petitions to officials (rather than depending on assemblymen or just voting for the best candidate or party)[c]	22	74	4	100	(916)
Think the best way to have people's opinions reflected in national affairs is through group activity (rather than through simply careful thought at election time)[d]	21	62	17	100	(660)
Would cooperate with a recall movement when a prefectural assemblyman is corrupt (rather than just vote against him or do nothing)[e]	15	71	14	100	(1,385)
Think the best way to have people's opinions reflected in local politics is through groups or movements (rather than simply electing someone who will reflect one's opinions)[f]	44	51	5	100	(475)
Best way to resolve hamlet or neighborhood problems is through community discussion (rather than by asking influentials or officials or waiting for things to work out)[g]	36	54	9	99	(195)
Would take an active role in resolution of local problems (rather than depend on influentials or do nothing due to apathy)[h]	26	70	4	100	(5,000)

SOURCES:
[a] Kōmei 1966/4, 54.   [b] Kumamoto 1962, p. 5.   [c] Miyazaki 1964, p. 55.
[d] Fukushima 1962, p. 173.   [e] Kōmei 1967A, p. 80 (national).   [f] Fukushima 1963, p. 169.   [g] Aichi 1964, p. 143. Figures are for urban portion of sample only.
[h] Kōmei 1958, p. 85 (national).

* "Yes" answers signify activist attitudes and orientations; "no" answers signify passive role orientations and attitudes. "Don't know" answers include "can't really say" and "no answer," as well as "other" where the content of this response was not clearly identifiable as pertaining to "yes" or "no."

been an increase over time in the public awareness of the need to be alert with regard to what goes on in politics at the expense of depending on "fine leaders."

TABLE 4-4. PARTICIPATION AND DEFERENCE ATTITUDES, 1953–1963

	Yes (%)	No (%)	Don't Know (%)	Total (%)	(N)
Better to depend on a fine politician to ensure Japan's future (1953)	43	38	19	100	(2,254)
Same question (1958)	35	44	21	100	(2,369)
Same question (1963)	29	47	24	100	(2,696)

SOURCES: Tōkei Sūri Kenkyūjo, *Kokuminsei no Kenkyū: Dainiji Chōsa* (Tōkyō: 1959), p. 95, and University of California, Survey Research Center Codebook for the 1963 survey.

What these kinds of responses represent, more than anything else, is simply the ease with which Japanese respondents subscribe to the ideals of democracy where these are operationalized in terms of fairly abstract commitments or general postures toward politics. This serves to illustrate again the degree to which the tendency which I have called formalism is operative, since, in reply to concrete questions, most respondents indicated preferences for passive forms of participation.

The general trend toward passivity was most clear when survey questions focused on the desirability or possibilities for active participation in matters relating to national or prefectural political processes. When asked about the best way to express opinions or articulate wants at the level of prefectural or national politics, or "politics" in general, Japanese voters were inclined to be especially passive in their attitudes. Accordingly, most persons would simply "rely on their vote," and comparatively little support was shown for more active political participation. In reply to a question on the "best thing to do to get one's wants from politics realized," 39 percent of those interviewed in a mixed urban and rural district near Tokyo said they would simply "elect a good Diet member," while an additional 18 percent felt they would best profit by "depending on the efforts of political parties." Only four percent were of the opinion that it would be a good idea to "form a group and try to realize our wants through its activities" (Chiba 1962, p. 297). Elsewhere, three-quarters of those interviewed said they would "depend on a politician" or "vote for the best candidate or party" rather than petition or work through a group to "improve our lives" (Miyazaki 1964).

Similar opinions were expressed in other districts. Sixty-two percent of the voters in one of Japan's northern prefectures felt that the best way to have some impact on national politics was by "thinking carefully at election time," while only 21 percent would form a group or use existing groups to accomplish their aims (Fukushima 1962).[17] In another survey voting was also seen as the best way to manifest one's opinions regarding prefectural as well as regional problems; only 13 percent of those interviewed would "depend on groups" and another eight percent reported, somewhat ambiguously, that they would "wait for the proper occasion to do something about it" (Ōita 1962, p. 28). Finally, one survey reveals that only 15 percent of the national electorate would join a movement to recall a corrupt politician, while in such a case two-thirds of the citizenry would simply "vote for another candidate" in the next election (Kōmei 1967A).

Where the focus of survey questions was on local affairs, proportionately more persons indicated a preference for active forms of political participation than was the case with national politics. However, even at the local level majorities showed an inclination to depend on others, or the vote, to get things done. In a certain region where interest in politics is exceptionally high 44 percent felt the activities of groups or movements were the best means to get people's opinions reflected in local political processes; still, just over 50 percent of those interviewed were of the opinion that it was best just to "think carefully at election time . . . rather than upset the peace of the community" (Fukushima 1963). In another district most voters reported similarly that they would "depend on influentials" or "wait until things work out" in order to resolve local issues, although 36 percent of this group did feel that community-wide discussions were the best option (Aichi 1964).

The inclusion in surveys of questions about voters' views on appropriate forms of participation in local affairs reflects the interest of

---

[17] This pattern is especially significant in view of other evidence which indicates that political interest is especially high in this prefecture. See Ch. 2, n. 37.

many scholars and officials in Japan in determining the realities of local government following the postwar reforms. Similar concerns have motivated researchers of the Fair Election League to ask direct questions about individual predispositions to take active roles in community affairs. Fortunately, substantially the same query has been used in investigations conducted in many parts of the country at different times. The content of the question is especially interesting in view of the findings. Respondents were asked if they were inclined either to "state my opinion as much as I can and try to get things done," "make some effort to solve these problems," "maintain some interest in local affairs but depend on others" or "feel apathetic about local problems." Although the distribution of replies to this particularly concrete question has varied somewhat from place to place — differences are particularly notable between urban and rural areas — generally only about one-quarter to one-third of the public reported that they were inclined to take active roles in solving local problems (Kōmei 1958).[18]

Participation Attitudes: Trends and Ambiguities. It is important to note that more Japanese are inclined toward collective participation in local than in national politics. Still, it is an inescapable fact that the typical Japanese voter is inclined toward passive political participation or dependence on others, despite the fact that majorities of the electorate find politics relevant, report an interest in public affairs and have instrumental expectations toward politics. Most citizens quite clearly would normally rely on their vote to get something accomplished in the public sphere, or they would depend on influentials or politicians to take care of their interests. More active forms of political participation such as working through groups or movements are generally eschewed, although these are preferred, or are plausible courses of action, more often at the local than national level. The only exceptions to this general theme — and these are noteworthy, both substantively and methodologically — occur wherever questions are comparatively abstract, permitting respondents to express simply their appreciation of norms regarding the value of an alert citizenry under popular government.

As was the case with evaluative attitudes, assessment of the significance of these trends is somewhat problematical. Even though we often

---

[18] See also Tōkyō 1958, p. 27; Miyagi 1962, Appendix, p. 7; Aomori 1962, p. 23; and Saitama 1962, p. 29.

assume that voluntary political participation is desirable and important to the functioning of democratic government, there are no obvious standards of what constitutes "high" and "low," or adequate and inadequate, levels of participation or participation attitudes.[19] It may also be somewhat unrealistic to anticipate high levels of preference for more active forms of political participation in societies which have become increasingly urbanized. Although urbanization has fostered higher participation levels in some societies, it is far from clear whether this is a general case or if massive urbanization will in fact favor such tendencies.[20]

It is further difficult to find standards to apply to the Japanese evidence by looking at participation attitude trends in other countries. According to the findings of Almond and Verba, relatively few voters in Western democracies outside the United States place a high value on activist forms of political participation. Although the data from this study are not literally comparable with those from Japan, we can at least infer that the Japanese electorate compares favorably with some other countries in preferences for activist participation. Certainly the fact that between one-quarter and one-third of the electorate in Japan favors either collective participation or activist roles in local politics can be favorably interpreted in view of the comparative evidence.[21]

These problems notwithstanding, it is still possible to speculate

---

[19] For a simple statement of the expectations of democratic theory on the question of participation — which, incidentally, raises some questions about the desirability of high intensities of popular political interest — see Bernard Berelson, "Democratic Theory and Public Opinion," *Public Opinion Quarterly* 16 (fall 1952), especially pp. 316–17. For other considerations of the desirability of passive majorities see Herbert Tingsten, *Political Behavior: Studies in Election Statistics* (Totowa, New Jersey: Bedminister Press, 1963), pp. 225–26, and Seymour Martin Lipset, *Political Man: The Social Bases of Politics* (Garden City, New York: Doubleday, 1960), pp. 32–33.

[20] This unconventional interpretation of the effects of urbanization is based on the Japanese findings reported in Ch. 6 here. It is not at all clear, moreover, whether these tendencies are confined solely to Japan. For a review of the contradictory state of recent findings on urban-rural differences in Europe, see Jurg Steiner, *Bürger und Politik* (Meisenheim am Glan: Anton Hain, 1969), pp. 147–50. For a more conventional view and supporting data see Lester Milbrath, *Political Participation* (Chicago: Rand McNally, 1965), pp. 128–130.

By "massive urbanization" I refer to the current population movements in Japan; comparable tendencies can obviously be seen in other places.

[21] Japanese patterns do not compare favorably, however, with those in the United States.

on the sources and meanings of Japanese preferences for largely passive forms of political activity. Several types of passivity can be proposed, and we can make what are essentially qualitative assessments of the importance of each type within Japan. In so doing, some potentially fruitful themes for future research can be suggested.

The fact that most voters in Japan are inclined to favor the vote or dependence on others over more active political participation could signify high levels of satisfaction with the current state of political affairs. Adoption of activist political roles might then seem superfluous, and simply registering one's opinions by voting would be felt as adequate. While this may be the case in some other places, it is doubtful this mood prevails in Japan. Although it is indeed difficult to say just what intensity of feeling is involved when Japanese voters answer questions about political satisfaction, it is quite clear that majorities of the electorate are only weakly satisfied or else dissatisfied with current politics. It would seem quite safe to assume that in Japan passivity does not originate in feelings of contentment.

Preference for passive political roles could also reflect the presence of feelings of personal inadequacy in public affairs.[22] In this case, a preference for voting or "depending on others" could suggest that little is expected from political action and that any activity beyond the morally approved act of the vote is viewed as a waste of effort. Opinions expressed in answer to survey questions in this area in Japan are, as has already been observed, somewhat ambiguous. Majorities of the electorate have indicated that they feel their vote is meaningful and that politicians and officials are responsive, despite the generally considerable pessimism in assessments of the behavior of elites and the value of elections. Probably some of this ambivalence does carry over into attitudes about participation, and in view of the prevailing negativism in perceptions of the conduct of politics, quite a few voters may be resigned to the feeling that voting is enough.

So far we have looked only at voter feelings of satisfaction and self-evaluations of personal efficacy as possible influences on preferences

---

[22] Somewhat complex relationships between feelings of satisfaction and those of efficacy may also occur. Widespread dissatisfaction could be a correlative of similarly widespread feelings of inefficacy. Or the two types of attitudes may not be closely related, as appears to be the case in Japan. This could imply that feelings of efficacy are simply a "learned" attitude, although the question of intensity and meaning of feelings of satisfaction is also important here.

for active or passive political roles. The normative connotations of preferences for different kinds of political participation are also important. It has been clearly shown that voting is seen by majorities of Japanese as a morally desirable thing to do. On the other hand, more active forms of political participation do not command the same degree of approval, since indigenous norms exist which encourage passivism even though the importance of participation is stressed in democratic ideas. Norms favoring community cooperation do exist in Japan, especially in the rural districts.[23] They may contribute to developing activist orientations toward politics in certain circumstances, as I will show later. But norms less favorable to high levels of activist attitudes can also be observed in Japan. At least in rural Japan, self-assertiveness in pursuit of political office has not been considered a desirable trait. Political activism in the form of movements and group efforts may also be considered disruptive of highly desirable states of collective harmony and consensus.[24] In view of the presence of this kind of normative

---

[23] Such norms can be inferred from the prevalence of cooperative neighborhood and community activities in accounts of rural life in Japan. In my own experience, the importance of these sentiments could be seen reflected in the excuses given when interview appointments were postponed because of community decisions to conduct some kind of cooperative activity on a particularly suitable day.

Some sentiments of this kind are even prevalent in the new residential districts of the large cities, where at least nominal attention is given to household association requests for cooperation.

[24] Some writers have placed special emphasis on the degree to which personal ambitions for office have been cloaked in statements and behavior which minimize individual ambition. I have observed similar tendencies among some local politicians. But others were much more open in their statements, sometimes "legitimizing" their ambitions by subsuming them under a commitment to represent some community or group.

The idea that harmony and consensus are a major goal of social behavior in Japan has been so widely discussed that further comment is perhaps unnecessary. But the wording of one question on participation attitudes provides intriguing evidence of appreciation of the continuing viability of this norm in the face of possibly contradictory values: "Even though it is said that democracy means the active expression of individual opinions, these may be hard to reconcile; do you agree with the idea that it's preferable to just depend on an exemplary politician or not?" (Kumamoto 1962, p. 5.) Similar concerns for "the peace of the community" are observable in a question used in Fukushima 1963, p. 169. (See Table 4-3, here, for findings.)

While accepting the importance of harmony as a dominant cultural goal, I cannot help but wonder on what occasions and on what premises groups or individuals engage in behavior which results in its violation. In my own field experience, it appeared that action was frequently taken on behalf of the interests of a smaller collectivity (hamlet or local district) which had the consequence of

climate, it is perhaps natural that many Japanese would content themselves with voting, "depending on others," or "going along." [25]

Future studies of participation attitudes in Japan, as well as elsewhere, should take into greater account the nature of certain cultural norms. Cultural values may indeed prove to be as important for participation attitudes as the diffusion of democratic ideas or popular feelings of efficacy and satisfaction. Moreover, future research should investigate not only the cultural values that appear most directly relevant for participation attitudes, such as those pertaining to social cooperation or participation, but also the *goals* that are sought through political or social action. If, for example, community harmony and consensus is preferred over satisfaction of the wants of any of its component units, as may be the case in rural Japan, quite different political styles will be observed than where some other hierarchy of goals prevails.

Studies of participation attitudes should also consider the character of popular beliefs about what kinds of action are most *effective*. It is entirely plausible that such beliefs will vary among political cultures. Feelings about the suitability of the vote may in fact determine Japanese opinions on forms of participation, while the preference of some voters for "dependence" on others presumably reflects underlying assumptions about effectiveness.[26] Finally, the latent purposes

---

disrupting the harmony of a larger collectivity (administrative unit). Similar patterns can be observed at the national level. To some degree, frustration levels are probably important also, and the sometimes especially intense political competition between collectivities in Japan may be a correlative of the "extremeness" of situations where the norm is finally violated. (The bitterness which accrues when others violate this norm is, in turn, sometimes the basis for high levels of frustration.)

[25] Although I do not differ with Dore's conclusions that dependency attitudes are less common in Japan than earlier, that they are still around is readily evident in the findings reviewed here. Consequently, we cannot altogether discount the importance for participation orientations of dependency attitudes, which are grounded in the hierarchical nature of personal relationships that has existed, and still exists to some degree, in some sectors of society in Japan. Reflections of this are clearly found in the paternalistic attitudes of some politicians. See Bradley Richardson, "Japanese Local Politics: Support Mobilization and Leadership Styles," *Asian Survey* (December 1967), pp. 872–73.

[26] Much of the economic protest activity of organized labor in Japan suggests to some degree the influence of cultural norms regarding the appropriateness of certain kinds of participation. The brevity and somewhat "ritualized" nature of many strikes suggests that their main purpose is to register feelings which will then be acted upon by industrial officials, viewed as being somewhat paternalistically respon-

for participation must be considered as well as the manifest ones. The degree to which active political participation may be a source of self-satisfaction should thus be considered. It is certainly plausible that feelings of this kind may underlie American participation attitudes.[27]

The fact that Japanese voters see active forms of political participation as more desirable or potentially more effective in local rather than national politics also merits some consideration. This tendency may in part reflect the expansion during the American occupation of opportunities for local political participation.[28] Even though important political reforms occurred at the national level as well, the effects of postwar changes may have been more immediately felt in the more intimate sphere of local affairs. But we have also seen that Japanese voters are more interested in local affairs and more positive in their evaluation of local political opportunities and the quality of local candidates. The social patterns which favor higher interest and confidence at the local level may themselves be directly associated with the observed tendencies in attitudes toward local participation. Although high levels of social interaction and collective life may be found at the community or neighborhood level in other countries, along with similar levels of activist participation attitudes toward local politics, it is still possible that the social setting in Japan is especially

---

sible to their employees. (Many of labor's political demonstrations also seem predicated on these assumptions, while the sustained nature of some political and economic confrontations suggest the presence of feelings of extreme bitterness in the face of perceived irresponsibility.)

[27] This was the implication of some of the Almond and Verba findings on voting attitudes.

It is also possible to look beyond the subject at hand and infer that the term "politicization" may have quite different connotations in different cultures, despite contrary assumptions in some writings. See, for example, Philip E. Converse and Georges Dupeux, "Politicization of the Electorate in France and the United States," in Angus Campbell, Philip E. Converse, Warren E. Miller and Donald Stokes, *Elections and the Political Order* (New York, London and Sydney: John Wiley and Sons, 1966), pp. 269-91.

[28] The expansion of opportunities afforded by institutional reform is obvious. But land reform also has had a considerable effect by changing community social structure in ways that supplement the effects of reforms in government institutions. See Dore, *Land Reform in Japan*, pp. 326-37.

It is also possible that local politics are popularly understood as an extension of the national political sphere in at least the rural sector, and that attitudes toward local affairs are accordingly affected. It is quite clear that people there are acutely sensitive to the capacities of their national representatives with regard to getting vital outside grants and subsidies for local projects. See also Dore's comments on the importance of this kind of representation to vote-getting, *ibid.*, p. 321.

congenial in this regard.[29] Thus, while several scholars have justifiably lamented the constraints of rural Japanese social structure on past development of democratic sentiments, it is eminently conceivable that today this sector plays a much more positive role in political socialization.

---

[29] Evidence from other countries on attitudes toward different levels of government does in fact suggest some comparabilities, even though the Japanese findings are much more complete and suggest the importance of local politics across a broader range of attitudes. In the findings of Almond and Verba, local governments were felt to have a slightly greater impact on "daily life" in the United States, the Federal Republic of Germany and Italy, although more persons in these countries and in Great Britain found national politics of "great" relevance. In all of these countries, moreover, voters felt that they could have slightly greater influence on local than on national decision-making. See *The Civic Culture,* pp. 46–47, and the codebook of the Inter-University Consortium for Political Research for this study.

5

VOTING ATTITUDES

A large part of political behavior research to date has been concerned with understanding the conditions underlying voting preferences and decisions.[1] This has been true for research conducted in the United States as well as the growing literature from Europe and elsewhere.[2] Yet despite the great attention to these matters in empirical research, there has been little explicit consideration of voting-choice behavior as a component of political culture. Investigations conducted within the United States employing both sociological and social psychological models have typically ignored the possibility that their conceptual frameworks might be culturebound, at the same time that scholars concerned with explaining cross-national variations in behavior have felt that differences were attributable mainly to institutional variables or contrasts in educational systems.[3] The possible significance of voting-

---

[1] For an early summary of the development of this research in the United States, which clearly shows the models underlying various major research efforts, see Peter H. Rossi, "Four Landmarks in Voting Research," in Eugene Burdick and Arthur J. Brodbeck (eds.), *American Voting Behavior* (Glencoe, Illinois: Free Press, 1959), pp. 5–54.

[2] The major voting research outside the United States, published in English, is David Butler and Donald Stokes, *Political Change in Britain* (New York: St. Martin's Press, 1969). For Japan, the reader is referred to Ichirō Miyake, Tomio Kinoshita and Toshiichi Aiba, *Tōhyō Kōdō no Kenkyū* (Tōkyō: Sōbunsha, 1967).

[3] See Angus Campbell and Henry Valen, "Party Identification in Norway and the United States," and Philip E. Converse and Georges Dupeux, "Politicization of the Electorate in France and the United States," in Angus Campbell, Philip E. Converse, Warren E. Miller and Donald E. Stokes, *Elections and the Political Order* (New York: John Wiley, 1966), pp. 245–268 and 269–291, respectively.

choice research for political culture analysis, and vice versa, has consequently been ignored.

In contrast with general practice, voting-choice behavior and voting attitudes will be dealt with here as a component of political culture. To be sure, there are important dimensions of voting-choice that do not readily fit within a political cultural model.[4] But it is equally likely that there are cultural dimensions to the socialization processes relevant to formation of the attitudes upon which voting choices are made. It is possible, for example, that the alienation factor in French political culture contributes to the lower levels of partisan identification reported there by some scholars.[5] Likewise, the reported importance of party loyalty in American voter behavior may reflect both the salience of politics as a popular topic and the degree to which persons get satisfaction from identifying with a particular "team" in the American political culture. Or, to pose a question of immediate concern, to what degree do Japanese voters express cultural themes of dependence on a "protector" in their frequent indication of the importance of candidate character in their voting choices?

Several models of choice behavior are found in empirical research. Sociological theories of the vote dominated earlier writings on electoral behavior in the United States as well as abroad, and their more sophisticated descendents are still present in analyses of social and political cleavages. However, more recent research has generally stressed attitudinal models of voting-choice, wherein long-standing political loyalties are treated as a major variable, along with other more transient aspects of campaigns.[6] Finally, some writers have presented

---

[4] One has to be careful with voting-choice motivations in terms of political culture. Clearly, one would not want to suggest that candidate perceptions in a particular election have cultural implications. But if the content of such perceptions were fairly standard over time, without regard to context — such is the case in Japan, according to my findings — then I believe a cultural dimension of voting motivations has been uncovered.

[5] See Sidney Tarrow, "The Urban-Rural Cleavage in Involvement: The Case of France," *The American Political Science Review* 65 (June 1971), pp. 349–51, for a discussion of antipartisan feelings and low identification levels in rural France.

[6] See, for example, Angus Campbell, Gerald Gurin and Warren E. Miller, *The Voter Decides* (Evanston, Illinois: Row, Peterson, 1954), and Angus Campbell, Philip E. Converse, Warren E. Miller and Donald E. Stokes, *The American Voter* (New York and London: John Wiley and Sons, 1960), as well as other publications from the staff of the Survey Research Center, University of Michigan.

For other seminal studies on party loyalty and related topics, see especially

analyses in which the main goal is evaluation of the rational component of individual choice behavior.[7]

Analogies to American research are found in the emerging Japanese political behavior literature.[8] But unlike recent American studies, with their emphasis on measurement of independent attitudes, most Japanese studies have employed closed questions in which respondents have been asked to report which consideration among alternatives was most important to their voting decision in a particular election. Included in the arrays of choices have been familiar objects such as candidates, parties and, in a few cases, issues.[9]

The Japanese studies have rather extensively explored the effect of campaigns in voting choices, as well as explicitly investigating the extent to which a concern for having interests represented is an independent factor underlying the vote. The Japanese studies thus present findings which can be analyzed according to an attitudinal model of voting-choice, but their mode of measurement is typically different from that of American studies. As will be seen, this has both advantages and disadvantages.

The orientations and preferences uncovered in these studies are called *voting attitudes* here. Voting attitudes represent self-assessments of personal considerations in voting choices. Thus, like participation attitudes, voting attitudes represent predispositions to behave in certain ways. As such, they are distinguishable from involvement and evaluative attitudes, since these attitudes are representations of mental

---

Herbert McClosky and Harold E. Dahlgren, "Primary Group Influence on Party Loyalty," *The American Political Science Review* 53 (September 1959), pp. 757–776, and Donald R. Matthews and James R. Prothro, "The Concept of Party Image and its Importance for the Southern Electorate," in M. Kent Jennings and L. Harmon Ziegler (eds.), *The Electoral Process* (Englewood Cliffs, New Jersey: Prentice-Hall, 1966).

[7] V. O. Key, Jr., *The Responsible Electorate: Rationality in Presidential Voting 1936–1960* (New York: Vintage, 1968), and Arthur S. Goldberg, "Social Determinism and Rationality as Bases of Party Identification," *American Political Science Review* 63 (March 1964), pp. 5–25, are two salient examples.

[8] Ichirō Miyake et. al., *Tōhyō Kōdō no Kenkyū*, is the best example. The authors' methodology differs from that of many Japanese studies and is consequently one of the notable exceptions to comments following in the text.

[9] There are studies outside of the Kōmei Senkyo Remmei series where issues have received considerable emphasis. Ichirō Miyake et. al., ibid., is one example; so, also, is Akira Tsujimura, et. al., "Tōhyō Kōdō ni okeru Ishiki Kōzō," *Tōkyō Daigaku Shimbun Kenkyūjo Kiyō* 8 (1959), pp. 55–125.

states rather than inclinations to engage in specific kinds of behavior.[10]

The attitudes identified by survey research constitute a major dimension in real individual election choices in Japan. We can see this from the extent to which response patterns in a large number of surveys conducted over a substantial period of time actually converge. In other words, common patterns in hundreds of surveys support the inference that something tangibly important to people's decisions is being measured by interviewers' questions. However, the implications of voting attitudes in Japan may be somewhat different than in the United States. Recent American voting studies have generally assumed that the individual makes his voting choice largely on the basis of various internalized orientations that can in fact be identified by survey questions. The same assumption may not be as valid in Japan. Voting-choice in Japan can be affected by many direct and overt attempts by local elites and others to influence the vote, responses to which are determined as much by the circumstances of immediate social relationships as by the kinds of voting attitudes tapped in most survey research.

It is a well-known fact that Japanese candidates often seek support through maintenance of informal ties with community or group influentials, or with other leading figures who regularly endorse particular nominees or are otherwise active in influencing the choice of their followers. Candidates also act through lieutenants, or helpers who endeavor to influence the ordinary citizen's decision by giving gifts, vote-buying, reputation-peddling and organization of support associations. With such activities, voters are not infrequently exposed to communications from many sources, ranging from community or group endorsements to personal requests from acquaintances and neighbors. Although the frequency of communication does vary among different kinds of elections, and between urban and rural districts, as many as 85 percent of the electorate have reported that they are aware of these kinds of efforts to gain their vote.[11]

---

[10] In fact, the attitudes reported here are in most cases based on questions about actual behavior in specific elections.

[11] The effects of efforts to affect voting decisions in Japan have been investigated in quite a few studies. But the results will not be reported in detail here, in view of substantial problems in analyzing different sets of findings.

See Kōmei 1961A, pp. 63–64; Kōmei 1961B, pp. 49–51; Kōmei 1964A, p. 114; and Shimane 1960, p. 135.

In addition to the high frequency of attempts to influence the vote — itself a factor complicating voting behavior analysis — there is also a certain complexity introduced into analysis by competing appeals for voter support. Appeals from competing candidates are not uncommon, and voters are sometimes pressured by endorsements or personal requests on behalf of different nominees.

The net effect of heavy dependence on this kind of electioneering in Japan is that many voters are exposed to requests for support involving social pressures not reflected in the considerations customarily identified in surveys of voting motivations.[12] In this situation, the attitudes identified here are best interpreted in many instances at least as indicators of some of the parameters within which attempts to influence the vote are communicated. There is a variety of evidence on the content of attempts to recruit the vote which supports this conception.[13] Thus, it should be emphasized that in the context I have described the individual is less of an independent actor, even though his perception of the reasons for his choices may be accurately reported.

Conceptual Considerations. The voting attitudes of the Japanese electorate, as represented in the findings from many surveys, can be pragmatically grouped into three core categories: candidate perceptions, instrumental expectations and party orientations. Evidence about voters' assessments of other grounds for voting-choice is available, but these other categories will not be treated as central to the analysis here inasmuch as the evidence is either fragmentary or inconclusive.

Voting for a particular candidate may be based on something connected with his individual character, ability or experience. These emphases are called *candidate perceptions* here.[14] While the expectation may be latent that a certain kind of candidate will do something for the voter, his group or community, the most salient or visible content of this type of response is a concern for the character traits or capabilities of particular candidates, without explicit reference to other considerations.

---

[12] American studies have not ignored the importance of campaign influences, but recent research has focused mainly on the effects of campaign events on voter attitudes, rather than attempting to trace more directly the complexities of individuals' campaign exposure.

[13] See p. 126.

[14] The concept is taken from the writings of the Michigan Survey Research Center staff. See, for example, Angus Campbell *et. al., The American Voter,* Ch. 3.

A second category of voting attitudes is that of *party orientations.* What is implied here is not party identification of the kind described and analyzed in American voting studies, but rather an expression of concern for "party" as a factor in making voting choices. Although party support or partisan identifications have been measured independently in Japan, what is significant here is simply the fact that voters cite party affiliation as the most important consideration in voting-choice. This may imply only that such a voter maintains loyalty to a particular party as a reference group, or it could mean that he favors a particular party's policy orientations. It might further mean that he considers "party" to be important because these are the perceived preferences of certain people, such as persons belonging to a particular social class, toward which he feels loyal.[15]

Voting attitudes in Japan also contain what are best described as *instrumental expectations.* Survey replies indicate that voters frequently choose a particular candidate because they think that he will do something for their community or occupational group, or that he will represent some other particular interest.

Of course these conceptual choices are determined in large part by the kinds of questions typically asked in the Japanese studies. The most common question — one that has been used in literally hundreds of surveys — calls for a quite simple differentiation between voting

---

[15] A hamlet politician I interviewed said: "Well, I wouldn't really say that political parties as such have much meaning around here. Everybody really votes for the person. But I suppose they wouldn't ever consider somebody outside the Liberal Democratic Party, except for maybe a few persons."

The meaning of "class" in Japan must be qualified, however. As Dore has observed, positive class identifications are generally rather weak in Japan — except perhaps among workers, where they are given focus and content through the efforts of union leaders and cadres. Still, some individuals in answers to open questions did speak of the Japan Socialists as the party of the working class. However, this may result more from the vocabulary of party rhetoric than from strong feelings of "we-ness" among workers. See R. P. Dore, *City Life in Japan* (Berkeley and Los Angeles: University of California Press, 1959), pp. 214–21.

The phenomenon in Japan of leftist party support among white-collar employees and other occupational categories characterized by high levels of education is difficult to identify in precise class terms. One may see "causes" in the nature of the university experience, while feelings of frustration associated with highly bureaucratized work situations and careers, or low salaries, may have some sustaining effect. Still, it is possible that many white-collar workers have acquired surrogate working class identifications through union membership.

decisions made on the basis of either candidate or party.[16] There are some obvious limitations to this kind of question. A choice is forced, where in reality *both* party and candidate may have been considered. This kind of question is also insensitive to potentially important variation in intensity of support for particular parties or candidates. These limitations notwithstanding, this question clearly taps an exceedingly important and central dimension of Japanese political culture.

A second type of query used in the Japanese studies has consisted of a larger array of closed alternatives, measuring party orientations, candidate perceptions and instrumental expectations respectively. Many studies have included detailed breakdowns of these general categories, in the form of closed alternatives regarding such perceptions as "the candidate could be trusted" or "the candidate was experienced," or expectations that the nominee would "represent this district" or "do things for my occupational group."

Voting Attitudes in Japan. Patterns in voting attitudes necessarily vary somewhat as a result of rhetorical differences among questions. But there are some consistent themes, and both the consistencies and variations afford insights into political culture.

For one, electoral politics in Japan is highly personalized, according to surveys of individual perceptions of the basis for voting-choice. Where survey response alternatives were simply "party" or "candidate," a majority of Japanese voters said they felt "candidate" was more important in their voting-choice in both national and local elections (Table 5-1).[17] This is the first major cultural theme that we see in

---

[16] This question has been used in most of the studies conducted by the Fair Election League, as well as in many newspaper public opinion polls. The origins of this item, as far as I can tell, lie in an appreciation on the part of researchers of the importance of "candidate," as well as in a self-conscious feeling among scholars and intellectuals that possession of partisan orientations among the electorate is an indication of modern outlooks.

In many ways it would be better to ask independent questions, such as those used in the Michigan studies. Separate queries about the importance of "candidate" or "party" could be more effective. There is some value, however, in forcing a choice between the two kinds of objects, even though underlying subtleties are consequently lost.

[17] Findings on this theme are so extensive that more citations are superfluous. For additional information the reader is referred to almost any of the Fair Election League reports, or the series of public opinion survey summaries, "Zenkoku Yoron Chōsa no Genkyō," issued annually by the Naikaku Sōridaijin Kanbō Kōhōshitsu (Information Office of the Prime Minister's Secretariat).

TABLE 5-1. Voting Attitudes

	National Election (%)	Local Election (%)
Made choice on basis of party or candidate:[a]		
Party	37	16
Candidate	47	64
Don't know/can't say	17	20
Total	101	100
(N)	(2,163)	(1,542)
Reasons for voting choice:[b]		
Candidate's fine character/honest	24	37
Candidate a strong politician	10	8
Candidate's party affiliation	14	4
Candidate represents local area	27	21
Candidate represents workers	8	6
Endorsements/requests	5	5
Other/don't know	13	18
Total	101	99
(N)	(431)	(517)
Reasons for voting choice:[c]		
Agreement on principles	31	32
Candidate's experience	9	5
Respect the candidate	16	18
Candidate from around here	7	26
Candidate represents our occupation	30	13
Other	7	6
Total	100	100
(N)	(530)	(—)
Most important thing about candidate:[d]		
Candidate was not haughty	26	—
Candidate was serious	26	—
Candidate's ability/experience	25	—
Other/don't know	23	—
Total	100	
(N)	(541)	
Thought about representation of occupational interest in voting choice:[e]		
Yes	54	—
No	34	—
Don't know	12	—
Total	100	
(N)	(214)	

Sources:
[a] Kōmei 1967BB, p. 22 (national) and Kōmei 1967A, p. 106 (national); "local" was city, town and village elections. [b] Kumamoto 1960, p. 63. [c] Niigata 1963, p. 9 and Niigata 1964, p. 7. "National" was national district of House of Councillors election, "local" was prefectural assembly election. [d] Iwate 1963, p. 78. [e] Shizuoka 1963, p. 92.

the findings. Nevertheless, variation in emphasis occurs at different election levels; consequently, candidate perceptions were felt by the electorate to be more important in local than in national contests (Kōmei 1967BB; Kōmei 1967A).[18]

However, underlying this simple emphasis on candidate or party was a somewhat more subtle and complex array of attitudes. In the findings of studies where questions included expanded alternatives, candidate perceptions were still stressed at the local level, but candidate perceptions and instrumental expectations (an attitude not measured in the party-candidate questions) received about the same degree of consideration in a national election (Kumamoto 1960). Elsewhere, candidate perceptions of a more specific kind — including the fact that "the candidate was from this area" — were stressed more than "agreement on principles" and instrumental expectations at the local level, but all of these considerations received about equal stress in a national contest (Niigata 1963 and 1964). In responses where several alternatives were available, party affiliation was substantially lower in importance than in simple "party" and "candidate" questions (Kumamoto 1960). From the evidence of these studies conducted in different places it can be clearly seen that in many cases electoral choices are based on sentiments that include more than simply loyalty to particular politicians.

Also, as might be anticipated from the earlier discussion of the importance of instrumentalism in political involvement, an instrumental factor is present in Japanese voters' decisions in many instances. Although any relationship identified on the basis of response patterns to different kinds of questions is necessarily tentative, the evidence suggests that some voters who prefer "party" in simple questions make choices elsewhere on the basis of instrumental expectations, at least where national elections are concerned. In other words, instrumental expectations seem to underlie the emphasis on party in

---

[18] There is, however, some variation in the degree of voter emphasis on either "party" or "candidate" within national elections. In a *few* cases "party" has been a more important consideration than "candidate" in House of Representatives contests. Regarding House of Councillors elections, "party" outweighed "candidate" considerations in specifically the national constituency, but not in local constituency decisions. See Kōmei 1964A, pp. 24–26; and Kōmei 1966, pp. 110–11.

some instances.[19] This relationship can in fact be directly seen where specific questions about voters' reasons for supporting a particular party have been asked.[20] A similar relationship can be inferred between instrumental concerns and "candidate" emphases in local elections. A direct correlation between these two kinds of voting attitudes was in fact visible in an analysis of the responses to my own 1964 survey. We can thus assume that there is some instrumental or representational content in both "candidate" and "party" considerations in replies to simple questions, with the nature of the relationship varying somewhat between national and local contests.

These observations notwithstanding, candidate perceptions did have specific content. Japanese voters were able to specify the kinds of things they felt were important about certain candidates, and their replies afford intriguing insight into the ways in which traditional and modern definitions of leadership interpenetrate. Candidate perceptions included, for example, feelings that a particular nominee was "sincere," "dignified," "honest," or, on one occasion, "not haughty or arrogant" (Iwate 1963). The first two of these qualities reflect earlier Confucian images, while preferences for candidates who are either nonarrogant or honest reflect reactions to earlier social practices and their vestigial influence today as well as to the visibility of corruption in politics.

Instrumental considerations of candidate character were also stressed by respondents to some surveys, while qualifications appropriate to ascriptive definitions of political roles were also found. Candi-

---

[19] See Ōita 1968, pp. 42 and 49, for evidence in support of this inference, as well as the relationship between instrumental concerns and candidate preferences at the local level. (While instrumental expectations remained constant at a fairly high level in responses to expanded questions, when simple choices were asked candidate perceptions were predominant in local contests and "party" the major concern in national elections.)

[20] "Agreement with policies" is the reason most commonly given to direct questions about party support. See, for example, Gumma 1963, p. 34. In the case of my own research, policy support and expectations of representation were the most important considerations taken together. See my unpublished Ph.D. dissertation, "Political Behavior and Attitudes in Contemporary Japan," University of California, Berkeley, 1966.

Still parties are not necessarily seen as the best instrument for implementation of wants. While 39 percent of the voters in the semiurban Chiba prefecture would "elect a good Diet member" to get things done, only 18 percent would "depend on party activities." See Chiba 1962, p. 297.

dates were thus seen as able, experienced or "influential in politics," while the fact that a candidate was simply "fitting" for Diet membership or public office was also sometimes important (Iwate 1965, p. 22; Gifu 1963, pp. 50–51). In one instance voters preferred a candidate who simply could "be respected" (Aomori 1963, p. 38). Question content occasionally imposed restraints on replies, but it is evident from the findings that Japanese voters are responsive to a great variety of leadership images. It should be noted, however, that where reasonably broad arrays of alternatives were included, respondents usually considered candidate character more important than more instrumental considerations such as ability, effectiveness, or experience.

Personalism, Partisanship, and Instrumentalism in Japanese Political Culture. Despite the presence of some cross-cutting patterns, the main emphasis in voting attitudes in Japan is the candidate. Images of candidate character and instrumental expectations are in turn present as the underlying dimensions of this consideration in voting-choice. These tendencies reflect in part the influence of prevailing campaign techniques in Japan. It is well-known among observers of Japanese elections that many candidates seek support through voter appeals which are independent of party control. This is shown both in studies of the content of candidate appeals and in the extensive literature on support mobilization and personal machine politics in Japan.[21]

---

[21] Two central themes can be discerned in the descriptions of support mobilization activities. Social institutions and groups are extensively used to get votes, and Japanese candidates display marked concern for stable, "structured" support bases and relationships. The kind of support mobilization given emphasis differs, however, both between national and local elections and between House of Councillors and House of Representatives contests at the national level. Major differences are also apparent between urban and rural districts.

The literature on support mobilization is extensive. For discussions of recent elections as well as citations of the literature in general, see Bradley Richardson, "A Japanese House of Councillors Election: Support Mobilization and Political Recruitment," *Modern Asian Studies* 1 (fall 1967), pp. 385–402, and "Japanese Local Politics: Support Mobilization and Leadership Styles," *Asian Survey* 7 (December 1967), pp. 860–75. See also Scott C. Flanagan, "The Japanese Party System in Transition," *Comparative Politics* 3 (January 1971), pp. 231–253. See also Ch. 6, n. 29 for relevant citations.

It is important to note that both the form and content of support mobilization in Japan differ substantially from the kinds of activities seen in American elections. Even though some of the events in a formal campaign period in Japan are similar to the content of campaigns elsewhere, this aspect of campaigns is supplemented by extensive efforts to gain support by personal contacts and machine organization. The only specific parallel to Japanese activities, to my knowledge, is found in

Students of Japanese political life have quite accurately observed that electoral arrangements in Japan favor individualized campaigns and intraparty competition between candidates at the constituency level. Japan does not have proportional representation; at the same time, there are multimember districts in the especially important House of Representatives contests and in some other kinds of elections. Under these circumstances it is possible for candidates to look for support at the expense of other nominees from the same party as well as by competing with persons from other political groups.

Electoral practices alone do not suffice as an explanation, however. There are a large number of single-member districts in House of Councillors and prefectural assembly elections, as well as one-man gubernatorial and mayoralty contests. While the evidence is still scanty, it is clear that candidate-oriented campaigns are also typical in these elections. It is important to recognize, however, that at all election levels this phenomenon is more common among conservatives than among leftist party candidates.[22]

The prevalence of candidate-oriented campaigns in Japan is ultimately connected to the character of the social structure. Important urban-rural differences notwithstanding, the nature of local community structure and personal relationships makes it possible in many cases for candidates to employ social institutions and personal ties to gain electoral support. This permits candidates of all parties, but particularly conservative candidates in small cities and rural hamlets, to mobilize support without extensive dependence on party symbols or organization.[23]

---

accounts of support mobilization by American city bosses, such as Harold F. Gosnell's *Machine Politics: Chicago Model* (Chicago: University of Chicago Press, 1937 and 1968). (It is possible, of course, that similar tactics are used elsewhere. One account of community life in Great Britain indicates some similarities between support mobilization in Japan and small communities in Ireland. See Ronald Frankenberg, *Communities in Britain* [Baltimore: Penguin Books, 1966], p. 43.)

[22] For evidence on these matters in one House of Councillors election, see Richardson, "A Japanese House of Councillors Election . . . ," *supra*.

[23] The extent to which party labels are used by candidates does vary substantially, however, between national and local contests. Ninety-seven percent of the candidates for the House of Representatives in 1963 ran as party nominees, while only five percent of those who sought office in town and village assemblies in the same year reported party ties. (The figure for city assembly contests was higher; 33 percent of the nominees claimed party affiliations there.) See Jichishō

The mechanics of these efforts are well-known; it will suffice here to observe that candidates' connections with local elites or the candidates' own organization of support associations provide networks of followers whose primary allegiance is to a particular person rather than to a partisan grouping.

To be sure relations between candidates and supporters of this kind are found in other places. Moreover, it goes without saying that candidate personality is stressed in campaigns in other political systems besides Japan.[24] But it is critical nevertheless to appreciate the degree to which ongoing social practices facilitate the kind of candidate-centered electioneering found in Japan. For the ongoing networks of personal influence and interpersonal connections that form the backbone of Japanese community life are extensively cultivated by individual candidates in order to build up support, and without them it is doubtful if individual candidacies could be as independent of party control as they are now.[25]

Clearly, other factors are also important. The institutionalized factionalism of the Liberal Democratic party in recent years has been associated with factional sponsorship of individual nominees, who in turn compete with each other within the umbrella of the same party affiliation. The absence of a strong ideological program among conservatives can be seen as another facilitating circumstance. Still, it is possible to see these as favorable but not necessary prerequisites for the intensity of candidate emphasis observed in campaigns in Japan; the character of the social setting, on the other hand, would seem a necessary condition.

Emphasis on candidate perceptions and the special concern shown for candidate character also conform to other tendencies in Japanese society. It is quite clear that many voters stress candidate character in their choices simply on the assumption that public officials should have

---

Senkyokyoku *Chihō Senkyo Kekka Shirabe* (Tōkyō: 1964), p. 5; and *Shūgiin Giin Sōsenkyo, Saikō Saibansho Saibankan Kokumin Chōsa Kekka Shirabe* (Tōkyō: 1964), p. 2.

[24] On effects of candidate and leader perceptions in the United States, see Angus Campbell, *et al.*, *The American Voter*, pp. 68–69; for Great Britain, see David Butler and Donald Stokes, *Political Change in Britain,* Ch. 17.

[25] The patterns in rural and small city constituencies are given greater emphasis here, since they are the most representative. For a discussion of the important differences in social structure and support mobilization between large cities and the rural areas, see Ch. 6, pp. 135–144.

exemplary personal qualities.[26] Preferences for candidates of high moral calibre also include concern for the election of representatives whose quality and behavior will favorably reflect upon the constituencies supporting them. The term "pride of the district" is sometimes used to convey sentiments of this kind, and it is clear that merely having a well-respected representative in the Diet is itself a source of satisfaction for many people.[27]

The high incidence in Japan of preferences for persons of good character is also an extension into the political sphere of more general cultural themes regarding the importance of primary relationships. As we have observed earlier, many kinds of activities are highly "personalized," and this "primordial" character of Japanese social patterns is important to the nature of voting attitudes.[28] Japanese typically depend on personal benefactors to a degree uncommon in most West-

---

[26] Images of preferred leadership traits may correspond to some extent to the concept of "statesman" in other countries—although the categories are not necessarily literal equivalents. The term "statesman" has the connotation of wise and able leadership, independent of partisan or group influences. To some extent this may be implied in Japanese concepts of leadership qualities, but it seems that the concern simply for persons of fine character is the dominant theme.

The importance of personal character in Confucian ideas about proper leadership, as well as the related feeling that paternal figures of fine character are responsible to popular interests, presumably play some vestigial role in popular attitudes today. It is actually quite difficult in some cases to separate candidate perceptions from instrumental expectations, given the somewhat diffuse nature in some instances of the conception of "character" and the concomitant presence of "instrumentalist" overtones.

[27] See, for example, Shimane 1963, p. 99, where respondents were asked to comment on the degree to which candidates fit the category of "kyōdo no hokori" or a "pride of the region."

Dore also reports that whether or not a representative's behavior will reflect favorably on the hamlet has also been a consideration in local nominations. See R. P. Dore, *Land Reform in Japan* (London, New York and Toronto: Oxford University Press, 1959), p. 339.

[28] The term "primordial" is used in more or less the same sense by Harry Eckstein in *Division and Cohesion in Democracy: A Study of Norway* (Princeton: Princeton University Press, 1966), pp. 112 ff. In Eckstein's usage it refers to the "intimacy and functional salience" of kinship bonds. The usage here extends the application to primary groups and important personal relationships, which are functionally important in Japanese society.

Usage of the term "primordial" should not be considered an assessment of Japan's state of political development. In addition to rejecting the utility of unilinear models of political development, I do not feel comfortable with the frequently parochial assessments of developmental tendencies made by many American scholars. When I use the expression "primordial" it is only for the purpose of precise description, and nothing else.

ern societies; they prefer to work through known intermediaries in many kinds of situations rather than deal with persons who are unknown. There are indications that these practices are much less important today than they were in the past. But the point here is simply that the importance of personal connections and benefactors in everyday life is still considerable, being reflected in political life by preferences for candidates who have the kinds of character desirable for intermediary roles. It is quite clear that here, and in other aspects of popular attitudes and behavior, the sphere of politics is only imperfectly differentiated from general social practice in contemporary Japan.[29] Thus the pervasion of personalism in Japanese life results in an attentiveness to the personalities of candidates that differs markedly from other societies, where the cultivation of "connections" is less of a cultural ethos.

Finally, the emphasis on "candidate" in voting-choice, specifically on character traits, presumably represents in many cases a vague instrumental concern for improving the quality of politics. As a natural consequence of the prevalence of pessimistic evaluations of the behavior of public officials, it is particularly apparent in the attitudes of some subgroups of the population — although it may be present to some degree in the electorate as a whole. Urban residents in my own survey, for example, felt that candidate character was more important than representation of their interests, an emphasis that could only be explained by their parallel concern for the problem of corruption in politics.

It is important at this point to note that the emphasis on candidate perceptions is not necessarily accompanied by strong affect for individual candidates. When respondents to my 1964 survey were asked if they especially "liked" the candidate of their choice, majorities an-

---

[29] Despite my assertion about the uniqueness of Japanese behavior viewed from the western perspective, there are still some parallels to be noted. It is thus likely that government is perceived as it is among residents of Boston's West End, who "conceive the governmental process to be much like *personal relationships* in the peer group society . . . ; government agencies are identified with the individuals who run them, and agency behavior is explained in terms of their *personal motives*." This conceptualization seems to fit with respect to rural Japan, where at least known aspects of politics are concerned. See Herbert J. Gans, *The Urban Villagers* (New York: Free Press of Glencoe, 1962), p. 164.

swered that they felt no affect or "didn't know." [30] Only 21 percent indicated that they liked the candidate they supported in the House of Representatives election, while this figure was only slightly higher in the case of local assembly contests. This tendency is even more surprising, perhaps, in that respondents who reported affect for a particular candidate cited the same kinds of candidate perceptions and expectations of representation in their choices as persons who did not feel warmly toward a particular nominee.

This apparent ambiguity should be viewed, however, in light of more general themes in Japanese political attitudes. As noted in earlier chapters, quite a few voters are pessimistic about politics, at the same time seeing it as "relevant" and even interesting. The importance of this general trend of pessimism in nonaffective candidate perceptions, as well as the special alienating effects of social isolation, was evident from the replies to a follow-up question in my survey. Majorities of the voters feeling no affect said they felt that way because they "didn't have a personal relationship with the candidate," "all of the candidates were remote," "all of the candidates were smooth tongued," or "politics wouldn't change even if you liked someone." Even though voters make choices on the basis of specific candidate perceptions, it is clear that an overall impression of politics in many cases still influences the levels of enthusiasm aroused by particular candidates.[31] The replies of people who did not particularly "like" the candidate of their choice also provided evidence in support of the contention here

---

[30] It would be good to compare these patterns with affect levels elsewhere, but I don't think a direct question of this kind has been used.
To some degree, the very wording of this question seemed odd in the context of Japanese culture (as seen in the surprised reactions of some respondents). This by itself was a clue to the nature of their sentiments, and provides additional insight into the nature of Japanese political attitudes. Some replied "that it isn't really a matter of liking or not liking somebody."

[31] The fact that comparatively few voters felt affect for the candidate of their choice does not contradict their reports of concern for "candidate perceptions" in replies to questions about voting attitudes (Richardson 1964). A preferred candidate might have been considered only marginally better than another, even in the absence of affect.
But it is also plausible that affect is simply not common in Japanese feelings about politics. Although it is extremely difficult to measure intensities of feelings, the fact that several voters felt "it was not a matter of liking or not liking somebody" suggests that this may be the case. Low levels of affect might also be a natural correlative of the formalistic tendencies discussed earlier.

(and earlier) of the importance of personal contacts in Japanese life in general, and politics in particular.[32]

It is also clear from numerous findings — and as a corollary of what I have just described — that the Japanese electorate typically deemphasizes partisan affiliations of nominees at the expense of candidate perceptions. It might be inferred from this that party symbols and party loyalty are meaningless to a large segment of the Japanese public. It is true, as research has shown, that Japanese partisan loyalty is typically less frequent than comparable attachments in the United States.[33] Still, in the vicinity of three-quarters of the population indicated that they like or support a particular party, in response to questions that are roughly comparable to party identification questions employed in American studies (Table 5-2). It should be noted, however, that markedly fewer people claim to support a party where the wording of survey questions makes support seem a more serious or self-conscious type of relationship (Table 5-2). In other words, fewer people indicated loyalties where the question was formulated in such a way as to query if a party were in fact supported. These frequencies of reported party loyalties in replies to more difficult questions reflect the fact that intensities of party attachments are typically quite weak in Japan, in contrast with the United States.[34] There are very few

---

[32] It is interesting to note that affect for candidates in both national and local elections was lower in urban Yokohama than in rural sectors.

There were some interesting variations within the rural sectors, however, and it is obvious that local conditions are important. Thus, more respondents "liked" the candidate they supported in rural Atsugi, where a "local son" incumbent was given solid backing by residents of the area. In Nita, on the other hand, support was less homogeneous and the candidate who received the most votes was not a local son and had spent most of his life away from the prefecture as an upper level bureaucrat. As a result, feelings of affect were somewhat lower than in Atsugi.

Other considerations, such as Atsugi's more favorable economic situation and more egalitarian social patterns, could also have been relevant. Average farm incomes were substantially higher, there were more opportunities for outside employment and at higher wages, and land ownership was more equitably distributed in Atsugi than in Nita. See "Political Behavior and Attitudes in Contemporary Japan," Appendix II.

[33] The figures for the United States are reported in Angus Campbell *et al., The American Voter*, p. 124. For representative findings on Japan see Miyagi 1962, appendix, p. 30.

[34] Ichirō Miyake and his colleagues concluded that intensities of party identification are weaker in Japan than in other countries where comparable research was conducted. (*Tōhyō Kōdō no Kenkyū*, p. 73, n. 3.) In the case of my own findings, two out of every five supporters felt that their feelings were best summarized in the

TABLE 5-2. PARTY IDENTIFICATION

Survey	Support a Party (%)	Tend to Support (%)	Don't Support (%)	Don't Know (%)	Total (%)	(N)
SYCR 1955	64	11	5	20	100	(2,500)
Asahi 1955	66	15	4	15	100	(3,000)
Asahi 1956	64	16	4	16	100	(3,000)
Asahi 1956	63	21	4	12	100	(3,000)
Asahi 1958	57	22	6	15	100	(3,000)
Asahi 1959	60	24	4	12	100	(3,000)
SYCR 1958	63	10	5	22	100	(2,500)
SYCR 1960	66	6	5	23	100	(3,000)
Asahi 1960	62	21	5	12	100	(3,000)
Asahi 1961	62	21	6	11	100	(3,000)
CCS 1961	66	10	7	17	100	(1,250)

SOURCES: Basic data sources were newspaper or commercial opinion surveys, specifically those of *Asahi Shimbun*, Shimbun Yoron Chōsa Remmei (SYCR) and Chūō Chōsasha (CCS). The figures presented here are from the 1956 (pp. 37 and 39), 1957 (pp. 52–53), and 1958 (pp. 105–06) issues of the periodical *Zenkoku Yoron Chōsa Kikan no Gaiyō*, issued by the Naikaku Sōridaijin Kambō Shingishitsu, and from the same office's *Zenkoku Yoron Chōsa no Genkyō* (Tōkyō: 1960), p. 131. 1961 data are from Naikaku Sōridaijin Kanbō Kōhōshitsu, *Zenkoku Yoron Chōsa no Genkyō* (Tokyo: 1962), p. 155.

persons in the contemporary Japanese electorate who indicate "strong support" or liking for a party, even though many people are nominal supporters.

The substantial levels of at least nominal party attachment would seem on the surface to contradict the evidence about the low saliency of partisan attitudes in the electoral decision. Several reasons for the singular importance of candidates in Japanese voting-choice have already been discussed, and it is obvious that these involve among other things a low stress on parties in campaign organization and communications.

But it should be pointed out that party labels and cues are not entirely absent from political campaigns in Japan. Most candidates in national elections run on the basis of party affiliations, even if their constituency campaigns in many cases focus on their own individually

---

statement, "I have no special interest, but just feel it's the best party." But a slightly larger ratio of the respondents reported feelings of "strong attraction" to the party of their choice and a few persons were party members.

tailored appeals and organization. Moreover, both conservative and leftist parties take positions on issues, and the leftist parties go to the electorate with ideological appeals that are reasonably clearcut. Party leaders also support candidates in districts which are seen as especially critical and make speeches on their behalf, while some parties attempt to assign voter quotas to candidates from among the groups which support that party. But dependence on party leadership and organization for support mobilization is still generally secondary in importance.[35] Since even in the leftist parties some candidates seek support more on the basis of their own individual efforts and contacts than by depending extensively on party labels or party help, it is safe to assume that political parties typically have a lower visibility than candidates.[36] However, the greater importance of parties in mobilization efforts in

---

[35] For both a discussion of how parties conduct campaigns and an assessment of the importance of party support of individual candidates by the distribution of party funds, see Arnold Heidenheimer and Frank Langdon, *Business Associations and the Financing of Political Parties* (The Hague: Martinus Nijhoff, 1968), pp. 181–88.

For evidence on the assignment of quotas of supporting groups by the Socialist Party in a House of Councillors election, see Bradley Richardson, "A Japanese House of Councillors Election," *Modern Asian Studies* 1 (October 1967), pp. 396–97. I also found evidence of quota assignment at the local level in Yokohama, although some Socialist candidates were nominees largely of a single group, in which case the candidacy reflected the influence in party circles of the supporting trade union. Even though individual effort plays a lesser role among some Socialist candidates than in the Liberal Democratic Party — reflecting differences both in party structure and in sources of support — individual Socialist candidates still campaign actively at election time.

The situation in Japan is vastly different from that which characterizes the relationship between candidates and parties in some European countries, where proportional representation systems exist. I have noted earlier that the extreme factionalism of most Japanese parties is a factor in the degree to which candidates mobilize support independently of party assistance. In many cases the factions are themselves sponsors of candidates, and have an interest in seeing that their own nominees are successful at the expense of candidates from other factions. Sometimes the efforts of party leaders to help individual candidates (which appear to be a "party" activity) are actually motivated by factional interests. The only cases where party organization seems clearly to dominate campaign activities in a systematic fashion is in the Kōmeito, the political wing of the Soka Gakkai religion, and at times in the Japan Communist Party.

[36] This was shown to be true according to the findings of my survey. Very few respondents mentioned "party" as a topic of political discussion, while the major theme was candidate perceptions and instrumental expectations.

However, city voters did mention party somewhat more often than did rural residents, and this reflects the comparatively greater importance of party symbols in urban campaign communications. As we will see in Ch. 6, urban voters also generally place more emphasis on party in voting-choice.

It is also important to differentiate somewhat between the role played by

the cities and in national politics should be recognized, along with the greater importance of party ideologies and symbols in campaigns by leftist parties.

Thus, while reflecting the influences which put stress on "candidate," tendencies concerning "party" in voting attitudes are largely attributable to the nature of electoral competition and support mobilization. But other influences are at work as well. There have been marked discontinuities in the recent history of political parties in Japan. The identities of the major parties substantially changed from the prewar to the postwar period, despite continuities among constituency level politicians. The postwar conservative parties bore different names and had different leaders from their prewar predecessors, while the postwar emergence of a viable Socialist movement had no real prewar precedent. The postwar period can also be divided into pre-1955 and post-1955 phases, in the sense that party labels and leadership were relatively more stable in the latter period than in the first.[37] In the presence of discontinuities of this kind it seems likely that fewer people will develop deep party attachments than would be the case in a more stable environment. For the same reason, it would be much harder for parents to pass on party loyalties to their

---

political parties in support mobilization and the importance of parties in general campaign communications, especially where national elections are concerned. While many candidates' efforts to get support are largely independent of party-coordinated campaign activities, candidates still talk about their partisan connections and issues in their speeches. As might be anticipated, this seems to be especially common among candidates from the leftist parties. Moreover, the news coverage of campaigns is largely couched in the language of partisan competition. Parties are also a highly visible campaign object where party elites make speeches in urban constituencies, wherever outcomes are critical or where favored candidates are running.

[37] Leftist parties became a viable force in Japanese elections and parliamentary politics only in the postwar period. Their emergence was due to a combination of favorable events, including occupation policies toward organized labor in the early postwar period, the land reform in some districts and the generally greater freedom of political activity in the postwar period.

Party labels changed rather frequently during the early postwar chaos, stabilizing only in 1955. This was especially true for the conservative forces, but there were important divisions among the left as well.

For a discussion of the development of the postwar party system, see Robert A. Scalapino and Junnosuke Masumi, *Parties and Politics in Contemporary Japan* (Berkeley and Los Angeles: University of California Press, 1962), pp. 28–41 and 47–53. The complex regrouping of parties is illustrated in a table in Asahi Shimbunsha, *Asahi Nenkan 1964* (Tokyo 1965), p. 242.

children in the fashion found in more stable systems.[38] Both of these consequences of discontinuities in party experience could contribute to the lower frequencies of concern for party in voting-choice.

Sizable numbers of Japanese voters also have negative images of political parties. This tendency has been reported in qualitative commentaries on Japanese politics but it is also found in some survey findings. For example, a substantial plurality of the electorate in one district agreed with the proposition that "today's political parties can't really be trusted" (Iwate 1963, p. 48). According to my own 1964 findings, a plurality of respondents in urban Yokohama also reported negative images of both major parties, although views were generally more favorable in the rural districts. Moreover, even among supporters of both major parties there were negative evaluations of their respective parties.[39]

---

[38] Findings from my own survey show that up to 55 percent of those who voted on the *basis* of party in the 1963 national election perceived that their parents had supported the same party. The ratios of persons reporting this kind of intergenerational conformity varied substantially by district; the influence of local community preferences was apparent, and it was quite clear that community homogeneity in partisan loyalties (as determined by voting records) favored higher levels of conformity between respondents and their parents. A markedly lower incidence of perceived intergenerational congruence was found among Japan Socialist supporters than among Liberal Democrat voters.

A somewhat higher incidence of intergenerational transfer of party loyalty has been reported in a study of the attitudes of school-age youths and their parents conducted at the time of the 1967 general election. See Akira Kubota and Robert E. Ward, "Family Influence and Political Socialization in Japan: Some Preliminary Findings in Comparative Perspective," *Comparative Political Studies* 3 (July 1970), pp. 140–175.

It is possible that the changes in party labels were not as important for the inhibition of development of deep loyalties as is believed, since transfer of loyalties *within* only the conservative and leftist *tendencies* is certainly plausible. Whatever the nature of party loyalty, and the conditioning factors at different times, it is clear that party orientation plays a limited role in actual voting-choice.

[39] The distribution of "impressions" of the two major parties were as follows:

	Liberal Democrats			Japan Socialists		
	Y(%)	A(%)	N(%)	Y(%)	A(%)	N(%)
Favorable	31	46	45	22	14	28
Unfavorable	37	16	9	34	29	21
Ambiguous	2	2	6	18	6	6
Didn't know	30	36	40	26	51	45
Total	100	100	100	100	100	100
(Number)	(202)	(129)	(67)	(203)	(108)	(67)

Y refers to Yokohama, *A* to Atsugi and *N* to Nita. The question was, "Just what kind of impression do you have of each of Japan's present political parties?"

Obviously, then, many factors contribute to the subdued role of partisan orientation in Japanese voting-choice. The nature of support mobilization, the incidence of negative party images and changes in party labels and identities are all potential factors. Social patterns contributing to the leading role of candidate perceptions may also be important, but in a way different from that noted earlier. It is certainly plausible that as a corollary of their intense commitment to personalized frames of reference, Japanese identify less commonly and intensely with remote secondary groupings than is the case, for example, in the United States. Although there is no direct evidence on this matter where other social groupings are concerned, the findings do suggest that this is a reasonable interpretation in the case of political parties.

It is apparent that attitudes toward political parties also have a special relationship to candidate perceptions in Japan. Where questions on simple "party" or "candidate" preferences were expanded to include the consideration "voted on the basis of candidate but considered party," the group of voters who replied that they had paid some attention to partisan considerations, either through considering candidate *and* party or simply "party," was now a majority (Richardson 1964). Partisan orientations seem to perform at least a minimal screening function for quite a few voters in Japan. In other words, party loyalties bring focus to decisions even if choices are ultimately made on the basis of candidate. It is safe to assume that many voters would not consider candidates from another party, even though they do decide between individual candidates once partisan considerations have been accounted for.

While partisan orientations were second in frequency to candidate perceptions in replies to simple questions about voting attitudes, instrumental expectations — the feeling that a particular candidate would represent one's interests — were second in importance in most cases where questions had a greater array of alternatives. The level of popular concern for instrumental representation was in fact notable (see Table 5-1), and the prevalence of this concern underscores the

---

The presence of negative impressions of parties has different implications for voting attitudes than the mere absence of affect in candidate perceptions. While quite a few voters clearly had negative feelings about parties, attitudes toward candidates were not clearly negative where affect was absent.

importance of pragmatic themes in contemporary Japanese political culture.

Furthermore, the degree to which instrumental expectations are relevant to voting-choice seems especially significant in light of the view that Japanese prewar political culture was largely "subject" oriented. To be sure, these two categories of political attitudes are not totally incompatible. Feelings of deference could have been accompanied by expectations that interests would be represented by paternalistic leaders. The existence of sentiments of this kind can in fact be seen today. But development of an articulate and intense consciousness of wants from politics, and expectations that these wants will be represented, does seem more plausible where democratic ideas are given major emphasis.

Indeed, it is highly probable that strains of pragmatism in Japanese postwar political attitudes are largely the result of the diffusion of democratic ideas. Nevertheless, it is also plausible that consciousness of interests is heightened by the character of social institutions, at least in rural Japan. Rural voters are more aware of their interests than urban residents, and this fact can be attributed to the nature of leadership and social structure in these areas. In rural communities influentials are inclined to discuss what can be obtained through political action and to stimulate an awareness of these matters in the community as a whole. Both in-group loyalties and competition with other communities, and the prevailing sense of economic deprivation in some rural districts at the time the studies analyzed here were conducted, are additional stimuli for increased awareness of interest. Although all of these conditions have parallels to some degree in labor unions in the cities, and in merchant and neighborhood groups in older urban districts, the urban environment does not generally encourage the same awareness of interests as do rural communities.

Varying emphasis on different expectations of representation was also important, according to the survey results I reviewed. Most common among the different instrumental expectations were hopes for representation of voters living in a *particular* district. Less frequent were concerns for representation of occupational categories or organized groups, although occupational interests were typically seen as more important in national elections than in local contests. However, concern for occupational representation was detectable as a major latent force where respondents were asked solely whether or not they had considered this in their vote (Shizuoka 1963).[40]

We should not overlook the importance of the emphasis given expectations about representation of local interests. The fact that more voters in the rural districts expected representation of some small geographical area than expected representation of farming interests in general reinforces the suggestion of the primacy in Japan of community ties over loyalty to more remote social groupings.[41] Moreover, these tendencies suggest themselves as natural correlatives of the higher levels of political involvement and confidence manifest in local affairs. Residence in intimate communities and neighborhoods in the country, and in small cities, provides many Japanese voters with a stimulation toward awareness of the opportunities for representation of popular interests as well as an appreciation of the importance of local affairs and confidence in the way they are handled.

To recapitulate briefly, the dominant themes in Japanese voting attitudes are personalism and pragmatism. Majorities or pluralities of the electorate typically make their election choice on the basis of candidate perceptions, while representational expectations are a secondary but significant emphasis. Political parties are of lower priority in most citizens' voting-choice, although they may play a latent screening role in some cases.

Both social and political factors are determining influences in Japanese voting attitudes. The primacy of candidate perceptions reflects the effect of prevailing support mobilization styles as well as the

---

[40] There were significant variations in nationwide surveys where a somewhat different combination of alternatives was used. Local considerations, including the fact that a candidate was from a particular area, were favored in rural districts, while occupational representation was sought in the large cities. Voters in small cities were inclined to place about equal stress on locality and occupation, although locality was heavily favored according to the results of one survey. See Kōmei 1961, p. 42 and Chūō Chōsasha, *Shūgiin Giin Sōsenkyo ni tsuite no Seron Chōsa* (Tōkyō: 1964), p. 36.

[41] It is also plausible that farmers' interests as an occupational grouping merge with concerns for local needs. The activities conducted on their behalf by occupational interest groups in Tōkyō may seem much more remote than tangible improvements in local transport or irrigation facilities. But the overall effects of narrow community identifications are naturally reflected in feelings of this very kind, too, and it is important to see that parochial definitions of interest outweigh a sense of common cause with farmers as a general category. Dore's comments on the effects of particularistic feelings on class identifications in Japan are relevant here, too. See n. 11.

importance of primary relationships in contemporary social life. These same influences are manifested in the low concern for political parties in voting-choice; but other more specialized considerations are also relevant, such as the substantial incidence of negative attitudes toward parties and the nature of party histories in recent times. Instrumental expectations have assumed considerable importance in popular attitudes through the favorable effects of expanded political opportunities and the parallel growth of an acute awareness of self-interests among some sectors of the population.

While it is quite clear that voting attitudes are important components of electoral decisions in Japan, some consideration should be given to the role they play in relationship to the matrix of outside influences to which many voters are exposed. It has often been assumed that many people's voting choices are determined primarily on the basis of appeals for their vote from superiors or individuals to whom obligations are owed; this assessment is probably accurate in many instances. But there is also a conspicuous link between the character of voting attitudes and campaign behavior of this kind. Although influence is undeniably exercised in Japanese election campaigns, it is still interesting that the most frequent themes in discussions about endorsements and requests for support do conform to the content of voting attitudes. Thus, voters who were aware of having been asked to vote in a particular way reported that these conversations more often focused on the candidate's character and expectations that he would represent a particular interest than they involved simply a request to vote for somebody (Richardson 1964).[42] The viability of voting attitudes, as well as the fact that efforts to influence the vote involve more rational appeals than has been sometimes assumed, can be seen in this evidence.

The significance of voting attitude patterns in Japan for comparative assessment of levels of "politicization" should also be noted. In at least one study the degree to which members of electorates identified with political parties was seen as an indicator of the state of

---

[42] There were, however, important urban-rural differences; Yokohama residents typically reported simply being asked to vote for someone. This, of course, testifies to the importance of instrumentalism in the rural, at the expense of urban, areas. See my Ph.D. dissertation, "Political Behavior and Attitudes in Contemporary Japan," p. 90.

politicization, along with correlative states of political involvement.[43] If we were to look only at levels of party identification in Japan, we would conclude that the Japanese electorate is substantially politicized. In contrast, if we were to confine our assessments to an examination of tendencies in voting attitudes, somewhat different conclusions might be drawn. The point that can be made is quite obvious: although levels of party loyalty may be one indicator of politicization, it is important for students of comparative politics to look at a variety of variables in their assessment. Other "styles" of politicization may exist, and the great importance of candidate perceptions in voting attitudes here suggests the appropriateness of more complex research designs in future studies of politicization levels and content.[44]

---

[43] Converse and Dupeux (see n. 3).

[44] Much of the discussion in Sydney Tarrow's article (see n. 5) is useful here; the value of multidimensional approaches to studying involvement and behavior is implicit throughout his comments.

6

CITY AND COUNTRYSIDE

Urban-rural residence has an ambiguous status as a variable in political behavior research. Empirical theory predicts that urbanization will result in higher levels of political involvement and participation. But this anticipated effect is only sometimes borne out by research findings. Urban-rural trends in political behavior, involvement and participation attitudes vary substantially from place to place.[1] Japan is one of

---

[1] There are three tendencies in the effects of place of residence. Urban residence is sometimes associated with relatively higher levels of psychological involvement, as reported in Angus Campbell, Philip E. Converse, Warren E. Miller and Donald E. Stokes, *The American Voter* (New York: Wiley, 1960), p. 412, and Edward N. Muller, "Cross-National Dimensions of Political Competence," *American Political Science Review* 64 (September 1970), p. 797.

Urban supremacy in voter turnout is reported in the United States in Angus Campbell, Gerald Gurin and Warren Miller, *The Voter Decides* (Evanston: Row and Peterson, 1954), pp. 128–130.

Higher turnouts were found in the rural districts in some countries but in the cities in others, according to Herbert Tingsten in *Political Behavior: Studies in Election Statistics* (London: P. S. King, 1939), pp. 211–214. Moreover, place of residence has no effect on activist forms of political participation in national politics, but local participation is favored in the rural districts of various countries, according to a reanalysis of the Almond and Verba findings in Norman H. Nie, G. Bingham Powell, Jr., and Kenneth Prewitt, "Social Structure and Political Participation: Developmental Relationships, Part I," *American Political Science Review* 63 (June 1969), p. 368.

Finally, voter turnout is higher today in the rural parts of several countries. These include France, the Federal Republic of Germany and Great Britain, as well as Japan. For Britain, see *Gallup Analysis of the Election 1966* (London: The Daily Telegraph, 1966), p. 27; and Jean and Monica Charlot, "Politisation et Dépolitisation en Grande Bretagne," *Revue Française de Science Politique* 11 (September 1961), p. 634. German trends are reported by Erwin Faul in Dolf Sternberger *et al.*, *Wahlen und Wähler in Westdeutschland* (Villingen: Ring, 1960), p.

the most notable cases in which actuality deviates from the expectations of theory, at least regarding political participation. This is a matter which has never ceased to fascinate students of Japanese politics, as well as attract attention from scholars concerned with comparative political behavior.

The most useful and interesting examples of theoretical or a priori projections, wherein residence figures importantly, are the center-periphery models of Milbrath and others and modernization theory. Milbrath tried to bring order to sociological analysis of political life by reducing the complexities of social structure to a unidimensional concept of center-periphery locations.[2] According to this view of political behavior, some individuals are more integrated than others into political communications channels, especially those which provide links with important decision-making centers. Variations in social location and communication involvement are in turn related to differences in overall political involvement and participation. People near the center of public life, in terms of social location, are thus expected to participate more than those closer to the periphery. Among the various factors defining social location is place of residence. Urban dwellers are considered to be closer to the center of society than their country counterparts, and as a result are expected to be more involved in politics.

Modernization theory also predicts fairly similar consequences

---

156; and, "Das Wahlverhalten verschiedener Bevölkerungsgruppen bei der Bundestagswahl 1965," *Wirtschaft und Statistik* 3 (1966), p. 165. French patterns are discussed in Alain Lancelot, *L'Abstentionnisme Electorale en France* (Paris: Armand Colin, 1968), pp. 195–97; Mark Kesselman, "French Local Politics: A Statistical Examination of Grass Roots Consensus," *American Political Science Review* 60 (December 1966), pp. 963–73; and Sidney Tarrow, "The Urban-Rural Cleavage in Involvement: The Case of France," *American Political Science Review* 65 (June 1971), pp. 344–46. Japanese voter turnout is discussed in detail in Jun'ichi Kyōgoku and Nobutaka Ike, "Urban-Rural Differences in Voting Behavior in Postwar Japan," *Economic Development and Cultural Change* 9 (October 1960), Part II, pp. 170–72.

Comparable rural tendencies are also found in some American states today, and also in earlier times. The main sources are James A. Robinson and William Standing, "Some Correlates of Voter Participation: The Case of Indiana," *Journal of Politics* 22 (February 1960), pp. 99–106; V. O. Key, Jr., *Southern Politics in State and Nation* (New York: Alfred Knopf, 1950), pp. 510–13; and Walter Dean Burnham, "The Changing Shape of the American Political Universe," *American Political Science Review* 59 (March 1965), pp. 15–16.

[2] Lester W. Milbrath, *Political Participation* (Chicago: Rand McNally, 1965), pp. 110–114 and 128–130. Robert E. Lane also used the concept of centrality in *Political Life: Why People Get Involved in Politics* (Glencoe, Illinois: Free Press, 1959), p. 196.

from urbanization. However, in contrast to the static and cross-sectional concerns of center-periphery conceptions, modernization theory focuses on the effects of urbanization as one of the central processes of social change in the contemporary epoch.[3] The connections between urban residence and behavior are thus slightly different than in the center-periphery model, even though there are some areas of comparability. Lerner's modernization model, for example, sees urbanization as one of the vital phases in a multistage process encompassing, among other things, sequential increases in education and media exposure. The various processes associated with modern social change were viewed as freeing villagers from their traditional parochialism, leading in turn to higher levels of mass participation in national life.

For Karl Deutsch the consequences of recent social change are similar. But here the critical nexus between modernization and increased political participation is the growth of political instrumentalism. According to Deutsch, as more and more persons are exposed to the combined influences of urbanization, industrialization and integration into a modern economy, their dependence on government grows, and awareness of their political interests increases. The growth in awareness of self-interests leads in turn to placing greater demands on government, and to higher levels of popular political involvement and participation.

Each of these theories offers important and useful perspectives for the study of urban-rural patterns of political culture in Japan. In Milbrath we are made sensitive to the importance of variation in individual proximity to political communication. Of particular interest here is the concern in this approach for the role played by personal as well as media communications networks.

---

[3] For the core writings in this area see Karl Deutsch, "Social Mobilization and Political Development," *American Political Science Review* 55 (September, 1961), pp. 493–515; and Daniel Lerner, *The Passing of Traditional Society: Modernizing the Middle East* (Glencoe: Free Press, 1958), especially Ch. 2.

Deutsch's analysis treats the various components of the social modernization process as a cluster of interrelated forces, and looks for their combined effects on social and political behavior. Lerner presents a sequential model wherein urbanization plays a special function in the early phases of modernization.

It should be made clear at this point that the following discussion addresses itself primarily to the question of the usability of the *participation* elements of developmental models. I am not concerned here with extending the discussion to include the more elaborate models of democratic behavior that have been developed from Deutsch, Lerner and other modernization analyses.

Modernization theories point up other concerns. (It should be emphasized here that my own concern at this point is mainly with explaining relatively simple cross-sectional differences rather than with the more global concerns of modernization theory.)[4] While residence is isolable as a variable in the center-periphery concepts, both Deutsch and Lerner emphasize the importance of linking urbanization with other influences. This latter approach encourages us to look at the urban-rural distribution and effects of such factors as education and group membership. We also learn from Deutsch a concern for the effect of residence on popular awareness of self-interest.

The lines of analysis pursued here will lead to consideration of the reformulation of these theoretical models, particularly as they apply to the realities of modern life in Japan. Despite the utility of these approaches, their fit with real conditions in Japan is still quite uneven in some places. Some revision is thus inevitable if prediction is to accord with the realities of experience.

I will also be deviating by and large from the interpretations of an earlier generation of scholars who dealt with Japanese political behavior. Earlier writings in this field have typically looked at single dimensions of political involvement, and presented findings or impressions which conformed to the tenets of modernization theory. Thus, Ike and Kyogoku saw urban dwellers as politically more conscious than rural residents, while Ward felt that the typical city dweller had a more developed awareness of what government could do for him.[5] Still, relatively lower levels of political participation were found among

---

[4] I am deviating from the intent of the modernization theorists in attempting to adapt their ideas to tests with contemporary survey data. Both Deutsch and Lerner are interested in processes that affected societies as a whole, and to them urbanization is part of a global process of change which affects parochial villagers as well as others. By applying this model to contemporary sectoral differences in attitudes or behavior, I am distorting the propositions in their theories to some extent. Nevertheless, both Lerner and Deutsch deal with hypotheses about the effects of global modernization which ultimately depend on predictions about changes at the individual level. Consequently, if we interpret these hypotheses in terms of their applicability to individual behavior, we should find among other things that persons who are residents of the urban sector of contemporary societies participate more than persons in the rural sector. For an example of this kind of application of the social modernization concepts see Norman H. Nie, *et al.* (see n. 1, above).

[5] See Jun'ichi Kyōgoku and Nobutaka Ike (see n. 1, above), p. 171; and, Robert E. Ward, "Urban-Rural Differences and the Process of Political Modernization in Japan: A Case Study," in *Economic Development and Cultural Change* (October 1960), Part II, p. 162.

urban residents in Japan by earlier researchers, despite the presumably inescapable logic of both theoretical and popular expectations about the "liberalizing" and favorable effects of city life, and the evidence on political involvement. High rural voter turnout levels were consequently seen as evidence of behavior that deviated from the tendencies in political involvement, presumably as the result of pressure from influentials and the honors associated with maintaining high turnouts.

An examination of urban-rural differences in Japanese political culture is inevitable, given the contradiction between theory and observed reality. In light of the earlier interpretations, some crucial questions also emerge. Were earlier explanations of the deviating findings on Japanese political participation on the right track in emphasizing primarily the mobilizing potential of rural social structure in their efforts to reconcile theory with reality? Or are there previously unresearched attitudinal dimensions that might help explain otherwise confusing sectoral participation trends? Is it possible that researchers in Japan, as well as elsewhere, have been so influenced by the obvious social and cultural contrasts between city and village that they have overlooked less obvious but significantly explanatory subcultural characteristics?[6] While accepting parts of these writers' analyses, I will consequently examine the complexity of the differentiation in urban-rural attitude structures here and the many implications of this complexity for behavior and for theory.

Before taking up these and other questions, there are some additional reasons for looking at urban-rural differences in Japan. A sizeable ratio of the national population still lives in small rural communities and is engaged in agriculture, even though the importance of this sector has declined since the end of World War II. Consequently, in discussing the rural sector in Japan we are talking about more than a residual element of the population, as would be the case were we discussing the United States or some other countries.[7] Secondly, the

---

[6] For an eloquent description of the characteristics of rural life that contribute to high participation levels in modern rural France—one which dispels some earlier interpretations of the superiority of urban life—see Sidney Tarrow (see n. 1, above), especially p. 353.

[7] The rural sector still remains quite large in Japan, in both internal and comparative terms. In 1963 nearly one-quarter of the labor force was engaged in agriculture, a ratio matched only by France and Italy among modern industrial na-

political importance of the countryside is exaggerated by over-representation in the Diet; this has been a central factor in Japan's unique kind of political stability.[8] Over-representation, and the fact that the rural districts gave much of their support to the conservative parties, which helped sustain conservative dominance of national politics throughout most of the postwar period.

There are also some caveats to keep in mind. In dealing with urban-rural patterns in Japan, it is important to remember that observable differences do not necessarily reflect a simple traditional-modern dichotomy. On the one hand, rural styles and norms are to some degree found in all sectors of society in modern Japan. The importance of personal ties in Japanese behavior (though perhaps considerably modified in urban districts) is but one example of the effect on urban life of patterns presumably originating in the rural sector. Many urban Japanese are especially conscious of differences between urban and rural behavior, yet, Japan is clearly like other modern nations in that residual effects of an earlier agricultural society continue to influence contemporary relationships and attitudes to a considerable degree.[9]

---

tions. See Rōdōdaijin Kanbō, Rōdō Tōkei Chōsabu, *Rōdō Tōkei Nenpō* (Tōkyō: 1963), pp. 332–36. See also Ch. 1 here.

Labor force statistics such as these, which show the relative importance of different occupational categories in the overall working force, are one of the best indicators of current tendencies in urban-rural population patterns. Many farmers live within the administrative area of small cities—sometimes even within larger conurbations—with the consequence that the customary statistics on the distribution of the population within cities and rural districts are misleading.

I also estimated population distribution using density of population as an indicator, and it appeared that about one-third of the population was located in the major cities and surrounding metropolitan districts, another one-third lived in smaller provincial cities and major towns, while the remaining third lived in rural communities. The relevant basic data can be found in Sōrifu Tōkeikyoku, *Nihon Tōkei Nenkan* (Tōkyō: 1967), pp. 18–19.

[8] For a discussion of the over-representation of the rural electorate, see Jun'ichi Kyōgoku and Nobutaka Ike, pp. 173–175.

[9] Identification of what is "modern" and what is "traditional" is also difficult at times. For example, "modern" content can sometimes be seen with more "traditional" frames of reference. Thus, many Japanese voters depend upon leaders, presumably a traditional orientation, for representation of popular interests, a sentiment that has modern connotations.

Interesting evidence indicative of higher levels of traditionalism in the rural sectors can be seen in some of the findings of the Japanese national character studies — although some measures of "traditional" and "modern" traits are somewhat arbitrary. But these findings also suggest the extent to which traditional and modern orientations are intermingled in both sectors. See, for example, Tōkei Sūri Kenkyūjo, *Kokuminsei no Kenkyū, Dai Niji Chōsa* (Tōkyō: 1959).

There is also an obvious reciprocal penetration of rural life by modern influences. The narrowness of the urban-rural gap in some cultural perspectives is shown by national character studies in Japan; this could have resulted only from marked exposure to stimuli common to both sectors. Although it is obvious that older customs often have greater relevance in rural than in urban life, these are best characterized as vestigial traditions that are rather complexly intermingled with newer behavior. Thus, while tradition is relevant in rural Japan, we must qualify its role.

Moreover, conditions in the two sectors have been far from static in the postwar period. While urbanization as a long-term trend continues, there have been significant changes within the urban and rural districts themselves.[10] Postwar land reform altered economic and social relationships in many parts of rural Japan, and its legacy is an important factor affecting the character of rural political attitudes today. More recently, the nature of rural life has been strongly influenced by technological changes in both farm practices and household life. Unprecedented prosperity and the expansion of industrial centers into some rural areas has also been important.[11]

It is highly plausible that the political attitudes found in rural

---

[10] Some of these trends were described very briefly in Ch. 1, but they are sufficiently important to be reiterated here. Both general population and labor force figures show the extent and pace of urbanization in Japan in the 1950s and 1960s. While the total population increased by 15 million between 1950 and 1965, the numbers of persons living in large cities alone grew by 12 million in the same period. In contrast, the ratio of persons employed in agriculture within the entire labor force declined from 41 percent in 1955 to 27 percent in 1963, and 23 percent in 1966. See Sōrifu Tōkeikyoku, *Nihon Tōkei Nenkan*, pp. 11, 19, and 56.

[11] For a discussion of the effects of land reform and some pertinent statistical data, see R. P. Dore, *Land Reform in Japan* (London, New York and Toronto: Oxford University Press, 1959), Ch. 15.

Disposable farm income doubled between 1955 and 1965, which meant a substantial increase in the affluence of the rural districts even in the face of inflation. (The price index for commodities used in farm production increased by 28 percent in the same period while the index for commodities consumed rose by 30 percent.) See Sōrifu Tōkeikyoku, *ibid.*, pp. 126 and 378–79.

Also contributing to the growing relative affluence of the rural areas, as well as being an indicator of social trends of major importance, has been the growing tendency for farmers to seek supplementary occupations. Thus, the number of part-time farmers mainly engaged in jobs other than farming increased by nearly 50 percent in the years between 1955 and 1965. See Tōkeikyoku, *ibid.*, p. 87. (Commuting to work was also becoming more common, according to the Ministry of Agriculture's 1964 White Paper. Both this trend and tendencies in outside employment reflect industrialization in areas outside established industrial centers.)

districts in the period under review were influenced by these events. The apparent increase in instrumental awareness in the rural sector is a case in point. But, at the same time, life in the cities has been changing through the effects of both suburbanization and population changes in older urban neighborhoods.[12] Although all political effects of recent social change cannot be directly identified at present, it is important that these dynamic tendencies be kept in mind.

Urban-Rural Social Differences. The formation of patterns of political attitudes distinctive to urban and rural districts reflects differences both in social context and individual socio-economic characteristics. Variations in community structure are of fundamental importance and contribute to major differences in political culture, despite the many integrating influences in Japanese society. Urban and rural voters also vary in important ways with regard to income, education and partisan preferences. This second axis of differentiation frequently accounts for political attitude patterns that are quite distinct from those resulting from differences in community life.

Distinctive patterns of community life in the countryside and the city are conspicuous in Japan.[13] Most rural residents live in small hamlets — long-established communities in which a large part of the residents' social contacts and activities are concentrated. Among neighbors and residents of individual hamlets there are high levels of interaction; accordingly, hamlet dwellers are less cosmopolitan than urban residents in their social contacts (see Table 6–1). Associations flourish and their activities are also centered in the hamlet, even where hamlet groups maintain connections with organizations outside the local community. Cooperation in carrying out various community and farm functions is also common, although its importance may be on the de-

---

[12] The population of districts adjacent to the established metropolitan centers increased dramatically between the middle 1950s and early 1960s; older neighborhoods in "downtown" sections also received new immigrants while losing residents to the suburbs. For a discussion of population shifts in metropolitan Tōkyō and their political implications, see Junnosuke Masumi, "A Profile of the Japanese Conservative Party," *Asian Survey* 3 (August 1963), especially p. 400.

[13] These and subsequent comments are based primarily on the writings of sociologists and anthropologists. The best summaries of the dimensions of rural society relevant to my discussion are found in Richard K. Beardsley, John W. Hall and Robert E. Ward, *Village Japan* (Chicago and London: University of Chicago Press, 1959), especially Ch. 10; R. P. Dore, *Land Reform in Japan*, Chs. 14 and 15; and, Tadashi Fukutake, *Japanese Rural Society* (London, New York and Tōkyō: Oxford University Press, 1967), especially Chs. 7 and 8.

TABLE 6-1. Social Characteristics of Urban and Rural Populations

	Metropolitan (%)	Urban (%)	Rural (%)	(N)
Education:[a]				
Lower/Middle School	52	61	75	(2,425)
High School/College	48	39	25	
Party Support:[b]				
Leftist Parties	31	22	16	(2,425)
Length of Residence:[c]				
Over 15 years	46	62	72	
15 years and less	54	38	28	(2,425)
Association with Neighbors:[d]				
Associate enthusiastically	28	37	50	
Associate without enthusiasm or don't associate	71	60	46	(1,794)
Scope of Acquaintanceships:[d]				
0–29 families	63	51	46	
30 or more families	15	23	36	(1,794)
Group Memberships:[e]				
No groups	31	—	8	
1–3 groups	67	—	49	
4 or more groups	2	—	43	(354)

Sources:
Figures represent percentages of all respondents in each response category.
[a] Calculated from Prime Ministers Office 1404, May 1963. Figures for education are typical of those in Japanese national surveys.
[b] Same as above. Leftist party support includes responses favoring the Japan Socialists, Democratic Socialists and Japan Communists.
[c] Same as above. Length of residence figures refer to specifically the "same ward, city or town." Length of residence data are also representative.
[d] Calculated from Prime Ministers Office 2060, March 1966.
[e] From Richardson 1964 survey.

cline in many places.[14] Hamlet life is thus characterized by typically high levels of intimacy and redundancy in both personal and group relationships.

---

[14] The observation that levels of cooperative activity may be declining in importance reflects the opinions of informants in several Kanto plain hamlets I studied in 1963–65. But my main concerns lay in other areas, and I made no attempt to investigate the validity of these opinions. Moreover, the places in question were atypical in several ways, due to the existence of nearby opportunities for industrial employment. Finally, a check of statistical data on formal cooperative activities and ownership of farm implements produced no clear indication of tendencies in any one direction.

Hamlet members typically have a highly developed sense of local tradition, reflecting the fact that these communities have existed in most cases for several centuries, while many local families can trace a similarly long ancestry. Pronounced community ethnocentrism is apparent in many cases, manifested in both positive perceptions of hamlet qualities and feelings of competition with other communities. Rivalries between communities are indeed one of the main features of local politics, despite the fact that hamlet norms stress the desirability of consensus and harmony within local community confines.[15]

These characteristics of hamlet life are found particularly in hamlets isolated from urban centers and main lines of communications. Although there are many hamlets with these traits today, the importance of social patterns that focus inward on the local community may be on the decline in some rural districts adjacent to principal rail lines or highways, or near metropolitan centers or developing industrial areas. In communities of this kind commuting to work has become increasingly common in recent years; some decline in community commitment and participation is an obvious corollary of this trend.[16] However, rural styles of life still prevail to a considerable degree in even these types of communities, and the characteristics of hamlets described above are still relevant where general comparisons between urban and rural life are concerned.

In contrast, city dwellers often live in a less socially integrated milieu and are commonly involved in quite different patterns of social interaction (Table 6-1).[17] Urban residents tend to be less involved in

---

[15] R. P. Dore has written an entertaining account of the consequences of hamlet rivalries in "The Day the Fire Brigade Went Fishing," *Japan Quarterly* (July 1956), pp. 347–355.

Local political processes in largely rural Atsugi were brought to a near standstill on two occasions in the early 1960s as the result of rivalries between different hamlets or districts. One controversy centered on the location of a new school, the other involved the location of a city sanitation plant.

[16] A difference in the degree of isolation from train lines was clearly relevant in the political attitudes of persons living in different communities in one rural prefecture. The inhabitants of an island hamlet showed higher percentages of "rural" tendencies than did persons in districts adjacent to train lines, even in what is generally viewed as an especially isolated and backward part of the country. See Kumamoto 1960.

[17] Although not explicitly comparative of urban and rural differences, Dore's characterization of urban life in a "mixed" downtown and residential neighborhood and Vogel's description of a middle class residential district contrast sharply with descriptions of hamlet life. See Ronald P. Dore, *City Life in Japan* (Berkeley and

community or neighborhood affairs and interact less with neighbors than do rural citizens. Indeed, among urban dwellers both the frequency and intimacy of social relationships within the areas of their residence are different. Urban residents also become members of groups far less often than rural people — this applies particularly to groups whose activities are concentrated within neighborhood boundaries.[18] Moreover, most urban dwellers live in districts which have a lesser sense of tradition or identity than is the case in the countryside.

There are some differences, however, between social patterns in large and small cities and between different kinds of districts within large cities. Both the "downtown" parts of large cities and neighborhoods in provincial cities manifest social patterns that are more comparable to those in the rural sector than is the case in the newly settled, or purely residential, sectors of large cities. But community life and sentiments in the older districts of large cities appear to be declining in importance as these areas are affected both by the departure of old residents for the suburbs and immigration from the countryside or other urban districts.[19]

Los Angeles: University of California Press, 1958), pp. 255–68; and, Ezra Vogel, *Japan's New Middle Class* (Berkeley and Los Angeles: University of California Press, 1963), especially pp. 102–13. Also relevant is Robert E. Cole, *Japanese Blue Collar* (Berkeley and Los Angeles: University of California Press, 1971), pp. 189–213.

It is clear that some urban residents, especially those living in white-collar neighborhoods in the cities, purposely avoid neighborhood and community obligations. Their desire for privacy is in some cases a factor contributing to feelings of isolation from contact with politics, as we will see later.

[18] This is shown by figures from my own study in Table 6-1. In Fukuoka prefecture 60 percent of the rural respondents were members of some group, in contrast with 46 percent among those living in a small city. See Fukuoka 1960A, p. 9.

My findings also showed that rural group members participated more frequently than city members in the activities of their groups. Elsewhere, in a survey of women's social participation, it was found that urban women participated much less often than rural women in the activities of groups to which they belonged. Urban women also reported enjoying these activities less often. See Rōdōshō Fujin Shōnen Kyoku, *Fujin no Seikatsu to Iken* (Tōkyō: 1957), p. 37.

[19] The "downtown" districts of large cities and neighborhoods in small provincial cities seem to have both a greater sense of identity and higher social participation levels than is the case for the "new" middle-class residential areas and some working-class districts. This was the impression I received from interviews with local politicians and household association heads I interviewed in Yokohama and Atsugi.

Some of these differences between different kinds of neighborhoods can also be inferred from comments in the works by Dore and Vogel cited in n. 17, although neither of these authors attempts extensive comparative statements. However, Dore

There are also important sectoral variations in mobility; city dwellers more commonly commute to work than rural residents. This is, of course, one of the factors contributing to the lower levels of neighborhood involvement generally found among city dwellers. But commuting to work involves more than simply a daily absence from areas of residence. It also brings with it interaction with a wider variety of people. Interaction patterns in the cities are thus much more cosmopolitan than among rural residents. Finally, commuting to work is often associated with employment in large organizations, where patterns of interaction, authority and communications are substantially more impersonal than those of rural communities, small firms and, to some degree, older urban neighborhoods.[20]

---

presents a clear summary of the popular beliefs about "downtown" and "uptown" life styles in City Life in Japan, pp. 11–13, and these have some relevance for my comments here.

My own figures on group participation for different kinds of urban districts confirm the presence of some differences between white-collar apartment residents and people living in an older part of the city, where men alone were concerned — probably because men who live in white-collar districts commute to work more commonly than their counterparts in the "downtown" areas. Some Japanese studies have also reported that membership in household associations in long-established neighborhoods was higher than was the case in new middle-class apartment blocks. See, for example, "Chiiki Shakai to Toshika," Kokusai Kirisutokyō Daigaku Gappō, No. IIA (Shakaikagaku Kenkyū No. 8), p. 132.

"Downtown" here refers to the mixed small business and residential areas found in certain parts of the large cities. Although the modern commercial and financial centers of some of Japan's large cities have in fact developed in some of these areas, the term here refers only to those kinds of districts that manifest some of the vestigial traits of the "little community" life found in earlier days of Japan's urbanization. For an extremely interesting account of the differences in life styles between these areas and the elite residential sectors in the development of Tōkyō, see Robert J. Smith, "Pre-Industrial Urbanism in Japan: A Consideration of Multiple Traditions in a Feudal Society," Economic Development and Cultural Change 9 (October 1960), Part II, pp. 241–54.

[20] Vogel's observations on the behavior of white-collar workers indicate that employment in large organizations at best involves infrequent interaction with a particular small group of colleagues. The range of frequent and intimate interactions is much smaller than in the country, or even perhaps in some old neighborhoods and small firms. See Ezra Vogel, Japan's New Middle Class, pp. 102–06.

Authority in large organizations takes many forms of course, ranging from the actions of immediate supervisors to the decisions of more remote persons or groups. There seems to be less opportunity for contact with high officials in large organizations than there is with influentials in small communities or "downtown" neighborhoods. Although the differences are more relative than absolute, there is probably less of a feeling of being involved in decisions that affect one's interests — even where the feeling of involvement is sometimes vicarious, as it is in many rural communities. Although expectations of corporate paternalism may be present, the absence of personal ties with some components of authority probably tends to weaken feelings

Urban and rural life styles also vary in regard to typical recreational activities. Urban residents more commonly attend audience-oriented performances, or eat and drink in the comparatively anonymous entertainment centers found in all the large cities of Japan. Most rural residents, on the other hand, still rely on group activities and participant-oriented recreation that either takes place within the community proper or involves community excursions to other places — although audience-oriented recreation is certainly not completely unknown in rural areas.

In addition to the urban-rural contrasts in community life in Japan, there are distinct sectoral patterns in individual socio-economic attributes which are of major importance to attitude formation. Residents of the farm areas generally have lower levels of educational attainment than do city dwellers, in part because many of the better-educated youth in the rural areas emigrate to the cities (Table 6-1).[21] Rural income levels also are lower than urban levels, although there are some important variations in rural levels.[22] Comparison of family incomes in the two sectors is somewhat distorted by the partial dependence of many rural families on their own farm production for food. Still, urban-rural differences in monetary income are meaningful, as is seen in the fact that patterns of visible consumption vary substantially between the two. This has been changing rapidly, however. For example, appliances have become more commonplace in the rural districts in recent years, even though an urban-rural disparity in own-

---

of self-confidence in dealing with authority in a more general sense. This may be especially common among blue-collar workers, although my information on their feelings on these matters depends solely on interviews with union activists.

The direct political relevance of being employed by a large organization is also certainly minimal when compared with that of residence in small communities, except where labor unions provide a nexus that encourages both political involvement and awareness of political interests. Participation in a group of company colleagues would appear to be of little importance, except where attitudes derived from other sources are reinforced. But more research on the role of such groups is needed, and it is clear that politics is discussed fairly often with working colleagues in the cities.

[21] For an extremely readable account of the emigration of high school graduates from a small town, see "Takehara: A Good Place to Be From," in Lawrence Olson, *Dimensions of Japan* (New York: American Universities Field Staff, 1963), pp. 54–63.

[22] Mean household incomes in Japan's large cities were nearly 50 percent higher than incomes in towns and villages in 1964. See Sōrifu Tōkeikyoku, *Nihon Tōkei Nenkan 1967*, p. 454.

ership of various kinds of household equipment was still present at the time the studies reviewed here were conducted.[23]

Urban and rural Japan scarcely contrast where the availability of mass media communications is concerned. Indeed, the modern media have considerably penetrated the countryside, and this is especially true for the broadcasting media. Ownership of television and radio sets is widespread in the rural areas and nearly matches that of the large cities and surrounding metropolitan areas.[24] Readership of the national daily newspapers as well as local publications is also fairly common in many rural districts. There are, however, some differences between the cities and the rural areas in per capita newspaper subscription levels; rural residents subscribe less commonly than city dwellers.[25]

These facts notwithstanding, there are still some urban-rural differences in political communications behavior (Table 6-2). Urban residents more commonly follow mass media accounts of politics than do rural people, both in newspapers and broadcasts. Rural voters, on the other hand, are more frequent participants in informal, word-of-mouth communications about political matters.[26] Rural residents also *depend*

---

[23] *Ibid.*, p. 161. This is especially true for urban-rural differences in the ownership of washing machines and vacuum cleaners.

[24] In a few prefectures, however, the number of radio sets falls substantially below the urban norm. See *ibid.*, p. 161.

[25] This conclusion is supported by a calculation of the per capita ratio of newspaper subscriptions in different prefectures. When subscriptions are compared with population figures it is seen that the per capita ratio is 1:2 in Tōkyō Ōsaka, while varying between 1:3 and 1:5 in most rural prefectures. Interestingly, Kagoshima conforms to the popular opinion in Japan about its relative backwardness with a ratio of 1:6. *Ibid.*, pp. 17 and 559.

[26] As can be seen from Table 6-2, there is also some variation in the urban-rural tendencies according to differences in the context of discussion. Urban and rural voters were most similar where discussion in the family was concerned, even though rural residents talked a little more within the family about politics than did urbanites. In contrast, rural residents were much more active in discussions with neighbors and in meetings; but urbanites participated more in discussions with colleagues at work. These tendencies are related to those urban and rural differences in social structure reported earlier and reflect differences in the possibilities for discussion in the respective social milieus.

Patterns in exposure to political influence and campaigns (Table 6-2) are not discussed in the text. Note that the evidence indicates higher levels of exposure in the rural areas only where local elections are concerned. Some findings from national studies show that rural voters are more aware than urban voters of attempts to influence their vote in the national elections as well, but there are no really consistent patterns in the various sets of findings. The situation may actually vary between elections, or the findings may be affected by sampling considerations that cannot be evaluated.

For evidence on influence communications supporting figures in Table 6-2 see

TABLE 6-2. POLITICAL COMMUNICATION

	Urban (%)	Rural (%)	Urban (%)	Rural (%)
	National Politics		Local Politics	
Discussion of politics:[a]				
At home	59	61	56	64
With neighbors	24	44	26	48
At place of work	42	35	40	36
At meetings	27	43	27	44
	Read Newspapers		Follow Radio/TV	
Exposure to political content of media:[b]				
Often	32	24	56	49
Sometimes	48	41	37	36
Not at all	20	34	7	15
Total	100	99	100	100
(N)	(772)	(1,555)	(772)	(1,555)
	National Elections		Local Elections	
Exposure to requests for vote and endorsements:[c]				
Yes	29	26	32	66
No	73	73	53	32
Total	102	99	85	98
(N)	(375)	(760)	(221)	(408)
	Read Election Pamphlet		Attended Speeches	
Exposure to campaign[d]				
Yes	62	74	13	20
No	11	16	59	71
Total	73	90	72	91
(N)	(428)	(1,026)	(428)	(1,026)

SOURCES: Note that figures for "urban" pertain to large cities only. Data for other cities, where patterns are frequently more like those in rural districts, are excluded here for purposes of simplicity.

[a] Kōmei 1958, p. 83. Totals and numbers were not shown; sample N was 5000. See also Table 4-6, for these and additional data on political discussions. [b] Kōmei 1962A, pp. 13–14. [c] National election data are from Kōmei 1964B, p. 54. Local election findings are from Kōmei 1964A, p. 114. [d] Kōmei 1961, p. 28.

more upon word-of-mouth communications than do urban residents.[27] Finally, urban dwellers not only report higher levels of exposure to politics in the mass media, they also depend more on the mass media.[28]

It is a well-known fact that among both urban and rural voters in Japan partisan preferences in voting patterns are somewhat homo-

---

Jichi 1966, p. 128. Contrary tendencies where national elections are concerned are found in Jichi 1958, p. 51, and Kōmei 1962B, pp. 50–51. The only thread of consistency on this point is related to time differences. As can readily be seen, perceptions of influence communications were comparatively more frequent in the rural districts according to the 1958 and 1962 studies, but more common in the cities in the 1964 and 1966 findings. This could reflect the presence of still unidentified changes in election tactics in the two types of areas — for example, increasing dependence in later years on long-term support mobilization through support associations (kōenkai) in the urban sectors.

Attendance at speeches is clearly not participation in informal discussions, but it does represent a different kind of contact than media exposure. (Differences between urban and rural districts where speech attendance is concerned presumably indicate a higher audience mobilization potential in the countryside; speech attendance should not be considered a voluntary activity in all cases. It is also important to note that candidates more often come to their rural audiences, while the reverse is true in the cities.)

[27] The relevant data are:

	Yokohama			Rural		
	HR(%)	LA(%)	Party(%)	HR(%)	LA(%)	Party(%)
Most important information source was:						
Media	44	28	58	31	8	46
Official announcements	16	19	3	14	16	11
Campaign	9	17	10	11	7	7
Discussion, acquaintance	25	31	14	36	61	14
Groups	4	5	12	2	2	3
Didn't know	2	—	3	6	6	9
Total	100	100	100	100	100	100
(Number)	(121)	(130)	(143)	(197)	(194)	(149)

HR is House of Representatives and LA is local assembly. The source is my 1964 survey.

[28] There is an obvious relationship between urban-rural differences in the distribution of radio and television sets and newspaper subscriptions and levels of exposure to mass media information on politics. But the habit of following the mass media may be more deeply ingrained among urban residents, especially in view of the higher levels of educational attainment found among city residents.

Although available data permit no extensive urban-rural comparison of levels of interest in mass media accounts of politics, one study of rural residents found that among the 44 percent of the respondents interested in any kind of newspaper stories, only four percent found political news "very interesting." See Hajime Ikeuchi, "Aru Nōson ni okeru Masu Komyunikeishon," *Tōkyō Daigaku Shimbun Kenkyūjo Kiyō* 2 (1953), pp. 126–27. (See Table 2-3 for slightly higher figures from surveys conducted in another rural prefecture.)

genous. With some local exceptions, the countryside has favored the Liberal Democratic party or its conservative predecessors, while the urban districts (especially the large cities) have given more support to the progressive parties (Table 6-1). This tendency reflects of course the greater concentration in the cities of labor union members and certain other categories of voters. In turn, the distribution of party preferences is sometimes related to sectoral patterns in evaluative attitudes.

Different kinds of political organization and contacts between politicians and voters are also found in the two sectors. In the rural districts and provincial cities candidates depend on campaigns that involve extensive contacts with ordinary voters — through hierarchies of personal ties or through their own individual support associations — more than they do in the large urban areas. Although the differences are relative (candidates in some older sections in the cities use techniques comparable to those employed outside the urban centers) there are still important overall differences.[29] As a corollary of these patterns, the role of political parties in campaigns is somewhat greater in the cities than in rural districts, with differences being most clear-cut during local elections. Because of these differences, it is accurate to say that rural residents have more personal connections with political leaders than do most city dwellers. Even though these connections are mediated by local influentials and ordinary voters "know" politicians on the basis of the contacts of local influentials rather than directly in many instances, there are meaningful sectoral contrasts in political linkages.

---

[29] For discussions of support mobilization and electoral processes in general in Japan see, particularly, Richard K. Beardsley, John W. Hall and Robert E. Ward, *op. cit.*, pp. 409–35; R. P. Dore, *City Life in Japan*, pp. 235, 269, 279 and 415; Dore, *Land Reform in Japan*, pp. 337–43; Kurt Steiner, *Local Government in Japan* (Stanford: Stanford University Press, 1965), pp. 409–31; Steiner, "The Japanese Village and Its Government," *Far Eastern Quarterly* 15 (February 1956), pp. 185–200; Paul Dull, "The Political Structure of a Japanese Village," *Far Eastern Quarterly* 12 (February 1964), pp. 175–90; Bradley Richardson, "A Japanese House of Councillors Election: Support Mobilization and Political Recruitment," *Modern Asian Studies* 1 (fall, 1967), pp. 393–96; Richardson, "Japanese Local Politics: Support Mobilization and Leadership Styles," *Asian Survey* 7 (December 1967), pp. 860–72; Robert E. Ward, "The Socio-Political Role of the Buraku (Hamlet) in Japan," *American Political Science Review* 45 (December 1951), pp. 1025–40; Ward, "Urban-Rural Differences and the Process of Political Modernization in Japan," *Economic Development and Cultural Change* 9 (October 1960), pp. 135–65; and Gerald L. Curtis, *Election Campaigning Japanese Style* (New York: Columbia University Press, 1971).

Methodology. Despite some strong integrating influences, it is clear that urban and rural Japan are still distinctive in several important dimensions of community organization and social structure. Obviously many of these urban-rural differences cannot be represented in a statistical analysis, simply because there are no readily available quantitative indicators for the kinds of qualitative differences I have discussed. In attempting to unravel just what underlies the urban-rural differences in political attitudes in Japan, I have incorporated systematic statistical analysis with less systematic qualitative explanations. In effect, I have relied on statistical analysis wherever possible, and supplemented the findings of this kind of research by other kinds of observations.

As will be seen, the statistical analysis shows quite clearly that urban-rural distributions of educational attainment are an important consideration underlying some of the differences in attitudes between persons living in the two kinds of sectors. Urban-rural distributions of group memberships are also important at some points. I have felt that in most instances levels of group memberships are really indicators of the qualitative differences in community life which I have already discussed. In other words, the high levels of multiple group memberships found in the rural districts do indeed provide some systematic evidence for the generally qualitative comments about the importance of differences in community life.

In considering the effects of such variables as education and group memberships on urban-rural differences in political attitudes, I have typically relied on Coleman's effect-parameter analysis.[30] As pointed out earlier, this technique is similar to multiple regression analysis. The Coleman approach has the added advantage of being suitable for use with attribute variables such as sex, age and place of residence. In its multivariate form, a single effect-index can be calculated indicating the contribution of each discreet variable *independent* of the effects of other influences. By manipulating different combinations of variables it will be possible to show just what accounts most for urban and rural differences and how much sectoral political culture variation is truly attributable to residual differences in community structure.

Before proceeding, it is important to note that the classification

---

[30] For works using this technique of analysis see Ch. 1, n. 25.

of respondents into urban and rural categories in the surveys reported here is different from the practice typically followed in other countries. Japanese surveys generally differentiate between urban and rural residents on the basis of residence within different kinds of *administrative units,* such as cities and counties, rather than size of place of residence. This method of classification is by and large acceptable, since the critical dimensions of population density and distribution of occupations varies substantially among different kinds of administrative categories.

There is however some concealment of primarily rural persons under the heading of "cities." As a result of the merger and/or incorporation of many small administrative units into larger entities during the middle and late 1950s, quite a few cities today actually have populations that are largely rural in character. Although the precise extent to which this has occurred on a nationwide basis is hard to estimate, it is obviously desirable to avoid misrepresentation of findings from urban samples where quite a few rural persons may be present in the population.[31] Accordingly, findings from *large* city samples are used wherever possible in order to minimize potential distortion. Elsewhere, occupation characteristics of the samples were carefully checked so as to avoid reporting evidence on urban tendencies from cities whose populations were primarily rural in character. In the case of my own 1964 postelection study, sample strata were selected to represent pure urban and rural districts.

Political Involvement. Expectations of modernization theory as to sectoral differences are largely borne out in Japan where feelings about

---

[31] Atsugi City in Kanagawa Prefecture, which I studied, was probably a typical case of municipal amalgamation in a largely rural area. The city of Atsugi was formed in 1955 by the merger of seven villages and a small town. The population of Atsugi remains primarily agricultural today, even though recent local industrialization and proximity to Tōkyō and Yokohama make it less representative of rural districts in general. Despite the effects of its location and growing industrialization, farmers account for 40 percent of the city's labor force and form the largest single category of employed persons. Municipal amalgamations are discussed at various places in Kurt Steiner, *Local Government in Japan.*

A rough idea of the scope of distortion in the statistics normally used to show urban-rural population patterns can be gained through an examination of official statistics pertaining to levels of concentration of the urban population. In 1965 the total urban population in Japan was 66,918,621 persons, but the number living in the cities in densely populated areas — places where there were more than 4,000 persons living in each square kilometer — was only 44,605,261 persons. See Sōrifu, Tōkeikyoku, *Nihon Tōkei Nenkan 1967,* p. 20.

involvement in national politics are concerned. This is shown first by the evidence on feelings about the relevance of politics (Table 6-3). Urban respondents found national politics more relevant than did rural voters in my 1964 five-district study. Similarly, residents of a small city in centrally located Aichi prefecture felt that there was a "direct connection between national politics and their lives" more commonly than did persons living in a small farming community (Aichi 1963, p. 188). Residents of towns within the suburban commuting area of Hiroshima city perceived some relationship between national political affairs and consumer price increases more commonly than did those who lived in a more remote, more conspicuously rural, part of Hiroshima prefecture (Hiroshima 1965, p. 82).

However, patterns in local involvement were substantially different from those where national politics was the focus. From this we can infer the existence of quite distinctive, but also internally complex, socializing forces in the two kinds of residential environments. The voters I interviewed in urban Yokohama and in several rural districts in 1964, for example, did not vary greatly in their feelings about the relevance of local politics. From this, it is obvious that rural voters were comparatively more aware of the importance of local than of national affairs. An analogous pattern was evident where respondents were asked simply to indicate whether they found national *or* local politics most relevant to their lives. In this case, urban voters throughout Japan tended to emphasize the relevance of national politics while persons living in the country found local affairs more important (Kōmei 1967A, p. 28).

Rural voters, moreover, found politics far more instrumentally important than did urban residents (Richardson 1964). Since this was the case for both national and local politics, it is plausible that feelings of political relevance among urban voters are substantially less grounded in self-interest than those of rural voters. This is a matter of some importance; various connotations of feelings of relevance may have different consequences for behavior. For example, different sectoral levels of feelings that politics is relevant in specifically instrumental terms could be a factor in urban-rural differences in participation.

Sectoral patterns in confidence in understanding public affairs were roughly similar to tendencies in the feeling that politics is relevant. Confidence in understanding politics varied between urban and

TABLE 6-3. INVOLVEMENT ATTITUDES

	Urban					Rural				
	Yes (%)	(Strong/Some) (%)	No (%)	Don't Know (%)	Total (%)	(N)	Yes (%)	(Strong/Some) (%)	No (%)	Don't Know (%)	Total (%)	(N)
National politics is closely related to our personal problems	78	(57/21)	14	7	99	(175)	69	(37/32)	15	16	100	(174)
Local politics is closely related to our personal problems	78	(49/29)	12	11	101	(175)	78	(44/34)	10	12	100	(174)
National politics is not difficult to understand	28	(3/25)	69	3	100	(175)	18	(3/15)	72	10	100	(174)
Local politics is not difficult to understand	30	(4/26)	64	6	100	(175)	43	(11/32)	49	8	100	(174)
Want our Diet member to do something for us	28	—	44	28	100	(179)	60	—	26	14	100	(178)
Want our local assemblyman to do something for us	36	—	36	27	99	(173)	67	—	24	9	100	(173)

SOURCE: Richardson 1964 postelection study.

CITY AND COUNTRYSIDE   149

rural citizens according to whether national or local politics was the object. Urban voters felt a little more commonly than rural residents that national politics was easy to understand, while the reverse was true regarding local politics. And, importantly, the ratio of rural voters who found *local* politics easy to understand was greater than the ratio of urban voters who found *national* politics easy to comprehend (Richardson 1964).

City dwellers were generally more knowledgeable than rural residents about politics; this tendency can be seen as evidence for the socializing processes forecast in the modernization models discussed earlier in this chapter (Table 6-4). Still, there were important urban-rural differences in the kind of political knowledge characteristic of each sector. Rural voters were especially deficient in abstract political knowledge, or knowledge of relatively remote matters such as the details of national political processes or general tendencies in election results. For example, substantially fewer rural than urban residents knew that the Election Law was being debated in the Diet (Miyagi 1962), that turnout rates in general elections were on the decline (Kōmei 1964B), or that partisan candidacies were on the increase in local elections (Kōmei 1964B).[32]

Where both important national institutions and more immediately relevant issues and processes were concerned, differences in political awareness among voters in the two sectors were much less noticeable. Almost as many rural as urban voters felt they knew how prime ministers were elected (Mie 1964), had opinions on the income doubling policy of the Liberal Democrats (Fukushima 1962), or were aware that national and local elections were scheduled (Kōmei 1962A; Kōmei 1967BB). Rural voters were actually more knowledgeable than urban voters in regard to at least one kind of political information: more residents of country districts could match House of Councillors candidates with their respective parties than was the case in a small city

---

[32] Differences in levels of awareness of turnout and partisanship trends were a reflection in part of variations in the nature of reality in the two kinds of sectors. Although rural election turnout had declined slightly in the years before this question was asked, greater declines were observed in urban constituencies. Moreover, tendencies of increasing partisanship in local elections were solely confined to the urban sector. See Jichishō Senkyokyoku, *Shūgiin Giin Sōsenkyo, Saikō Saibansho Saibankan Kokumin Chōsa Kekka Shirabe* (Tōkyō: 1964), p. 4; and, Jichichō Senkyobu, *Chihō Senkyo Kekka Shirabe* (Tōkyō: 1964), p. 5.

TABLE 6-4. POLITICAL KNOWLEDGE

	Urban				Rural			
	Yes (%)	No (%)	Total (%)	(N)	Yes (%)	No (%)	Total (%)	(N)
Knew how Prime Ministers are selected[a]	71	29	100	(240)	69	31	100	(160)
Knew that Election Law revision was an issue in Diet[b]	70	30	100	(187)	36	64	100	(87)
Had opinions on income doubling policy[c]	82	19	101	(249)	77	23	100	(411)
Knew tendencies in voter turnout in General Elections[d]	60	40	100	(490)	39	61	100	(885)
Knew that ratio of partisan candidacies in local elections was increasing[e]	52	48	100	(221)	42	59	101	(893)
Knew that House of Councillors elections were scheduled[f]	80	21	101	(772)	76	24	100	(1,555)
Knew that local elections were scheduled[g]	84	16	100	(433)	82	18	100	(788)
Could identify all or some candidates' party affiliations in House of Councillors election[h]	70	30	100	(249)	82	18	100	(411)

SOURCES:
[a] Mie 1964, p. 93. Figures were calculated from selected subsamples on the basis of the ratio of farmers in each sampled population. [b] Miyagi 1962, appendix, p. 41. Figures for rural respondents were calculated.
[c] Fukushima 1962, p. 178. [d] Kōmei 1964B, p. 67 (national). "Urban" here and in subsequent national studies refers to large cities only. [e] Kōmei 1964A, p. 126 (national). [f] Kōmei 1962A, p. 16 (national). [g] Kōmei 1967BB, p. 83 (national). [h] Fukushima 1962, p. 184.

(Fukushima 1962). Comparative political ignorance in the rural districts was consequently not systematic across categories of knowledge, and voters in these areas compared favorably with city dwellers in knowledge about more intimately relevant and experientially proximate political objects.

From this, and the evidence on feelings that politics is relevant, it would seem at first a good idea to recast our thinking about center-peripheral relationships in political involvement. Admitting the possibility that in reality there are multiple political "centers" would accommodate the distinctive urban-rural trend in Japan in respect to national and local political frames of reference. Urban residents in Japan could then be characterized as closer to national affairs, while rural residents were closer to the centers of local political life. But altering the center-periphery model of socio-political structure does not help in explaining urban-rural variations in political awareness. Urban-rural patterns of awareness largely reflect differences in the felt relevance of particular political objects. In other words, the center-periphery model might explain the relative ignorance among rural residents of national political processes in general, but it could not explain the fact of a much higher awareness among rural voters of national affairs when broadly relevant issues are involved.

Urban-rural patterns of interest in "politics" and election outcome were similar to patterns of other aspects of political involvement. Where the focus was "politics" or "elections" (both of which terms in Japan evoke the connotation of national affairs), sectoral patterns conform to the expectations of the theoretical models reviewed earlier (Table 6-5). This was the case both in nationwide studies and surveys conducted in particular regions of the country (Nihon 1961; Kōmei 1966/2; Kumamoto 1960, p. 23). But reverse tendencies were again demonstrated when the focus shifted to interest in *local* politics. Regardless of variations in question format and survey location, surveys uniformly showed rural voters more interested in local political life than urban voters, especially those living in the major metropolitan areas (Richardson 1964; Kōmei 1967A, p. 2; Fukushima 1962, p. 164; Aichi 1963, p. 41; Miyagi 1962, appendix, p. 33; Saga 1964, p. 12; Fukuoka 1961, p. 19; Kumamoto 1960, p. 39).

Respondents to my 1964 survey conformed to these same patterns with regard to feelings of concern about election outcome. More voters in Yokohama than in the rural districts were concerned about how the 1963 House of Representatives election would turn out. At the same time, rural voters cared more than urbanites about the outcome of the local assembly elections held in the spring of that same year. This finding is particularly interesting in view of the fact that local political competition (measured by the ratio of candidates to assembly

TABLE 6-5. INTEREST IN POLITICS

	Urban						Rural					
	Yes (%)	(Strong/Some) (%)	No (%)	Don't Know (%)	Total (%)	(N)	Yes (%)	(Strong/Some) (%)	No (%)	Don't Know (%)	Total (%)	(N)
Interest in politics[a]	60	(9/51)	40	—	100	—	50	(7/43)	50	—	100	—
Daily interest in politics[b]	71	(27/44)	27	2	100	(124)	65	(20/45)	34	1	100	(170)
Interest in election[b]	86	(47/39)	14	—	100	(124)	84	(47/37)	15	1	100	(170)
Concern about national election outcome[c]	73	(32/41)	27	—	100	(175)	70	(28/42)	28	2	100	(174)
Interest in local politics[c]	58	(14/44)	42	—	100	(174)	76	(29/47)	24	—	100	(174)
Concern about local election outcome[c]	64	(26/38)	34	2	100	(175)	68	(31/37)	30	2	100	(173)

SOURCES:

[a] *Nihon no Seijiteki Mukanshin* (Tōkyō, 1961), p. 41. "Urban" refers here to Japan's six largest cities of that time. [b] *Kōmei 1966/2*, pp. 141 and 144. The urban district in this case was Fukuoka City. [c] Richardson 1964 postelection study.

seats) was higher in Yokohama in 1963 than in the rural districts. Many observers of Japanese politics have felt that community loyalty and intercommunity rivalry contribute to high levels of rural concern about local election outcome; their impressions are obviously confirmed by these findings.

Educational attainment is clearly the major factor that contributes to urban-rural variation in levels of *national* political involvement. Trends in education alone do not account for all variations, but the higher educational level in the cities is of primary importance. In a Coleman multivariate analysis controls for the effects of education reduced the level of urban-rural differences in feelings that politics is relevant and confidence in understanding politics to negligible proportion (see Table 6–11).[33] Underlying these patterns is of course the fact that education enhances feelings of familiarity with national politics, both directly and by its part in determining levels of exposure to the mass media. It is also possible that better-educated voters more commonly feel that being informed about national politics is an imperative of citizenship, although evidence for this is not clear. It is clear, however, that education is the major factor in urban-rural differences in nationally oriented involvement. The importance of this fact for theory will be discussed later.

Some other characteristics of the urban environment have a comparable effect to that of education on involvement attitudes where

---

[33] An initial index .098 of urban-rural difference for feelings about the relevance of national politics was reduced to .025 by controlling for the effects of urban-rural distributions of educational attainment. A sectoral difference rate of .098 in feelings that national politics was easy to understand was reduced to .043. (Boldface figures indicate the index is significant at the 0.5 level of confidence. Italic figures indicate significance at the .01 level. Regular figures indicate indexes that do not meet the .05 confidence criterion. In reality, significance tests are inappropriate here, given the stratified nature of the sample. They are employed in accordance with emerging conventions in survey research on political behavior.)

The Coleman effect parameters, or indexes, are extremely simple to understand. In the bivariate case they represent simply the difference between the left and right cells of a normal two-by-two contingency table. In the case at hand they are equivalent to the difference between "yes" categories for rural and urban respondents in Table 6–3. In the analysis here no sign in the tables will always mean higher urban frequencies and a minus sign will indicate higher rural frequencies.

In multivariate analysis the indexes are based on more complicated calculations, but they can be compared to differences in the various tables when controls are introduced in contingency table analysis. In this case, the residual-index for the effects of residence is the average of differences attributable to urban-rural residence, with the different educational categories held constant.

specifically national politics are concerned, although the degree of impact is not as certain in these cases. The fact that there are more voters in the cities who support leftist parties is probably a factor, since leftist party support has been shown to be a correlative of feelings that national elections are most interesting (Kōmei 1967A, pp. 3–4). Furthermore, voting-choice based on "party" is more common in the cities than in the rural districts, and voters reporting partisan considerations in their decisions are inclined toward higher levels of involvement in national politics (Richardson 1964).[34] Research outside of Japan has observed the importance of party loyalty as a socializing agent, and the evidence at this point would seem to affirm a similar phenomenon among at least some categories of people in Japan.

Differences in people's social and political characteristics which generally favor higher levels of national political involvement among urban voters are less important with respect to local politics. Here variations in community structure have a more direct effect on involvement levels. The comparatively greater intimacy, frequency and redundancy of social interaction among rural residents favors sensitivity to local problems, and is certainly of major importance in the comparatively higher rural levels of involvement in local politics. In this respect, the nature of group life in the two kinds of areas is particularly important. Proportionately higher group membership among rural voters is directly associated with more opportunities for interaction. Moreover, group activities overlap with community social patterns and concerns more commonly in the country than in the city. It is precisely in this sense that group activities complement and reinforce the various qualities of rural life described earlier.

In the statistical analysis levels of group membership played a significant role in determining sectoral trends in local political involvement. Controls for the effect of group membership resulted in a substantial decrease in urban-rural differences in interest in local politics, concern about local election outcomes and understanding of local affairs (Table 6–11).[35]

---

[34] See also Fukushima 1964, pp. 160–161.
[35] Control for group membership reduced the urban-rural difference in interest in local politics from $-.181$ to $-.106$, concern about local election outcomes from $-.044$ to $.008$ and comprehension of local politics from $-.132$ to $-.056$. The relative importance of the higher group involvement levels found in the rural sector, as well as the importance of residence in the compact rural communities as a residual influence independent from group membership, can be seen quite clearly from these

Other aspects of community life in the two sectors may also be important, even though their effects are less directly demonstrable. Community influentials have different roles in the two kinds of areas; their articulation and promotion of local interests presumably has a wider impact in rural communities than in cities. This is partially the result of the ease of interpersonal communications in the more intimate rural social setting. But the fact that residents of particular rural communities perceive community differences of interest more commonly than most urbanites, and that these sometimes lead to open rivalries with other communities, is also a factor.

The effects of community structure, both explicit and inferred, are of the greatest importance then to the formation of attitudes toward local politics — in contrast with the importance of education for sectoral variations where national politics was concerned. Differences in responsiveness to mass communications between urban and rural residents are also relevant to differences in involvement attitudes at some points. Differences in levels of mass media attention exist, but it is hard to see these as causes of urban-rural difference in involvement since mass media exposure could actually be dependent on political involvement rather than the contrary being the case. Moreover, urban and rural tendencies in involvement in national politics and mass media exposure are both typically the result of educational differences. What I do find important about urban-rural differences in mass media consumption is the fact that the mass media which people follow in the cities devote greater coverage to national and international news than is the case in the country. The major national dailies, with a largely cosmopolitan focus, are read more commonly in the cities than in many rural districts. The regional press, favored in quite a few country areas, pays much greater attention to prefectural and local news.[36] This is

---

figures. Interestingly, length of residence — an important variable in some Japanese studies — did not effect the basic urban-rural differences, despite the fact that far more persons had lived all of their lives in the rural sector than was the case in the cities (Table 6-1).

[36] Tendencies in readership are based on calculations of the ratio of subscriptions to national and local newspapers in each of Japan's prefectures. The information on subscriptions totals for different newspapers was provided by the United States Embassy, Tōkyō, and was compiled from a variety of Japanese sources.

The national press was favored in most of the metropolitan prefectures and in neighboring districts, including Tōkyō, Ōsaka, Kyōto, Hyōgo, Fukuoka, Chiba, Kanagawa and Saitama. The national press was read more often in 19 predominantly rural prefectures, but local newspapers exceeded 60 percent of all subscriptions in 36 other rural prefectures.

not terribly surprising, of course. Indeed, these patterns appear to be duplicated to some degree in national and regional radio broadcasting.

More research is needed before the effects of these variations in mass media content can be spelled out with any certainty. But it is highly possible that mass media *content* is a prior conditioning factor despite the unclear relationship between involvement attitudes and overall levels of mass media exposure. In this case, the character of mass media content in the two sectors can be assumed to reinforce tendencies toward involvement in national politics in the cities and a concern for local politics in the rural areas.

The fact that levels of wanting something done by political representatives were much higher in the rural areas than in the city was particularly interesting, since this was contrary to quite a bit of relevant theory. When a multivariate analysis of the tendencies in instrumental awareness between the two sectors was conducted, it was clear that there was something about rural life above and beyond simply the higher frequencies of group membership that facilitated the development of heightened feelings of self-interest (Table 6-11). This was a little confusing, but what I think it means is simply that the ease of communication in the rural areas facilitates development of this kind of awareness above and beyond the mere fact that many people interact frequently in group settings.[37] Whatever the case, it is important to see that forms of social organization native to the rural sector of Japan favor the formation of an awareness of self-interest more than the growth of cities and educational increases that are seen as essential by some theorists.[38]

Evaluative Attitudes. Most discussions of the relationship between

---

[37] The basic index for the effects of residence was *−.304*. When controls for group membership levels were introduced this was reduced to *−.244*.

The role of organizational involvement here is somewhat analogous to that reported for France by Sidney Tarrow (see n. 1), pp. 353–355. However, in Japan the chief focus is locally oriented instrumentalism, and this would appear to be different from the more generalized rural pragmatism in France.

[38] The fact that over 80 percent of all rural families own their own homes (in contrast to about 50 percent of urban families) may also be important, although no surveys have attempted to measure the effects of this variable on awareness of self-interest. See Sōrifu Tōkeikyoku, *Nihon Tōkei Nenkan 1967*, p. 434, for relevant data. (Slightly over 80 percent of all first-class farm households — those cultivating over one-half hectare of farmland, or having annual sales of over 100,000 yen from sericulture, livestock or poultry breeding or the operation of hot houses — also own their own land or facilities. *Ibid.*, p. 87.)

residence and political behavior focus on the effects of country or city life on involvement or participation attitudes. The possible impact of residence on the evaluation of politics has received less attention, although the idea that urban life enhances people's feelings of control over public affairs is surely a natural corollary of both social modernization and center-periphery theory. The theory of mass society also addresses itself to these issues, and in fact links social circumstances with feelings of political alienation. But in this view the specific effects of residence depend primarily on the quality and pace of urbanization rather than on the fact of urban residence itself. Indeed, people in both urban *and* rural areas may become socially or politically alienated depending on the situation, and there are no specific expectations about the effects of place of residence alone.[39]

Sectoral patterns in evaluative attitudes in Japan are especially interesting, given the fact that theory in this area is comparatively undeveloped. In general, rural voters were more positive than urban voters in their appraisal of politics. This was the case in a wide variety of locales and with somewhat diverse topics (Table 6–6), although it must be remembered that these were relative tendencies and that the national trend in most instances was one of pessimism.[40] Persons living in the rural parts of Kumamoto prefecture were more content with "the way contemporary politics is carried out" than were people who lived

---

[39] See William Kornhauser, *The Theory of Mass Society* (Glencoe, Illinois: Free Press, 1959), pp. 143–150.

[40] The urban-rural trends in evaluative attitudes thus confirm Robert Ward's observation that urban residents may be more cynical about politics; see "Urban-Rural Differences and the Process of Political Modernization in Japan," *Economic Development and Cultural Change* 9 (October 1960), p. 162. In contrast with the general lack of attention to these matters in empirical theory, some writers have speculated about the nature of political cynicism in large American cities, and have anticipated effects of the kinds observed in Japan. See, for example, Robert E. Agger, Daniel Goldrich and Bert E. Swanson, *The Rulers and the Ruled: Political Power and Impotence in American Communities* (New York, London and Sydney: John Wiley and Sons, 1964), p. 761, as well as the growing literature that links urbanization with political violence in Latin America.

The fact that "don't know" answers were more common in many cases among rural respondents is a potential contaminating factor of some significance in trends in evaluative attitudes. However, the trends in evaluative attitudes among urban and rural voters were consistent in cases where this was a problem as well as where there were no great differences in levels of "don't know" answers in the two sectors, so it is assumed that the problem is less important than might otherwise be anticipated.

TABLE 6-6. EVALUATIVE ATTITUDES

	Urban				Rural			
	Positive (%)	Negative (%)	Don't Know (%)	Total (%)	(N)	Positive (%)	Negative (%)	Don't Know (%)	Total (%)	(N)
---	---	---	---	---	---	---	---	---	---	---
Satisfaction with politics[a]	12	66	23	101	(102)	18	50	32	100	(68)
Satisfaction with elected Councillors[b]	51	28	20	99	(421)	56	13	31	100	(905)
Quality of recent local assembly candidates[c]	20	33	48	101	(421)	35	21	44	100	(780)
Politics improves by holding elections[d]	30	42	28	100	(773)	37	36	27	100	(2,205)
Law violations in Representatives election[e]	37	41	22	100	(453)	35	36	29	100	(788)
National politicians and officials are concerned about our needs[f]	51	35	13	99	(175)	55	20	25	100	(174)
Local politicians and officials are concerned about our needs[f]	57	29	14	100	(175)	75	10	14	99	(174)
Effect of people's vote and interest on national politics[f]	74	13	13	100	(175)	73	9	18	100	(174)
Effect of people's vote and interest on local politics[f]	81	9	11	101	(175)	80	7	13	100	(174)
Candidates keep their election promises[g]	10	70	20	100	(333)	15	59	26	100	(167)
Politics moves by our power[h]	57	39	4	100	(163)	44	51	5	100	(312)

SOURCES:

[a] Kumamoto 1960, p. 34. [b] Kōmei 1962B, p. 88 (national). [c] Kōmei 1967A, p. 133 (national). [d] Kōmei 1958, p. 72 (national). "It depends" is included in "don't know" responses. [e] Kōmei 1967BB, p. 43 (national). [f] Richardson 1964 postelection survey. [g] Fukuoka 1960B, p. 48 (recalculated). [h] Fukushima 1963, p. 176. Included in negative answers are perceptions that only national or only local politics is "moved by our power."

"Positive" responses were those which indicated satisfaction, optimism about elections, feelings of efficacy and favorable perceptions of politicians' responsiveness. "Negative" answers included manifestations of dissatisfaction, pessimism about elections (including the feeling that "politics stays the same"), perceptions that "many" or "all" candidates violated election laws, feelings of inefficacy and perceptions that politicians were not responsive. "Urban" in national survey findings refers to large cities, and "rural" is counties or towns and villages; data on intermediate level population units from national surveys were omitted for the sake of simplicity.

in small cities in the same district (Kumamoto 1960).[41] Compared to urban voters, residents of rural communities throughout the nation reported higher levels of satisfaction with the quality of the successful candidates in a House of Councillors election (Kōmei 1962B). Paralleling these findings was the higher rural rate of disagreement with the idea that "the quality of candidates in local elections has deteriorated in recent years" (Kōmei 1967A). Also, on one occasion rural voters were more commonly inclined to believe that "politics is getting better" than were residents of a small city (Saga 1964, p. 6).

Perhaps the tendency among rural voters to feel satisfied is brought about in part by the effectiveness of candidate efforts to mobilize support. The assiduous cultivation of personal reputations in rural areas could lead to higher levels of voter satisfaction, at least where appraisal of some particular politician was more or less directly implied by the wording of survey questions. However, support mobilization is presumably less influential where more general assessments of political life are sought.

Where question content focuses on dimensions of politics other than frames of reference where feelings about particular politicians might be evoked, it could be anticipated that different patterns would occur in the urban and rural areas. In particular, the presence of more well-educated persons in the cities could lead to greater optimism there, by virtue of the fact that higher levels of schooling involve greater cumulative exposure to the formal norms of democracy. It was surprising, then, to see that popular assessment of elections and electoral processes reflected the same tendencies as feelings of satisfaction. In response to an often asked question about the basic value of elections, consistently more rural than urban voters said that "politics improves by holding elections," or disagreed with the proposition that "it worsens" or "just stays the same" (Kōmei 1958; Miyagi 1962, appendix, p. 39).[42] In response to the same question, proportionately more urban

---

[41] This finding is supported by the results of Shimane 1963 (p. 46), which like Kumamoto 1963 was also a study from a single prefecture.

[42] These findings are also supported by the results reported in Kōmei 1962A, p. 45. Like Kōmei 1958, this was a national survey; the "urban" tendencies reported here are for large city residents only. In the case of the Miyagi data "urban" referred to residents of Sendai, one of Japan's major provincial cities.

Urban-rural differences in specific regions regarding voter opinions about the consequences of holding elections which deviate from the national survey findings

voters were pessimistic about elections. This was also the case with questions on illegal and corrupt activities in elections. People in the rural districts felt that the 1958 House of Representatives election had been conducted "fairly and cleanly" more than did urbanites (Jichi 1958, pp. 15–16), or reported less often than urban voters that "many" candidates violated the election laws in regard to both national and local contests (Kōmei 1965BB; Kōmei 1964A, p. 127; Nagasaki 1962, p. 43). Somewhat analogous trends were apparent when more urban than rural voters reported that they considered corruption a vital issue when voting in the 1967 local and prefectural elections (Kōmei 1967A, pp. 74 and 110).[43]

Rural optimism was repeated in evaluations of the performance of politicians. Slightly more voters in rural areas than in urban Yokohama felt that Diet members and national officials were responsive to their needs (Richardson 1964). Much greater differences in the same direction were registered with respect to local politics. Elsewhere, urban and rural voters were similarly pessimistic about the responsiveness of national politicians, but rural voters were comparatively more optimistic about the performance of local representatives than were residents of a small city (Shiga 1962, p. 47). Similarly, more voters in the rural parts of Miyagi prefecture felt that their interests were satisfactorily represented in local political processes, while respondents from urban Sendai were somewhat less favorable and more often felt that their interests were represented only "to some degree" (Miyagi 1962, appendix, p. 67). Finally, in three southern prefectures rural residents felt more often than small city dwellers that candidates kept their election promises (Fukuoka 1960B; Kumamoto 1960, p. 100; Saga 1964, p. 45).

---

are reported in Kumamoto 1960 p. 97; Aichi 1963, p. 51; and, Kagawa 1965, p. 26. Presumably, local influences were important in these cases, especially since in all cases "urban" residents came from the populations of small cities. (Inhabitants of small cities showed attitudes more similar to those of rural voters in the results of both the 1958 and 1962 national studies. Consequently, the chance of local deviation from overall urban-rural differences is probably greater where small city population samples are used.)

There were also some interesting urban-rural differences in voter assessment of the reasons for feeling that politics "stays the same" or "worsens" through holding elections. Urban residents tended to base their pessimism on such beliefs as "you can't trust politics," "election law violations are bad," and "the people's consciousness is deficient," while rural citizens were generally less able to identify any reason for their feelings. See Miyagi 1962, appendix, p. 40.

[43] Corruption had been a major issue in Tōkyō metropolitan politics between the 1964 and 1967 local elections.

There is probably no simple cause for the general tendency among rural voters toward comparatively more favorable evaluations of political performance. One explanation for these patterns was suggested above. Various other kinds of evidence, and my multivariate analysis, suggest additional explanations. The first thing to be considered is the nature of political norms in urban and rural communities. Although more research is needed to establish clear definitions, some important differences between the two sectors are apparent. Urban political norms include higher levels of idealism and the expectation that politics should be free from corruption, especially among well-informed persons. This is shown specifically by urban attitudes toward election violations and feelings about corrupt candidates (Table 6–7). In contrast,

TABLE 6-7. Attitudes Toward Election Corruption

	Urban (%)	Rural (%)	
Feelings about illegal election practices:[a]			
Can't be helped or "natural"	22	32	
It's a bad thing	75	66	
Unclear	3	3	
Total:	100	101	(N = 1,734)
Action in the event a supported candidate was found to have bribed voters:[b]			
Would not vote for him under any circumstances	71	58	
Would vote for him if no other suitable candidate	11	19	
Would vote for him as he's still an outstanding person	2	6	
Doesn't bother me as bribery is common		3	
Don't know	16	14	
Total:	100	100	(N = 985)

Sources:
[a] Kōmei Senkyo Remmei, *Kōmei Senkyo no Jittai*, 1958, p. 78.
[b] From secondary analysis of Prime Ministers Office 1898.

rural voters are more permissive, although it is not very clear just why this is the case. It is possible that rural voters have a different definition of corruption, or they may be more aware of the benefits accruing from having effective politicians and thus tend to overlook the way in which these officials gain influence.[44]

The contrasting character of community life in the city and the country is also important for the sectoral trends in evaluative attitudes I have described. Various kinds of evidence suggest that rural voters either know candidates personally more often than urbanites, or they are more familiar with their reputations.[45] Differences of this kind might be expected in local elections, given the great interest of rural residents in local politics at the local level. But rural voters are more knowledgeable at other levels as well. It can be assumed that this reflects more than anything else the fact that rural voters are more often in face-to-face contact with influentials who endeavor to build support for particular candidates, as well as the fact that candidates in the less populous rural constituencies can also more readily establish their own direct contacts with the electorate. Whatever the case, it is my contention that the higher frequency of more intimate kinds of contact facilitates feelings of optimism and trust in the rural areas, particularly in view of the importance of personal connections in Japanese society. Finally, it can be argued that these feelings carry over into interview situations where there is no direct reference to a particular political

---

[44] It is also possible that centuries of acceptance of *ascriptive* status in many areas has led rural citizens to be less concerned with the way in which persons of high *achieved* status actually get there. This type of response may also be found among low status persons in the cities, particularly where the expectation of paternalistic behavior among elites still exists.

[45] Direct questions about acquaintance with candidates have been asked (Saga 1962, p. 22; Fukuoka 1964, p. 27), but the results were not tabulated according to residence.

Urban-rural differences in levels of direct or mediated acquaintanceship can, however, be inferred from the following findings:

	Urban		Rural	
	Local(%) *(Election)*	*Prefecture*(%) *(Election)*	*Local*(%) *Election*	*Prefecture*(%) *(Election)*
Knew about candidate of choice "ordinarily"	47	60	80	65
Didn't know about him until election	21	37	7	28

The source is Kōmei 1964A, p. 116, for local election figures, and Kōmei 1967A, p. 63, for data on attitudes during a prefectural assembly election. The questions in the two studies were identical.

figure, thus accounting for the pervasiveness of favorable evaluations in the rural districts.

There was some interesting evidence regarding the effects of rural residence and its connection with other variables in the multivariate analysis of voter appraisals of politicians' responsiveness. In most nations people of higher educational attainment are more optimistic about the responsiveness of persons in public life, either through the effects of their higher status or by virtue of their greater cumulative exposure to discussions of the formal norms of democracy in school and university. Well-educated people in Japan are also more optimistic than their educational inferiors, although they are not infrequently less clearly optimistic and more ambivalent in comparison with their counterparts in other countries. But the important point here is simply that well-educated people more often live in the urban areas and, as a result, it can be anticipated that at least some portions of the urban public will be optimistic about politicians' behavior.

When I analyzed the findings on evaluations of politicians' reponsiveness using the Coleman technique, a particularly intriguing interplay between education and residence was uncovered. Once the effects of education were removed — education was important as a contributing factor where specifically favorable appraisals of national politicians were concerned — the effects of living in the rural areas were even greater than they had been before. In other words, by excluding the optimistic evaluations of some well-educated persons (who also lived in the city) the basic urban-rural distinctiveness was actually enhanced.[46] In addition to showing how different kinds of variables contribute to the development of favorable impressions of politicians, this analysis demonstrates the importance of rural residence alone when other kinds of influences are removed.

Additional evidence in support of the interpretation that rural community life is favorable to the development of positive evaluations is found in the response to open questions in my survey. Urban resi-

---

[46] An urban-rural index of −.034 for evaluations of responsiveness of national politicians increased to −.088 when education was controlled; assessments of local politicians increased from a −.184 to −.242 with controls for education.

Something was clearly different about rural residence in these instances, although sectoral differences in organizational involvement were not the contributing factor, according to the analysis.

dents indicated on several occasions that they felt inadequate or pessimistic about politics because they "didn't know any of the candidates" or "didn't feel close to the politicians." Views of this kind were expressed in the rural areas, too, but less often than in the city and mainly in places where there was no native son candidate.

The fact that there is more identification with leftist parties among urban voters contributes to the effect of residence on evaluative attitudes in yet another way. Several studies show that leftist party supporters are more negative in their evaluative attitudes than Liberal Democratic Party adherents.[47] This may be a reflection only of the critical posture of leftist party leaders toward the conservative party's conduct of politics, or it may manifest other, more personal, considerations. Whatever the case, controls for party support reduced urban-rural differences in some instances.[48] From this we can say that sectoral trends in party support are an important factor in urban-rural differences in popular assessment of politics.

Another explanation of these differences is the possibility of variation in attitudes about speaking out critically. Many Japanese are reluctant to express critical opinions about known persons, especially in comparatively formal face-to-face encounters such as interviews. Although there are undoubtedly differences among individuals and communities on this point, it is plausible that rural residents are generally more reluctant than urban residents to speak critically.[49] This would

---

[47] See, for example, Kōmei 1962B, p. 88, for attitudes toward national politicians, and Kōmei 1967A, p. 135, for attitudes toward local politicians. My 1964 survey demonstrated similar left-conservative trends.

While party preference certainly is a factor in the formation of negative evaluative attitudes in some cases, it is also possible that many voters with negative evaluative attitudes support the leftist parties *because* of their attitudes. Furthermore, there is some overlap between such characteristics as high education, high mass media exposure and leftist party support, so that a hierarchy of causal forces cannot be conclusively defined here, where analysis is based on secondary sources.

[48] More details on this consideration, based on a reanalysis of various Japanese Prime Ministers Office Surveys, are included in "Urbanization and Political Behavior: The Case of Japan," to be published in *American Political Science Review*, June 1973.

[49] According to the results of Shimane 1960, p. 97, rural voters indicated that they felt free to talk about politics with other people in the community less often than urbanites. But contrary patterns are found in Gumma 1963, p. 26.

Nevertheless, we know that rural residents are more sensitive than urban residents to the opinions of others where politics is concerned, and this could be important in determining (conscious or unconscious) willingness to express unfavorable opinions. For example, rural residents felt more commonly than city resibe especially important where questions are worded in such a way that they appear to refer to *particular* politicians. In such a case, personal relationships with politicians or with persons who support particular politicians, as well as perceptions that a particular politician is supported by many people in the community, might lead rural voters to feel that they *should* express satisfaction (since it might be felt that any negative opinion would seem to reflect on the politicians best-known to the respondent).

There is one final factor in the sectoral differences in evaluative attitudes. The evidence in several places indicates that rural voters are more often inclined to depend on politicians to take care of them than are urban voters. In this regard, rural residents manifest what is best characterized as expectations of paternalism. This clearly implies trust in the motives of their "betters" that contrasts with, or exceeds that of urban residents; such trust is a natural correlative of favorable assessments of performance.

There were a few exceptions to the general tendency of rural voters to manifest more optimism about politics than urban residents. These are interesting for the light they throw on the underlying meanings of different kinds of questions. In two separate instances where voters were asked questions about their own efficacy there was either less distinctiveness between urban and rural voters than was the case where other kinds of questions were asked (Richardson 1964), or, urban voters felt more efficacious than their rural counterparts (Fukushima 1963). What this indicates is again connected with the special role of education as an underlying influence in urban-rural patterns where some kinds of evaluative attitudes are concerned. The question about people's efficacy touched directly on a formal norm (that people ought to have real political powers in a democracy), and increases in education were clearly linked with more positive evaluations in this kind of situation.[50] A multivariate analysis of the relationships between educa-

---

dents that their voting preferences were known by others (Kōmei 1967BB, p. 74), and substantially more often that they considered other people's opinions in making their voting choices (Kōmei 1958, p. 59).

[50] Persons of higher educational backgrounds felt more *effective* toward politics, according to both my own study and Fukushima 1963. Interestingly, where feelings about the responsiveness of politicians were concerned, well-educated persons in my own sampled populations were also more optimistic than voters whose education was limited. But the relationship was much weaker than in the case of feelings of popular efficacy, and as a result had less of an effect on urban-rural patterns.

tion, place of residence and feelings about voter efficacy showed not only that education contributed more than residence to the development of attitudes about the effectiveness of the vote, but that urban-rural tendencies in evaluative attitudes with the effects of education removed were actually more like those I have been describing.[51] Thus, we can see again the special complexities introduced both by the optimism found in some instances among educated people and by the fact that well-educated persons more commonly live in the urban areas.[52]

It is also possible to believe that the greater sensitivity to formal democratic norms among educated people contributes in still another way to urban-rural differences where evaluative attitudes are concerned. Thus some of the dissatisfaction generally shown by people in the cities probably stems as much from the sensitivity to democratic ideas and rejection of earlier value systems among well-educated persons as it does to some other kinds of influences. Just as some French respondents repudiate party loyalties as a matter of principle, educated Japanese living in the urban areas may repudiate dependence on politicians and favorable assessments of their accomplishments in order to demonstrate the modernity of their outlooks.[53] In other words, well-educated voters can be seen as espousing both the view that the only legitimate politics operates on the basis of ordinary people's influence on politicians and

---

[51] In this case an original urban-rural index of .006 became −.060 once education was controlled. But the overall emphasis in my comments on the role of education is based on the size of the bivariate index for education, which was *.157.*

[52] Data with a higher incidence of negative evaluative attitudes among persons of high educational attainment is also available, in Kōmei 1967A, p. 135, and Kōmei 1958, p. 71, as well as in several regional studies where questions on evaluative attitudes have been asked.

There is no research on the nature of attitude formation among persons of different educational backgrounds, but presumably many postwar graduates of institutions of higher education have had some exposure to the critical political attitudes of some student groups and faculty members, and the higher levels of attention to mass media and political awareness of well-educated persons either reinforces attitudes acquired at some earlier point in time or fosters negative attitudes without reference to earlier experiences. It is also possible that highly bureaucratic white-collar careers nurture negative attitudes in some instances. But, of course, these same kinds of persons often live in the looser structure of urban environments where contacts with politicians are less common, and are acutely sensitive to the kinds of urban norms discussed earlier. Definitive identification of causal patterns is obviously impossible on the basis of the available evidence, and more research should be conducted on this extremely important tendency among better-educated Japanese voters.

[53] See Tarrow (see n. 1 above), pp. 350–351.

the complimentary position that dependence on the benevolence of paternal representatives is in itself both undesirable and ineffective.

Participation Attitudes. Identification of the character and sources of popular participation in political life is obviously one of the core concerns of empirical political theory. As noted earlier, current theory typically anticipates that urbanization and participation are positively linked, even though the status of residence has been ambiguous in the overall findings of empirical research. The fact that voter turnout in Japan is higher in rural districts than it is in the cities has therefore attracted special attention. Several writers have been concerned with analysis of the causes, and have speculated about the significance of the Japanese trends. However, with the exception of the seminal work of Jōji Watanuki, little has been done to explore the attitudinal basis of urban-rural trends in political participation in Japan.[54]

The general lack of attention to the possibility that urban-rural differences in turnout actually may be based on complementary differences in underlying attitudes makes it particularly imperative that we look into the available evidence on sectoral trends in participation attitudes here. Unless Japanese urban-rural trends in participation are largely an effect of the mobilization capacity of influence channels within communities, there should be some connection between participation attitudes and actual participation in politics. In fact, the latter is the case, and we do see attitude tendencies that parallel turnout trends. In the first place, rural residents manifest feelings of obligation about the vote more often than urban residents, while a sense of duty has been positively linked to voter turnout.[55] Rural voters are also generally more inclined than urban voters to express attitudes favoring activist participation in political affairs, a fact which is of some im-

---

[54] See Jōji Watanuki, "Social Structure and Political Participation in Japan," Laboratory for Political Research, Department of Political Science, University of Iowa, Report No. 32, May 1970, pp. 4–5.

[55] Voter feelings of duty have been positively related to turnout in Yamaguchi 1964, pp. 26–27 and 30.

In contrast with the direct linkage between attitudes about the obligation to vote and actual participation, involvement attitudes are more complexly related to behavior. In the city involvement in politics leads to voting, but in the country both people who are interested in politics and those who are apathetic turn out in elections (Aichi 1963, p. 37), presumably because of the overriding importance of duty there. I have tried to unravel some of these relationships using my own findings in Ch. 8.

portance to the theoretical expectations about the effects of urban residence on political attitudes and behavior reviewed earlier.

The tendency to regard voting as a duty was more prevalent among rural than urban residents regardless of variations in location and question content among different surveys. According to the results of several local studies, rural voters cited "duty" more often as an explicit reason for going out to vote, while persons living in the cities more often said that they went to vote on the basis of their "possession of the franchise right" or the feeling that the vote was a "chance to express one's views directly" (Aichi 1963, p. 59; Aichi 1964, p. 46; Shizuoka 1963, p. 55). In response to questions about the legitimacy of abstention (Table 6–8), more rural voters than persons in the cities felt that it was "bad to abstain from voting" (Gumma 1963; Niigata 1963, p. 14), "better to vote for the next best candidate than abstain" (Gifu 1963) or "bad to abstain even when there's no desirable candidate" (Fukuoka 1960B; Wakayama 1962, p. 20).[56] Finally, nearly twice as many rural as urban respondents agreed with the proposition that "it's everybody's duty to go out and vote" (Richardson 1964).

It was argued earlier that socialization in the prewar period favored the attitude that voting is an obligation somewhat more than is the case at present. If this view is valid, it would appear that the residual force of tradition is somewhat greater in the rural districts than it is in the cities. But it is also possible that, where influences conducive to attitudes of duty toward the vote are concerned, differences between urban and rural environments go beyond simply differences in the viability of older beliefs. When we examine the tendencies among age groupings in each sector, we see that majorities or near majorities of even young voters in the rural areas manifest attitudes of duty, in contrast with much lower ratios for young persons in the cities.[57] This does

---

[56] It should be noted that most of the urban samples were drawn from the populations of small cities. Somewhat greater urban-rural differences might be the case were large cities the base.

[57] Thus, more rural voters in their twenties and thirties felt they had voted on the basis of duty alone, or the compound belief that the vote was both a right and a duty. Persons in the same age group living in small cities felt that they voted because the vote was a "right" or because of a "chance for expression of one's opinions." See Aichi 1963, p. 60, and Shizuoka 1963, p. 56.

Majorities of older voters in both urban and rural sectors reported motivations of duty, although this emphasis was still a little more common among rural than urban voters in the respective age groups.

TABLE 6-8. ATTITUDES TOWARD THE VOTE

	Urban					Rural				
	Yes (%)	No (%)	Don't Know (%)	Total (%)	(N)	Yes (%)	No (%)	Don't Know (%)	Total (%)	(N)
It's everybody's duty to go out and vote[a]	30	43	28	101	(174)	62	26	12	100	(174)
It's bad to abstain from voting except under special circumstances[b]	48	41	11	100	(—)	64	30	7	101	(—)
It's better to vote for the best candidate rather than abstain, when a person you prefer isn't running[c]	54	26	20	100	(172)	68	27	5	100	(79)
Disagree with idea that it's all right to abstain when there is no appropriate candidate[d]	43	49	8	100	(333)	60	29	11	100	(167)

SOURCES:
[a] Richardson 1964 postelection study. [b] Gumma 1963, pp. 63–64. [c] Gifu 1963, p. 69. The urban sample was drawn from Gifu city. [d] Fukuoka 1960B, p. 51. The urban respondents lived in Fukuoka City.

not completely negate the importance of possible sectoral differences in the effects of tradition. But it does cause us to look for contemporary socialization mechanisms in the rural environment which favor feelings that the vote is a civic obligation.

To begin, rural voters have a stronger sense of obligation to participate in community activities than do city voters.[58] This is the conclusion of many community studies (and is supported by data to be presented shortly). It is certainly plausible that these sentiments are carried over into feelings about the vote. The very appeals by election administrators for increased turnout strike an especially receptive chord among rural voters, since they are not infrequently expressed as requests to "get together and vote." The practice of some communities of competing for the honor of high turnouts and the practice of encouraging voters to turn out in support of locally endorsed candidates are additional modes for translating feelings of obligation toward the community into the attitude that the vote is a duty. Finally, multivariate analysis shows that the higher incidence of group membership found in rural areas is directly associated with urban-rural differences in the frequency of attitudes of obligation.[59] Since group membership levels can be interpreted as an expression of community structure, this gives additional weight to the above comments.

At the same time, urban socialization specifically favors the attitude that the vote is either a right or an "opportunity for self-expression." Although democratic ideas have been widely diffused among the general population since the war, the comparatively higher ratio in the cities of voters who are well-educated and who follow politics in the mass media is a factor in the greater acceptance among urban residents of explicitly democratic concepts of the vote — just as it con-

---

[58] Urban-rural differences in feelings that one should be active in community life can be seen from the results of interviews with hamlet heads and urban household association officials. Among the former there were references to the frequent "cooperative" feelings of local people, while the latter deplored the fact that few people took community activities seriously any more.

Differences in feeling about the obligation to participate are also evident in various accounts of urban and rural life. See especially Tadashi Fukutake, *Man and Society in Japan* (Tōkyō: University of Tōkyō Press, 1962), pp. 93–94.

It should be noted that a few rural respondents to my survey felt they had turned out "because everybody was going out to vote." Perhaps high turnout itself has some socializing and reinforcing effect on attitudes in many rural areas.

[59] An initial urban-rural effect index of −.089 was also reduced to −.072 when controls for group membership were introduced.

tributes to greater awareness of ideals in regard to other aspects of politics.[60]

It is hardly surprising that rural residents are more inclined to have attitudes of duty toward voting, given the various influences that favor such circumstances. It is less obvious, however, that conditions in the rural areas favor a comparatively greater preference for activist forms of political participation (Table 6-9).[61] When asked about the best way to have "one's opinions reflected in local and prefectural politics," preferences for "working through a group," or willingness to submit petitions or participate in recall and dissolution movements, answers reflecting activist predispositions were proportionately greater among rural than among urban residents. The latter would more often just "think carefully at election time," vote for someone who would "take care of our interests" or simply "depend on elections" (Fukushima 1962; Fukushima 1963; Ōita 1962, p. 37).

Rural voters would also take a more active role in local decisionmaking than urban voters, according to the findings from a variety of locales. Rural residents said they would "take the lead" or "actively assist" in efforts to resolve local problems more often than did city dwellers, while urban residents more commonly felt that they would "depend on influentials or officials" or didn't care about local problems

---

[60] For evidence of a strong positive relationship between high educational attainment and attitudes that the vote is either a right or an instrumental opportunity, see Aichi 1963, p. 61, and Aichi 1964, p. 47. (Whether the relationship was especially strong among well-educated *young* persons, as the result both of contemporary socialization and the special receptiveness of persons in this category to political idealism, could not be determined inasmuch as there were no controls for age.)

There was also a positive relationship in some cases between educational accomplishment and feelings of duty in replies to questions about specifically the legitimacy of abstention. But the effects here were much less pronounced than in the case of direct questions about turnout motivations, with the result that the distribution of education did not effect urban-rural differences so greatly here (and more rural voters showed attitudes of duty).

[61] In all instances the urban samples were drawn from small city populations, and the differences shown in Table 6-9 might have been even greater were large city samples included.

Preferences for collective solutions to political problems are interpreted here as an indicator of activist participant orientations (following the practice of Almond and Verba, *The Civic Culture* [Boston: Little, Brown, 1965], Ch. 5). There may be some question whether preferences for collective activities have the same voluntaristic connotations among Japanese voters as are asserted for those attitudes elsewhere, but it was still felt that urban-rural differences on this point are important enough and worthwhile noting.

TABLE 6-9. PARTICIPATION ATTITUDES

	Urban				Rural			
	Yes (%)	No (%)	Don't Know (%)	Total (%)	(N)	Yes (%)	No (%)	Don't Know (%)	Total (%)	(N)
Would stress group activity to get people's opinions reflected in national affairs[a]	17	77	6	100	(249)	24	53	23	100	(411)
Would stress groups or movements to have opinions reflected in local politics[b]	35	61	4	100	(163)	49	46	5	100	(312)
Would take an active role in the resolution of local problems[c]	32	67	1	100	(187)	43	52	5	100	(44)
Best way to resolve local problems is through community discussions[d]	36	54	9	99	(200)	38	39	23	100	(121)
Better to pay attention to politics than just to follow leaders[e]	72	12	15	99	(412)	49	30	19	98	(53)
Same question[f]	77	11	12	100	(124)	76	14	11	101	(170)

SOURCES:
[a] Fukushima 1962, p. 172. [b] Fukushima 1963, p. 168. [c] Miyagi 1962, appendix, p. 7. The urban sample was from Sendai City. [d] Aichi 1964, p. 143. [e] Kōmei 1966/3, p. 35. The urban sample was from Kōfu City. [f] Kōmei 1966/2, p. 143. The urban sample was from Fukuoka City.

(Miyagi 1962; Aomori 1962, p. 23; Saitama 1962, p. 29).[62] Rural voters also saw "discussing things together" as the best way to resolve local issues, while urban voters would more commonly "let things work out naturally" (Aichi 1964).

The higher rural frequency of willingness to undertake active roles in decision-making, or of preference for collective forms of political activity in specific situations, simply reflects in part respective differences in attitudes toward the value of cooperation and active participation in community affairs. The tradition in rural Japan of dependence on collective action at the community or neighborhood level is well-established, and is clearly the natural way of doing things even today — substantially more than is the case in the cities. Some kinds of land are still held and used in common in many rural communities, mutual help is common between neighbors and community residents, irrigation facilities are owned and managed in common at various local levels, and agricultural cooperation is formally organized by local groups.[63] Indeed, no small part of the rich organizational life of the rural communities is related to these kinds of activities. No one would argue that all collective activity in the rural districts is spontaneous, or egalitarian in leadership, so that reservations are in order about the degree of voluntarism implicit in participation norms. Still, it is obvious that rural life favors an appreciation of the value of collective activities more than does residence in the cities, and feelings of this kind carry over into political attitudes and participation.

Patterns in participation attitudes in the country and in the cities nevertheless present some interesting contradictions. Although rural voters indicated a greater propensity for active roles in local affairs, they were more disposed to depend on leaders at the national level.

---

[62] With the exception of the Miyagi findings, urban voters were small city residents. The results of a survey conducted in metropolitan Tōkyō offers further evidence in support of these tendencies among urban and rural voters, since preference of activist roles was less common than that reported for rural voters in the Miyagi and Saitama studies; see Tōkyō 1958, p. 27. (Tōkyō voters were a little more inclined than Aomori residents to become active, however. Even though urban-rural differences conformed to the general trend in Aomori, the overall tendency in that area was toward levels of activism lower than are seen in many other rural districts.)

[63] For a description of the kinds of collective activities which are still of importance in rural hamlets, see Tadashi Fukutake, *Japanese Rural Society*, pp. 89–95. Professor Fukutake also discusses prewar and postwar trends in collective ownership and cooperation.

When voters were asked whether the public should "follow the leadership of Diet members and ministers, whose ways of doing things are generally all right" or "pay attention because the government and Diet members sometimes do bad things," rural voters were comparatively more inclined toward dependence than were residents of cities (Kōmei 1966/2; Kōmei 1966/3).[64] This trend is compatible with earlier evidence, and most of the rural characteristics just discussed would seem to be more operative with respect to local politics than to national affairs.

Urban-rural differences in basic attitudes toward leadership and in internalization of democratic norms are also involved here. The effects of urban-rural distribution of education and mass media exposure are once again evident, and contribute here to the relatively greater emphasis on alertness and skepticism among urban residents toward national affairs. By contrast, rural residents put their faith in ambassadors to the "outside world," men who represent them in areas beyond the impact of their own locally focused collective activities.

Voting Attitudes. Differences in community structure are clearly one of the major factors in the existence of political subcultures in urban and rural districts in Japan. On the basis of our observations thus far we might expect these contrasts in community relationships and their attitudinal correlatives to contribute to parallel trends in voting motivations. It might be expected that persons residing in hamlets vote more commonly on the basis of candidate reputation, with special consideration given to a candidate's record or promise as a representative of local interests. City dwellers, on the other hand, might place more weight on party labels and national issues.

These expectations were largely borne out by the data I collected. Where questions about voting attitudes were dichotomized into the simple alternatives of "party" or "candidate," urban voters reported more often than rural voters that they voted on the basis of "party."

---

[64] The Yamanashi findings (Kōmei 1966/3) are also supported by data in Fukushima 1962, p. 172, but findings on urban-rural differences in Fukuoka prefecture indicated less sectoral distinctiveness than was the case in either Yamanashi or Fukushima. It would seem that the Yamanashi and Fukushima samples are more representative than the Fukuoka sample (Kōmei 1966/2), which manifests lesser urban-rural variation. Fukuoka is a more industrialized prefecture and there may be less of an actual difference between its urban and rural sectors.

Rural voters placed proportionately greater emphasis on "candidate" (Table 6-10). There were some important differences, however, where either national or local affairs were concerned. While "party" was the main focus in the large cities in national elections, there was greater emphasis on "candidate" in local contests. Rural voters considered "candidate" of major importance in both national and local elections, but "candidate" was even further emphasized in local elections (Kōmei 1967BB; Kōmei 1967A).

Some variation on these patterns occurred where questions with a greater number of closed alternatives were used. This variation gives greater insight than that afforded by skeletal "party-candidate" patterns alone. In this case, voters living in the cities reported that they considered candidate character *or* party labels more commonly than any other considerations in national elections. Persons interviewed in rural areas said they stressed expectations of representation of local interests, and candidate character was only a secondary consideration in this context (Kumamoto 1960; Shiga 1962, pp. 34–37; Okayama 1962, p. 30).[65] Party affiliations were relatively unimportant to voters in both sectors in local assembly elections. Candidate qualities received major emphasis by urban voters in local contests, while representation of local interests was important to rural residents (Ōita 1962, p. 39; Ōita 1964B, pp. 22–23).

We may say, then, that urban voters cast their vote more in terms of responses to comparatively diffuse symbolic objects (party label or candidate reputation), whereas rural voters make their choice on more pragmatic and personally immediate grounds.[66] This contrast, of course, obviously parallels many of the attitudinal patterns discussed previously. In particular, the relative absence of instrumental expecta-

---

[65] The findings cited here pertained only to tendencies among persons living in small cities. There was no evidence for residents of large cities. Presumably, large city voters would give some greater thought to instrumental expectations relating to occupational interests, given the apparently higher concentrations of union members in the large cities, and this would effect the overall urban trends. (The ratio of union members to total population is higher in the more urbanized *prefectures* than it is elsewhere, but it was impossible to compare large cities and small cities on this point. See Sōrifu Tōkeikyoku, *Nihon Tōkei Nenkan 1967*, pp. 17 and 414.)

[66] This has all the appearances of deviating diametrically from Gabriel Almond's expectation that the attitudes in more traditional sectors or states will be diffuse. See G. Almond and G. Bingham Powell, Jr., *Comparative Politics: A Developmental Approach* (Boston: Little, Brown, 1966), p. 87.

TABLE 6-10. Voting Attitudes

	Urban (%)	Rural (%)
Party or candidate in national election:[a]		
Party	55	30
Candidate	35	50
Don't know	10	20
Total	100	100
(N)	(368)	(700)
Party or candidate in local election:[b]		
Party	30	4
Candidate	44	77
Don't know; both the same	26	19
Total	100	100
(N)	(185)	(398)
Reasons for voting choice in national election:[c]		
Fine character/honest	25	19
Strong politician	10	12
Party affiliation	17	3
Represents local area	17	54
Represents workers	8	4
Endorsements/requests	6	
Other/don't know	17	8
Total	100	100
(N)	(77)	(74)
Think about representation of occupational interest in making national election choice:[d]		
Yes	51	71
No	36	29
Don't know	13	
Total	100	100
(N)	(47)	(14)

Sources: [a] Kōmei 1967BB, p. 22 (national). "Urban" was large cities. [b] Kōmei 1962A, p. 196 (national). [c] Kumamoto 1960, p. 60. "Rural" was a small, isolated island farming community. Concern for local representation there was somewhat greater than in rural districts adjacent to communications lines. [d] Shizuoka 1963, p. 31. "Urban" was office workers and "rural" was farmers. (Blue-collar workers in this mixed industrial and farming prefecture showed a somewhat lower awareness of occupational interest than persons in either of the above categories.)

tions and a greater concern with the events of comparatively remote political processes among urban voters seem obvious correlatives of the above trends in voting considerations.

Somewhat comparable tendencies were shown where different and more narrowly focused questions pertaining to instrumental expectations were asked. More rural than small city voters in one prefecture felt that they considered representation of their occupational interests in voting-choice (Shizuoka 1963). Similarly, in a national study where identification of concern for either occupational or local interests was the focus, persons living in rural areas reported making choices based on these considerations more commonly than did urban residents (Kōmei 1961, p. 42).[67]

In sorting out the factors that underly the urban-rural differences in stress on alternatively "party" or "candidate," important differences between the two sectors in political stimuli should be noted. To begin, the cumulative exposure of rural voters to parties in election campaigns is lower than is the case for people living in the cities, since candidates for local office in the rural areas typically prefer to run as independents. Although it is true that nominees in most other kinds of elections in Japan report their ties in both rural and urban districts, still the degree of exposure to parties is considerably lessened in the rural areas by virtue of the independence of candidates in local elections.[68]

Added to this imbalance in exposure to party labels is the fact that urban voters are more interested in national politics and elections where parties are comparatively more salient, while rural voters tend toward higher involvement at the local level, where parties rarely (and specifically in rural areas) assume important roles. Involvement surely is a factor in awareness. Urban-rural differences in attention to mass media coverage of politics may also have some effect on awareness of parties, since urban voters are more inclined to follow the mass media, and parties are a common topic in coverage of public affairs. It seems

---

[67] Respondents were asked to assign relative importance to concerns for the fact that a candidate was a native of the constituency or local district, was doing his utmost for local interests, or acted on behalf of occupational or organizational concerns. Multiple answers were permitted, and replies indicating concern for representation of all kinds of interests totalled 64 percent in the cities and 97 percent in the rural districts.

[68] See Ch. 5, n. 23.

safe to conclude that many urban and rural voters have different cognitive maps of politics with respect to parties.[69]

Somewhat analogous differences in awareness of "candidates," or individual politicians as political objects, also exist. At the risk of harping, the effects of differences in social structure and related tendencies in political communication should be considered here. It is easier in the typical rural community to know a politician directly, or know someone who personally knows a politician, than in the more loosely structured urban neighborhoods. Direct relationships with politicians are more common of course at the level of local politics, but even where national politics is concerned rural voters at least know somebody who directly knows a candidate more often than is the case in the cities. This is reflected most directly in the emphasis on "candidate" in discussions of politics in the rural areas, as well as in the higher frequencies of rural voter familiarity with candidates cited at earlier points.[70]

The distribution of education and leftist party preference is important as well in voting attitudes. The proportionately greater number of well-educated persons in the cities is again a factor, and controls for education erased quite a bit of the urban-rural cleavage in specifically partisan voting.[71] Underlying this trend, of course, was the fact that well-educated people in Japan tend to consider "party" in voting-choice more than do citizens of more limited education.[72] This partisanship may result from their greater involvement in specifically national affairs, as well as their substantially higher levels of mass media exposure. But it is also possible simply that their greater overall political awareness results in a heightened sensitivity to the significance of parties in politics. Obviously, it is difficult on the basis of analysis of the kinds of data available here to sort out these relation-

---

[69] This is reflected in part in the fact that there are more party supporters among urban residents than in the rural districts, although it is true that some other causal factors I shall discuss in the text with regard to voting attitudes are undoubtedly also relevant to the formation of party loyalties. For information on tendencies in party support see Miyagi 1962, appendix p. 30.

[70] See Ch. 5, n. 36; and, n. 45 of this chapter.

[71] The net effect-index for place of residence in this case was smaller than that for education alone, and was only .003.

[72] See, for example, Tōkyō 1958, p. 38; Saga 1962, p. 14; and, Nagasaki 1962, p. 40.

ships and determine their direction. But the relationship between education and emphasis on "party" in urban voting-choice is quite clearly established.

There are also more leftist party supporters in the cities, and a positive relationship between leftist party support and emphasis on "party" in voting-choice is also clear. Presumably, this is because the leftist parties have typically presented more coherent *party* positions than have the conservative parties.[73]

We have attempted to explain urban-rural differences in voter concern for "party" and "candidate" largely on the basis of replies to simple questions about voting-choice. In replies to more elaborate questions, the fact that rural residents tended to emphasize instrumental considerations is simply a correlative of comparatively higher rural levels of instrumental awareness. At the same time, the tendency among urban residents toward even greater emphasis on the "objects" of election campaigns (candidates and parties) is a little more difficult to explain. We know that urban voters are less sensitive to representation of local, and in some cases occupational interests. Still, something besides merely an abstract response to candidate or party may be involved in their calculations. Fragmentary evidence from several places indicates that urban voters place more emphasis on national issues and "principles" in their support for parties *and* candidates than do rural residents.[74] These alternatives were not present in questions from the surveys referred to earlier in this chapter. Obviously, the findings I reported were chosen for their representative character. A concern for principles and issues could have been the *real* criteria among persons who answered that they voted on the basis of either party label

---

[73] However, the fact that well-educated persons in Japan are more inclined to support leftist parties means that there is some overlap in the effects of education and party support. For recent findings on party preferences among persons of different educational backgrounds, see Jōji Watanuki, "Patterns of Politics in Present-Day Japan," in Seymour Martin Lipset and Stein Rokkan, *Party Systems and Voter Alignments* (New York: Free Press, 1967), p. 449.

[74] More small city than rural voters felt that a candidate's "principles" were important to their choice, according to the results in Niigata 1963, p. 9. Moreover, party support — more common in urban than in rural areas — is based more on agreement with "policies" than on other kinds of considerations. See Miyagi 1962, appendix p. 30, for information on tendencies in party preferences, and both Gumma 1962, p. 17, and Gumma 1963, p. 34, for typical examples of findings on voter-assessed reasons for support of a particular party.

or candidate reputation, but this would not have been revealed simply because of the nature of the questions which were asked.

Sectoral Differences and Empirical Political Theory. In the discussion here I have departed somewhat from the usual focus of studies of political life in urban and rural Japan. I do not deny the fact that the pressures for conformity in rural hamlets which so many writers have stressed do have a lot to do with the character of political choice and levels of participation. Indeed, it would be unrealistic to ignore the mobilizing potential of rural influence structures and community norms even in today's rapidly changing circumstances. Still, I have tried to show here how the character of the sectoral variations in the quality and intensity of social interaction and associated norms have contributed to subcultural political differences in a variety of unanticipated ways.

Secondly, and relatedly, I have broken down sectoral differences into their component parts wherever possible. In other words, I have sought to evaluate through statistical analysis the degree to which residence alone contributes to variation in political attitudes, and the instances where sectoral differences are actually attributable to underlying patterns in the distribution of individual educational accomplishment or some other factor.

At this point, I want to juxtapose the results of these analyses with some of the propositions from empirical political theory noted at the beginning of the chapter. This will serve as a convenient vehicle for summarizing some of the main findings, as well as for establishing links between analysis of Japanese subcultural characteristics and some of the more general concerns of comparative political science. In so doing, I will inevitably have to ignore some of the more idiosyncratic factors discussed earlier, even though at various points they are clearly important with respect to specific Japanese patterns.

Thus far I have looked primarily at the effects of single control variables on urban-rural differences in political attitudes. In other words, I have examined the effects (otherwise attributable to residence) of such factors as education or group membership, using the proper control techniques. In this way, specific influences underlying sectoral patterns could be discerned most clearly.

The results of these analyses are summarized in Table 6-11. In reading this table, it should be remembered that the effect of living in

TABLE 6-11. PLACE OF RESIDENCE AND POLITICAL ATTITUDES, MULTIVARIATE RELATIONSHIPS

	Residence	(Sex)	(Education)	(Group Membership)
Interest — National	−.040	−.037	**−.108**	−.001
Concern — N	.023	.027	−.031	.027
Responsiveness — N	−.034	−.032	−.088	−.056
Efficacy — N	.006	.008	−.060	.003
Relevance — N	**.098**	**.101**	.025	**.113**
Comprehension — N	**.098**	**.104**	.043	**.119**
Civic Duty	**−.089**	**−.089**	**−.093**	−.072
Wants from Politics	*−.304*	*−.303*	*−.313*	*−.244*
Interest — Local	*−.181*	*−.179*	*−.195*	−.106
Concern — L	−.044	−.043	−.056	−.008
Responsiveness — L	*−.184*	*−.183*	*−.242*	*−.187*
Efficacy — L	.006	.007	−.036	.040
Relevance — L	.000	.002	−.049	.012
Comprehension — L	**−.132**	**−.127**	*−.168*	−.056

These figures are from a Coleman effect-parameter analysis. The indexes listed under "residence" indicate the simple differences between urban and rural residence groupings output by a bivariate Coleman analysis. Negative indexes indicate simply that higher frequencies were found in the rural areas.

The indexes listed under various socio-economic attribute headings in parentheses are for place of residence *after controls* for the effects of urban-rural distributions were introduced. With high and low education held constant, for example, the effects of residence, independent of urban-rural distribution of education, can be seen. As indicated in the text, the resulting indexes indicate the residual effects of residence, and comparison of these with the bivariate effect-index gives some idea of the effect of urban-rural differences in social structure and group life.

Index figures in italic are significant at the .01 level of probability; bold figures indicate the .05 requirements are met. Tests of significance are used here simply to provide some idea of levels of confidence, even though the fact that the sample was stratified militates against assuming that they are literally appropriate indicators.

the city or in the country is reflected in a single index under the heading "residence." In other columns I have included the revised index of the effect of residence after the contribution of some other relevant variables have been considered. If there is no relationship in fact between the urban and rural distribution of some characteristic (such as educational attainment), the index under the relevant heading (education, in this case) will remain the same. But if the distribution of education in the cities and rural areas were the *real* consideration, rather than mere residence in one or another kind of environment, then the index will be changed. Change, to be meaningful, must also be in the direction of zero, regardless of whether the initial index was positive or negative. In a few cases, however, the index actually crosses the zero point and assumes a contrary value, which is still quite consistent with the substantive meaning of the indexes. Finally, it should be repeated at this point that a negative sign implies that rural residence is the stronger of the influences where a particular attitude is concerned. Correspondingly, a positive index (which has no sign) indicates that urban residents report higher frequencies of a particular attitudinal orientation than rural residents.[75]

Looking first at the evidence pertaining to nationally focused political attitudes, we can readily see that residence is typically of little residual importance as a variable. This is best seen in the case of feelings about the relevance of national politics and expressions of competence in one's understanding of national public affairs. Education was responsible for the urban-rural attitude distributions in these cases; in other words, education was the main factor in the positive relationship between urban residence and political involvement attitudes in the untreated findings.

Exceptions to these overall tendencies occurred with regard to voter feelings about the responsiveness of politicians at the national level, and also to some degree with regard to feelings of political efficacy. In this case, education was important but rural residence was also associated with optimistic appraisals after other variables were controlled (and these obviously affected urban trends); the actual contribution of rural residence was "enhanced" in this instance.

Interest in national politics also deviated from the general pattern with regard to psychological involvement in national politics. I did not discuss this earlier simply because my findings differed in this one instance from those of most other studies conducted in Japan. In this case, there were slightly more persons in the rural districts than in the

---

[75] I have also included in this analysis a variable which, on the basis of the discussion so far, does not seem relevant. Sex had to be included simply because there were fewer men in the urban portion of the sample than in the rural group, and this might have biased the results of the analysis in undetermined ways. In Table 6-11 we can see that the urban-rural distribution of men and women in the sample was of no special importance as factors underlying the urban-rural tendencies in political attitudes. For that reason they are not discussed in the text, even though I felt they should be included for the sake of an honest analysis.

cities who were interested in national affairs, a factor which I believe was associated with the presence of important national leaders in both of the rural constituencies I studied. In other words, it seemed reasonable to believe that people in these districts were more "politicized" than is typically the case in the rural areas by virtue of the presence of very prominent political leaders. This interpretation was suggested to me by observers of politics in both areas, and agrees with the importance I have assigned to personalism in Japanese behavior. Finally, I did look at two other examples of findings where people living in rural areas were more interested in national politics than persons in the city, and did find one instance where conditions paralleled those in the areas I studied. Suffice it to say at this point that this is the pattern reflected in the initial negative index for residence; in this case education was of some importance, but the remaining contribution of residence is indicated by the strengthened negative index.

From this multivariate analysis of the effects of residence and other social variables, we can infer that the Japanese patterns of psychological involvement in national politics conform to the expectations of modernization theory in a very special sense. Generally, it is education rather than residence which is the most important of modern influences relating to development of cosmopolitan political involvement attitudes in contemporary Japan. Since this is the case, my results have some resemblance to those of Nie, Powell and Prewitt, who found nonvoting political participation in national political processes particularly sensitive to patterns in the distribution of social status (which included education) and to certain mediating attitude structures, including psychological involvement. Although actual participation in Japan clearly does not fit the modernization model, it seems highly plausible that cosmopolitan psychological involvement in Japan is affected by the same kinds of influences as is participation in some other advanced societies. Indeed, if it is legitimate to evaluate theories of aggregate social change by looking at contemporary political behavior, the Japanese evidence supports the interpretation advanced by the above authors to the effect that changes in social status are more critical than urbanization in the processes of social and political change associated with the concept of "modernization."

It is always possible that residence was actually of greater importance to attitude formation in an earlier period, when integrating forces were less identifiable, than is the case today. Indeed, an even greater cleavage in earlier times between urban and rural political styles (presumably, also in underlying social dimensions) can be inferred from various comments about the prewar political system. Bloc voting was believed to be more widespread prior to the equalizing effects of postwar land reform and, perhaps, later increases in rural affluence.[76] What Scalapino has called agrarian primitivist sentiments were also to be found and were indicative of formerly wider gulfs between subcultures. As indicated above, it is clearly possible that the effects of urbanization and the growth of the mass media actually have penetrated the rural areas to such a degree in recent years that residence has diminished in direct importance for some kinds of attitudes.

The findings under review also have some other direct implications for modernization theory, or for any other hypotheses about the effects of residence which predict that either urban or rural life will be associated with completely consistent tendencies in political attitudes. The effects of living in the cities or in the countryside in Japan are clearly multi-dimensional, and no simple pattern of directionality can be found. The patterns are largely reversed with respect to involvement in either national or local politics, while complexity and even ambiguity pervade sectoral patterns in evaluative and participation attitudes. Living in the cities is associated with high levels of awareness of national politics alongside high frequencies of feelings of pessimism about the behavior of politicians. Rural residence is associated with parochial tendencies and feelings of optimism in a similarly complex manner.

It is also readily apparent that developing a less parochial rural sector depends on an array of facilitating, or contributing circumstances in Japan somewhat larger than is forecast by modernization theory. Karl Deutsch, it will be remembered, explicitly stated that one of the consequences of modernization might be the development of strong feelings of self-interest among farmers who were most affected by the commercialization of agriculture. Clearly, strong feelings of self-interest have developed in the rural areas in the Japanese case, and

---

[76] See Ward's comments on the Inukai "iron" *jiban*, in Richard Beardsley et al., *Village Japan*, pp. 424–435.

this is one of the major indicators of deparochializing tendencies among rural residents in contemporary Japan. But this has depended on influences other than the commercialization of agriculture alone. Moreover, Deutsch's theory in no way anticipated the kinds of imbalance in instrumental attitudes observed in Japan today, where rural residents are more sensitive to questions of self-interest than persons in the urban industrial centers.

What is especially significant is the fact that variables not included in modernization theory prove important. Traditions of parochial cohesion and self-consciousness in the rural sector of Japan have been a well-spring of awareness of self-interests, particularly after the formerly divisive effects of differences in interest between landlords and tenants were substantially eliminated through land reform. Other aspects of rural life, such as the widespread presence of community leaders who are extremely conscious of the needs of their areas, rising expectations about the chances for improving one's lot as a result of land reform, and the comparative affluence of the postwar period following a tradition of poverty, are all presumably important to the development of rural instrumentalism in Japan.

In addition to ignoring the potential importance of such things as patterns of community social organization in shaping people's political consciousness, it seems that modernization theory also places undue confidence in the positive effects of mass media exposure — at least this is true in the Japanese case. Lerner, in particular, interpreted mass media exposure as primarily a route to identification with wider, more cosmopolitan worlds of experience. What he failed to forecast is that this could be alienating as well as integrative, depending on the specific character of mass media content. If sectoral patterns are at all similar elsewhere, and if these are related to the effects of mass media, then the effects of urbanization specified by Lerner are not found in reality in some instances.

It will be remembered that center-periphery approaches to the conceptualization of the sources of political attitudes postulated that people who are near the "center" of political life would be more aware of politics and more involved psychologically in political processes than persons on the periphery of public affairs. Urban residence was one of the several factors believed to be associated with proximity to the center of politics, and was seen rather simplistically as contributing to greater involvement and awareness. My findings show that this is true in Japan as far as involvement attitudes about national politics are concerned. But urban-rural differences in educational attainment, rather than the direct effects of urban residence, are the main factor in national involvement attitudes.

Exposure in higher frequencies to the mass media presumably is the main thing that distinguishes urban residents from rural voters where "proximity" to the "center" of political life is concerned. In contrast, rural voters are in close proximity to the myriads of local political centers (governments at the city, town and village level) found throughout Japanese society. This is reflected in rural voters' high involvement in local political life, which, we have seen, is heavily influenced by the character of local social structure and the intimacy of local community relationships (see Table 6-11 for a summary of these relationships). What this suggests to me is extremely simple: the center-periphery concepts of political attitude formation leaves out the possibility that politics in reality has many "centers," and that proximity to a particular center may be influenced by quite different social characteristics than that which favor proximity to another center.

It is difficult to say at present whether tendencies in political attitudes among urban and rural voters in Japan have many parallels in other industrialized nations. Some common tendencies can be observed between voters in Japan and the United States where attitudes toward national political involvement are concerned. But urban American trends are believed to be associated with the mutually reinforcing effects of higher levels of both educational attainment and group membership, while Japanese urban patterns are more the result solely of the distribution of educational accomplishment. Japanese tendencies in group membership have other kinds of effects.

Research on other countries suggests tendencies in urban-rural differences in political attitudes both comparable and noncomparable to those of Japan. In an especially interesting study on political involvement and participation in France, Sidney Tarrow has reported patterns that sometimes compare with those in Japan. The French peasant, like his Japanese counterpart, is less involved in national political life on some abstract dimensions but, at the same time, has a strong awareness of his own self-interests and typically participates more in political life than his city cousins.[77] Since there are both similarities and differences between Tarrow's analysis of France and the interpretations here — the importance of community structure and local leadership in developing an awareness of instrumental issues seem more important in Japan than in France — the comparabilities of the two cases should not be overdrawn. Nevertheless, both discussions draw attention to the possibility that under certain conditions the rural voter can be mobilized into an acute awareness of what goes on in national politics when it affects him most. That this can and does happen draws our attention in turn to the deficiencies of present theory on urban-rural differences.

Elsewhere, in a reanalysis of the Almond and Verba survey findings, it has been shown that place of residence has little effect on involvement and evaluative attitudes in certain industrialized countries.[78] Only in the Federal Republic of Germany were significant patterns attributable to residence, and in this case people in large cities felt more effective and were more involved in politics than persons living in small communities.[79]

These findings are relevant to our analysis in an important way: they should alert the student of politics to be aware of cross-national differences that do exist. While it has been my purpose here to afford new insight into sectoral differences in the case of Japan, we must not overlook the compelling task of developing a viable comparative theory of sectoral political socialization and behavior. In order to do so, we will have to admit the possibility that urban and rural social patterns have quite different implications for political attitudes in different societies.[80]

---

[77] See Tarrow (see n. 1, above), pp. 353–355.

[78] See Edward N. Muller (see n. 1, above), pp. 797–799.

[79] The Muller findings on the United States contradict comments in *The American Voter* (Angus Campell, et al.), p. 412. The former show that involvement flattens out in communities of 20,000 and above, while the latter posit an urban-rural continuum (without supportive findings).

The Muller findings are also contradicted in part in the case of Germany by subsequent research by the DIVO organization. Where Muller reports that feelings of efficacy (based on an index that includes comprehension competence) increases in urban and metropolitan centers, the DIVO findings show that comprehension competence is higher in intermediate-sized cities than in large metropolitan areas. See *Pressedienst*, November 1964 (I/II), pp. 12 and 14.

[80] There is a growing awareness, at least in Europe, that urban and rural residence may mean different things in different countries. See, for example, Jurg

It is also somewhat problematical whether the urban-rural patterns in political attitudes in Japan will be duplicated in the near future in less developed parts of the world. Although some of the tendencies reported here may be found in some places, presumably the rural sectors in these lands are less closely linked with national politics than is the case in Japan today. As we have observed, rural levels of national political involvement in Japan compare favorably in many cases with those found in the cities, and rural voters are quite perceptive of close relationships between national politics and local affairs where local interests are involved. Obviously, the fact that Japan has been politically integrated for some time is important here, and in the less integrated political systems of the newly independent states of Africa and Asia quite different patterns may be found among rural residents.

On the other hand, the rapid internalization of democratic ideas, and its corollary, unrealized idealistic expectations regarding political performance, may be found in other countries. A more precise evaluation of the impact of the Japanese patterns on empirical research and theory (in both behavioral and developmental theory) must await more extensive comparative evidence. But the nature of the Japanese experience should suggest some fruitful lines of exploration in both highly industrial nations and in less developed countries where democratic ideas have only recently been introduced.

Steiner, *Bürger und Politik* (Meisenheim am Glan: Anton Hain, 1969), p. 147, and an excellent critique of the notion of an urban-rural continuum in Franz Urban Pappi, *Wahlverhalten und Politische Kultur* (Meisenheim am Glan: Anton Hain, 1970), pp. 90–101.

7

AGE AND POLITICAL CULTURE

The concept of political generations, first prominent in the work of Karl Mannheim, has found increasing acceptance in recent empirical literature on mass political behavior.[1] The term has been used to characterize age groupings within the general population who have been exposed to particularly dramatic political events, events associated with major discontinuities in political practices or beliefs. A concept of this kind proved especially appealing to students of nineteenth and twentieth century political history. The concept has been used explicitly in recent empirical research, as well as implicitly, as when the authors of *The American Voter* attributed the issue dispositions of the electorate in the 1950s to lingering memories of the depression period.[2]

---

[1] For a discussion of the concept of political generations and bibliography, see Robert E. Lane, *Political Life* (Glencoe, Illinois: Free Press, 1959), p. 219.

[2] For a discussion of the permanent effects of the depression period on the party loyalties of voters who were young in the early 1930s, see Angus Campbell *et al.*, *The American Voter* (New York: Wiley, 1960), pp. 153–154.

Cohort analysis of attitudes and behavior is a special methodological application of the generational concept. By this technique the outlooks of persons in a particular age grouping are examined at different times to see, in effect, what continuity or discontinuity may be found. Examples of this kind of research are found in John Crittenden, "Aging and Political Participation," *Western Political Quarterly* 16 (June 1963), pp. 323–331; and Norvell D. Glenn and Michael Grimes, "Aging, Voting and Political Interest," *American Sociological Review* 33 (August 1968), pp. 563–575. The use of cohorts as an analytical concept is dealt with in Norman B. Ryder, "The Cohort as a Concept in the Study of Social Change," *American Sociological Review* 30 (December 1965), pp. 843–861; technical aspects are treated in William M. Evan, "Cohort Analysis of Survey Data: A Procedure for Studying Long-Term Opinion Change," *Public Opinion Quarterly* 19 (winter 1959–60), pp. 64–72.

The idea of political generations is readily adaptable to the concept of mass attitude systems in the political culture approach. Different generations, by virtue of their exposure to particular kinds of socialization processes or experiences, can be seen as manifesting the traits of a political subculture. Furthermore, where a nation has experienced multiple political discontinuities over a short period of time, it is possible that several distinct subcultures of generations may exist. It is particularly likely that this phenomenon would exist in postwar Japanese political life. Japanese who were between the ages of 35 and 45 at the time most of the surveys used here were conducted constituted the first postwar generation politically. Voters in this age grouping were in their twenties at the time of the major postwar reforms and political realignments, and thus came of political age at a time of especially heightened interest in new ideas and new political formulas.[3]

By contrast, voters over 45 in the early 1960s had come to maturity during or before the war, and were thus exposed to the different kinds of political socialization influences which characterized parts of the prewar period in contrast with the postwar epoch. Finally, persons under 35, although perhaps less clearly a political generation in some terms, were socialized during the more stable but less self-consciously innovative postoccupation period. Persons in these different age groupings can be expected to show the effects of exposure to different political institutions and styles in the form of distinctive subcultural perspectives.

It must be remembered, however, that empirical research has shown that there are normal life cycle patterns in political attitudes, whose presence may confound the problem of tracing the residual effects of generational experiences. Studies of the effects of aging in various countries have shown that some kinds of political involvement reach a peak among persons in their fifties or sixties, following which there is a decline in political commitment and activity. Recent research in the United States, however, has produced an alternative picture of the effects of aging, demonstrating that the curvilinear patterns attributed to life cycle in earlier research were, in some instances, the result of historical changes in the distribution of educational accom-

---

[3] Women form a special subcategory where generational effects are concerned, since they received the franchise only after the war.

plishment as well as the sex composition of older age groupings.⁴ Interestingly, variations of the social disengagement hypotheses have been used to explain both the presence of declining involvement among older persons as well as the contrary findings.⁵

Despite the implications of this recent analysis of age and political attitudes in the United States, the bulk of the evidence from studies of aging in different political systems indicates that life cycle effects are typically present. For this reason any analysis of the political outlooks of persons in different age groups in Japan can hardly afford to ignore the possibility that life cycle influences may be operative.

The plausibility of this perspective is enhanced if we examine the social characteristics of persons in different age groupings in Japan. For one thing, some kinds of social status increase with age, at least until age 60, and status differences are typically important where political attitudes are concerned. To be sure, some measures of social status such as education and occupation may remain constant over the life span of most people beyond the age of twenty. Still, some people acquire wealth with age, or move up in positions at their place of work either on the basis of achievement or through the consideration typically given to seniority in many organizations. These kinds of status changes are reflected in increases in income levels among persons in successively older age cohorts in Japan, with the exceptions of persons over sixty years in age.⁶

---

⁴ Campbell *et al.*, *The American Voter*, p. 494; and Glenn and Grimes.

⁵ The social disengagement hypothesis asserts that older people are typically less involved in social interaction, and are consequently prone to be less concerned about political matters and less motivated to participate in politics at any level. Glenn and Grimes (n. 1) present an alternative analysis in which old age is viewed as a disengagement from activities that otherwise, at earlier points in life, detract people from attentiveness to political affairs.

⁶ For figures on monthly wage earnings among persons in different age groups employed in different industrial sectors, see Sōrifu Tōkeikyoku, *Nihon Tōkei Nenkan 1967* (Tōkyō: 1968), pp. 398-99 — the data are from a 1966 study. Since advances in wages among middle-aged and old persons in Japan sometimes reflect the effects of the practice of giving increases on the basis of seniority and family size, the tendencies in incomes do not always reflect variations in achievement. Still, the fact that some individuals have higher incomes as they become older is presumably of some importance to status.

Declines in wage levels among persons in their sixties may be due in part to the fact that some individuals are employed after formal retirement at wages lower than before retirement. Most people retire at 60 in private industry, but in civil service retirement comes at age 55. The decline in earned wages among persons over 60 may also reflect the present effect of wage scales established a few years back, or simply the reduced income from pensions received by persons who have retired.

Participation in community leadership also varies substantially with age in Japan. Only a small percentage of the adult population achieves the status of being elected to local public office, regardless of age considerations. But this privilege accrues much more commonly to middle-aged and old persons than to persons in their twenties and thirties, even though there are improved opportunities for active leadership by younger persons in the postwar period. However, it should be noted that men in their fifties are more commonly found in local leadership positions than persons from any other age group.[7]

Achievement of both higher economic and community status may result in feelings of greater political efficacy, as well as perhaps greater satisfaction with the way politics is carried out. Obviously, this is true for persons who become community leaders or are elected to political office, but it may be that those with comparatively higher incomes also conform to some of these tendencies, even though they may be more remote from the actual arena of public affairs.[8] Higher economic status may also result in a more intense interest in politics and greater political knowledge, as the result both of development of close ties with influentials or public officials or simply through the perception that the actions of officials (such as tax collectors) are now more relevant.[9] Persons of higher economic status may also develop feelings of

---

[7] For information on the ages of elected local assemblymen and mayors, see Jichishō Senkyokyoku, *Chihō Senkyo Kekka Shirabe* (Tōkyō, 1963), p. 7. Interestingly, there were more comparatively young office holders in the rural areas than in the cities. Roughly two-thirds of all assembly members in the cities were in their fifties and sixties, while in town and village assemblies two-thirds of the membership were in the age group of 40–69.

Dore reports that nearly one-third of a sampled group of rural residents had held office at the village level, and two-thirds had held positions at the hamlet level. But we have no general information on age distribution in positions other than those of local assemblyman and mayor, or town and village head. See R. P. Dore, *Land Reform in Japan* (London, New York and Toronto: Oxford University Press, 1959), p. 324.

[8] In my own findings, there was a positive relationship between income and most measures of involvement. The tendencies, however, were somewhat irregular in the higher income categories, possibly because of the effect of low numbers.

[9] Age alone — at least in the rural sector — may also result in more intimate contacts with local influentials and politicians, by virtue of the fact that such persons are more often peers of elder citizens. It must also be kept in mind throughout the ensuing discussion that age by itself has normally been believed to confer higher status in Japan. Still, in view of the findings I will present, I prefer to deal with the relationship between age and status in more specific and narrow senses wherever possible.

responsibility toward community or neighborhood, and participation in politics may seem more natural to them than to persons of lesser status.[10]

In addition to the links with changes in status, growing old is accompanied by increases in social integration for many Japanese, as evidenced by trends among middle-aged and older persons toward higher levels of membership in organized groups (Richardson 1964). Patterns in group membership are actually much like those of income, with a systematic increase in the average number of memberships being found in each successive age group, with the exception of persons over sixty. However, persons in their sixties and older are still more active than those in their twenties; we can conclude from this that social disengagement is present as in other countries, but only relative to the peak levels of involvement in middle age.[11] Further, it can be assumed at this point that the implications of increases in social participation for political attitudes are similar to those of increased status, especially where attitudes about local politics are concerned; obviously, however, the two conditions may also have overlapping and reinforcing effects in quite a few cases.

There are some additional important age differences in the degree of exposure to communications about politics (Table 7-1).[12] Mid-

---

[10] Age may also bring more intense feelings of responsibility by virtue of long residence in a community. Naturally, this would be more common in the rural areas than in urban neighborhoods.

[11] The decline in the average number of group memberships among persons in their sixties and older (in comparison with the trend among those in their fifties) presumably reflects disengagement associated with retirement and infirmity.

There is one more social correlative of aging in Japan that is of some importance to trends in political attitudes. Young respondents were better-educated than the old persons I interviewed in 1964, reflecting the effects both of postwar changes in compulsory education requirements and the tendency in the postwar period for more people to go to high school and college. Although we will look later at the effects of this trend (in multivariate analysis), there were no data in the evidence used in many of the tables on the possibly confounding effects of educational differences among persons in the various age groupings. For enrollment tendencies over time in institutions of higher education see Tatsumi Makino, "Japanese Education," *International Social Science Journal* 13 (1961), p. 49.

[12] In Table 7-1 and all subsequent tables, unless otherwise indicated, young voters are persons in their twenties, middle-aged citizens are people in their forties, and old voters are people in their sixties and older. Generally, the attitudes of persons in their thirties and fifties (which were omitted from the tables for the sake of simplicity) were more like those of voters in their forties, although voters in their thirties were sometimes more like those in the young grouping.

Since the surveys were conducted at different times, there are obviously some

TABLE 7-1. POLITICAL COMMUNICATION, BY AGE

	National Politics			Local Politics		
	Young (%)	Middle (%)	Old (%)	Young (%)	Middle (%)	Old (%)
Discussion of politics:[a]						
At home	65	73	51	64	71	58
With neighbors	41	54	37	44	56	40
At place of work	59	56	28	57	55	27
At meetings	52	56	41	52	55	44
	Read newspaper			Follow Radio/TV		
Exposure to political content of media:[b]						
Often	25	28	23	49	53	44
Sometimes	53	44	28	41	35	34
Not at all	22	28	49	10	11	23
Total	100	100	100	100	99	101
(N)	(993)	(942)	(584)	(1,008)	(948)	(585)
	National Elections			Local Elections		
Exposure to requests for support and endorsements:[c]						
Yes	46	44	23	56	54	49
No	54	56	77	44	46	51
Total	100	100	100	100	100	100
(N)	(314)	(445)	(261)	(304)	(308)	(199)
	Read Election Pamphlet			Attended Speeches		
Exposure to campaign:[d]						
Yes	67	77	51	17	22	17
No	13	14	25	63	69	60
Total	80	91	76	80	91	77
(N)	(620)	(567)	(346)	(620)	(567)	(346)

SOURCES:

[a] Kōmei 1958, p. 82 (national). Figures are for men only; tendencies for women were similar, but women's participation was substantially lower. Absolute figures were not provided, so the trends for both sexes could not be calculated (sample N was 5,000).

[b] Kōmei 1962, pp. 13–14 (national).

[c] National election figures are from Jichishō 1966, p. 128 (national). Local election data are from Kōmei 1964A, p. 115 (national). In both cases questions were asked only of persons who had actually voted. The national election was a House of Councillors contest.

[d] Kōmei 1961, pp. 21 and 28–29 (national). Figures are for voters only.

dle-aged voters are generally more commonly exposed to such communications than are persons in the other groupings. They talk about politics at home, with neighbors and at meetings more often than do other voters, read the newspaper or follow radio and television accounts of politics more often than others, and read election pamphlets and attend speeches more frequently than both youths and older citizens. Persons in their twenties are generally less attentive or active in communications about politics than their immediate elders, although they talk a little more about politics at work, are slightly more often "targets" of influence and reported a higher level of "some" attention to the media.[13] Voters in their sixties and older are overall the least exposed to communications about public affairs, regardless of the type of communication.

These variations in communications exposure are potentially important to political culture at some points. Although it must be acknowledged that political involvement attitudes are in many cases best seen as motivating exposure to the media or participation in discussions about politics, it is still possible that other kinds of attitudes are in fact dependent on levels of political communications exposure. In particular, it can be anticipated that greater exposure to the media will be associated with higher frequencies of cynicism about politics. Also, both feelings of competence about comprehending politics and actual awareness of political processes are undoubtedly facilitated in many instances by media exposure or access to other channels of communication about political life.

In the proceeding discussion, major attention will be paid to sorting out the "normal" effects of aging from those of generational experiences. This is especially important since the possibility does exist

---

problems with regard to the precise comparability across surveys between the respective age groupings; in other words, the group of people in their forties in 1960 would have had different kinds of experiences in some cases than persons who were in their forties in 1967, even though they obviously would be at approximately the same point in the life cycle. I tried to minimize this problem with regard to the analysis of the effects of age by including data from surveys conducted in the early 1960s as much as possible. Also, since the group of respondents in their forties is the median grouping where tendencies among middle-aged persons are concerned, some of the effects of time were not so important in this grouping.

[13] This resulted in higher levels of overall media attention when the response categories of "often" and "sometimes" were totaled.

Differences among age groupings where influence attempts are concerned could reflect simply differences in *awareness* as well as patterns of actual attempts.

that these two socializing forces may be complementary. For example, the residual effects of early exposure to norms appropriate to "subject" orientations toward politics may to some degree be intermingled in Japan with the ordinary effects of old age. Some comparative decline in political involvement among voters in their sixties might be expected as a result of diminished *social* involvement, but the presence of lower levels of interest in politics among persons in this age group might also be attributed to prewar political socialization. Similarly, the political attitudes of voters in middle age, which presumably reflect the special effects of formative experiences in the early postwar period, may at the same time be influenced by their comparatively higher collective status, social involvement and political communications exposure. While it may sometimes be impossible to rule out completely the existence of unmeasurable, mitigating factors, at least through multivariate analysis we can fairly well control for the visible influences of the individual's position in the life cycle. Consequently, it will be possible to state with some certainty what actual effect generational differences in political experience had on Japanese political attitudes in the early 1960s.

Involvement Attitudes. Patterns of involvement attitudes conformed markedly to the above expectations. Middle-aged citizens were generally more involved in politics than both youths or old persons. But in some cases young people tended to be more like middle-aged persons, or to even exceed the involvement levels of middle age where questions had something to do with national politics. Old voters also showed comparatively high levels of involvement in a few instances.

Both the general tendencies and some typical patterns of deviations were shown in feelings about the relevance of politics (Table 7-2). Young and middle-aged citizens found national politics more relevant (Richardson 1964) than old persons, or felt that the way national politics is conducted has some effect on consumer prices (Hiroshima 1965, p. 82). Elsewhere, middle-aged voters showed the highest level of feelings that "politics" or elections had some special impact on people's lives (Saga 1963; Aichi 1963, p. 49), or had the highest level of perceptions that politics is "very" relevant (Richardson 1964).

Old voters were comparatively more involved where questions focused on local politics or feelings of instrumentalism, and in some

TABLE 7-2. INVOLVEMENT ATTITUDES, BY AGE

	Young					Middle					Old				
	Yes (%)	No (%)	Don't Know (%)	Total (%)	(N)	Yes (%)	No (%)	Don't Know (%)	Total (%)	(N)	Yes (%)	No (%)	Don't Know (%)	Total (%)	(N)
National politics is closely related to our daily problems[a]	69	13	18	100	(71)	69	17	13	99	(75)	62	17	21	100	(47)
The outcomes of elections have many effects on our lives[b]	54	44	7	105	(—)	58	30	10	98	(—)	50	43	7	100	(—)
Local politics is closely related to our daily problems[a]	68	21	11	100	(71)	72	11	17	100	(75)	74	2	23	99	(47)
Want our local assemblyman to do something for us[a]	41	32	28	101	(69)	56	28	16	100	(75)	45	30	26	101	(47)
Something wanted from local politics[c]	49	51	—	100	(63)	75	25	—	100	(59)	49	51	—	100	(63)

SOURCES:
[a] Richardson 1964 postelection study. [b] Saga 1963, p. 21. [c] Tokushima 1962, p. 82.

cases actually exceeded the levels of middle-aged respondents. Thus, older voters expressed the opinion that "local politics is closely related to our daily problems" a little more commonly than others (Richardson 1964). They also said, according to the findings of a nationwide study, that local politics was more relevant to their lives than national affairs, while youths felt national politics was more important (Kōmei 1967A, p. 28). Still, an awareness of wanting a Diet member or local politician to represent one's interest was most common among middle-aged voters, although old voters showed a little more awareness than did youths (Richardson 1964; Tokushima 1962).

In contrast with the complex trends in feelings about the relevance of politics, tendencies in knowledge of public affairs were more coherent; young and middle-aged voters were consistently more knowledgeable about political affairs than their elders (Table 7-3). Still, there were some differences between young and middle-aged voters where different types of political knowledge were concerned. Young voters, for example, knew more about formal institutions and some national processes than others. These topics included the content of the constitution (Miyazaki 1962B), the fact that election funds were limited by law (Kōmei 1967BB, p. 53), turnout trends in House of Representatives elections (Kōmei 1964B), and the fact that partisan candidacies in local elections had increased (Kōmei 1964A). Young voters more often knew that the basic election law was a topic of Diet debate (Miyagi 1962 and Saga 1963, p. 47). But middle-aged voters knew more about other kinds of political events. In particular, they were more knowledgeable about contemporary issues, such as the military base question (Miyazaki 1964, p. 36), the education costs problem (Miyazaki 1964), and Prime Minister Ikeda's income-doubling policy (Fukushima 1962). Finally, young and middle-aged voters were equally knowledgeable about the scheduling of national elections (Kōmei 1962A), although middle-aged citizens more often knew that local elections were scheduled and were best able to match candidate names with partisan affiliations (Kōmei 1967BB; Fukushima 1962).

It is already evident that attitude patterns among age groupings show consistency, particularly with regard to the tendencies for middle-aged persons, even though there is also considerable complexity. Much the same observation can be made in regard to levels of interest in politics. In general, middle-aged voters were more interested in politics

TABLE 7-3. POLITICAL AWARENESS, BY AGE

	Young			Middle			Old			
	Yes (%)	No (%)	Total (%)	(N)	Yes (%)	No (%)	Total (%)	(N)	Yes (%)	No (%)	Total (%)	(N)
Knew all or part of the constitution[a]	90	10	100	(208)	77	23	100	(200)	57	43	100	(98)
Knew tendencies in voter turnout in General Election[b]	55	45	100	(565)	53	47	100	(510)	33	67	100	(422)
Knew the ratio of partisan candidacies in local elections was increasing[c]	58	42	100	(594)	48	52	100	(491)	32	68	100	(372)
Knew that election law revision was an issue in the Diet[d]	67	33	100	(87)	53	47	100	(89)	48	52	100	(113)
Had opinions on education costs increases[e]	80	20	100	(199)	96	4	100	(207)	78	22	100	(111)
Had opinions on income-doubling policy[f]	84	17	101	(121)	90	10	100	(138)	77	23	100	(81)
Knew that House of Councillors elections were scheduled[g]	78	22	100	(1,003)	79	21	100	(942)	65	35	100	(583)
Knew that local elections were scheduled[h]	81	19	100	(488)	88	12	100	(541)	76	24	100	(398)
Could identify all or some candidates' party affiliations in a House of Councillors election[i]	76	24	100	(121)	81	19	100	(138)	64	36	100	(81)

SOURCES:

[a] Miyazaki 1962B, p. 93.   [b] Kōmei 1964B, p. 67 (national).   [c] Kōmei 1964A, p. 127 (national).   [d] Miyagi 1962, appendix, p. 41. "Old" were persons 50 years and over.   [e] Miyazaki 1964, p. 122.   [f] Fukushima 1962, p. 178.   [g] Kōmei 1962A, p. 16 (national).   [h] Kōmei 1967BB, p. 83 (national).   [i] Fukushima 1962, p. 184.

and elections than were youths and elder citizens (Table 7-4). Middle-aged respondents reported more commonly than others that they were "very interested" in politics, according to the results of all the studies I reviewed, while a majority of these investigations also show that middle-age voters having the highest frequencies of overall interest (combining "strong" and "some" interest) in public affairs and elections (Kōmei 1966/2; Kōmei 1966/3, p. 64; Chiba 1963, pp. 76 and 86; Saga 1964, p. 2; Aichi 1963, p. 39; Ōita 1962, p. 7). But in a few instances younger voters had the highest levels of overall interest in politics, specifically during the period of the 1960 Mutual Security Treaty controversy (Nihon 1961) and after the 1963 general affairs (Richardson 1964).[14] Interest in mass media coverage of public affairs and Diet debates was also more commonly reported by youths than by persons in the other groupings (Tokushima 1958; Kumamoto 1960, p. 46).

Both youths and middle-aged persons showed comparatively high levels of concern about the outcome of the 1963 House of Representatives election (Richardson 1964). Similar patterns were shown in regard to local election outcomes in 1967, although the question in 1967 pertained only to concern about the partisan results (Kōmei 1967A, p. 18). By contrast, middle-aged and old voters reported more often than youths that they thought about the candidates at the time of the 1962 House of Councillors election (Miyagi 1963).[15]

Middle-aged persons also had the highest levels of interest in local politics and elections (Richardson 1964; Fukushima 1963, p. 132), as well as being comparatively most concerned about local election outcomes (Richardson 1964). Also, middle-aged voters and old voters reported more interest in local elections than national contests, while the reverse was true for youths (Saga 1964, p. 12; Miyagi 1963, appendix, p. 33).[16]

---

[14] In both cases this reflected the fact that reports of "some" interest were especially high among young voters, even though "strong" interest was still more common among middle-aged voters.

[15] These tendencies reflect the greater familiarity and concern for the importance of parties in elections reported by young and middle-aged voters, while old voters reported greater familiarity with and concern for "candidate." This point will be amplified later.

[16] These same patterns are shown in many other surveys conducted at different places and at slightly different points in time.

TABLE 7-4. INTEREST IN POLITICS, BY AGE

	Young				Middle				Old			
	Yes (%)	No (%)	Don't Know (%)	Total (%)	(N)	Yes (%)	No (%)	Don't Know (%)	Total (%)	(N)	Yes (%)	No (%)	Don't Know (%)	Total (%)	(N)
Daily interest in politics[a]	62	36	2	100	(—)	75	24	2	101	(—)	52	45	2	99	(—)
Interest in politics[b]	60	40	—	100	(—)	55	45	—	100	(—)	35	65	—	100	(—)
Interest in national politics[c]	76	24	—	100	(71)	68	32	—	100	(75)	51	49	—	100	(47)
Interest in political articles in the press[d]	33	60	8	101	(92)	28	65	6	99	(81)	15	58	28	101	(80)
Interest in Diet debates[e]	25	75	—	100	(92)	16	84	—	100	(81)	6	94	—	100	(80)
Concern about national election outcome[e]	71	27	3	101	(71)	69	29	1	99	(75)	68	32	—	100	(47)
Thinking about and comparing the candidates in the coming election[f]	10	83	7	100	(87)	20	74	6	100	(89)	20	73	8	101	(113)
Interest in local politics[e]	65	35	—	100	(71)	72	28	—	100	(74)	60	38	2	100	(47)
Concern about local election outcome[e]	57	40	3	100	(70)	76	23	1	100	(75)	64	36	—	100	(47)

SOURCES:

[a] Kōmei 1966/2, p. 65. "Young" were respondents in the 20-24 age category. [b] Nihon no Seijiteki Mukanshin (Tōkyō, 1961), p. 37. "Young" were voters between 20 and 24 years. [c] Richardson 1964 postelection survey. [d] Tokushima 1958, p. 69. [e] Tokushima 1958, p. 52. [f] Miyagi 1962, appendix, p. 35.

Responses were dichotomized for the sake of simplicity of presentation. Replies indicating the presence of "strong" and "some" interest were grouped under "yes"; those reflecting the existence of "little" or "no" interest were grouped under "no."

Age patterns in political involvement attitudes obviously are slightly complex, but some central trends are clearly observable. In the first place, surveys conducted in many different places show that middle-aged voters were consistently more involved in public affairs than any other age group. With the exception of their lesser interest in some special aspects of national affairs, and the comparative deficiencies in their knowledge about formal institutions and some national political processes, the middle age grouping clearly was more involved in politics (in most attitudinal dimensions) than either of the other two groups.

Young voters had the relatively highest level of involvement in certain, fairly special kinds of situations. For one, they were more knowledgeable about national institutions as well as some kinds of national political processes. Their reported interest in media accounts of politics was very high, and they were highly interested in politics when dramatic issues were being debated. They were also fairly strong in their concern about election outcomes. Finally, old voters were typically lowest in overall involvement, even though they were comparatively more like persons in the middle age category where feelings about local politics and representation of interests were concerned.

Both generational experiences and the effects of aging are factors in the higher levels of political involvement among middle-aged persons. Persons in middle age have a comparatively higher status (where income levels are used as a measure), while they were also more involved than other ages in groups. According to a multivariate analysis (summarized later), it is quite clear that these tendencies in status and group involvement did have some impact in the directions anticipated.[17]

There is evidence in the multivariate analysis of generational influences as well. It will be remembered that middle-aged persons were in the early years of their political maturity at the time of the political and social reforms of the American occupation. Their exposure to the political currents of the time presumably contributed to formation

---

[17] Since a presentation of the consolidated evidence from the multivariate analysis is more advantageous in determining the overall impact of generational differences, this will be presented at the end of the chapter. As a consequence, the evidence supporting various comments in the text — such as that about the effects of status and group membership — is shown in Table 7-9.

of particularly strong interest in politics. It is indeed possible that generational influences are of the greatest importance specifically with respect to persons who are now in early middle age as a result. The factors of status and social involvement often had only trace effects on political involvement, while sizable residual effects were associated with middle age alone.

Other kinds of evidence support this same line of interpretation about the importance of generational experiences for persons in the middle age group. This age cohort, which was in its forties at the time the studies I reviewed were conducted, showed the strongest interest in politics in comparison with other age groups in studies conducted a decade earlier. In other words, if we look at the responses of persons who were in their thirties in the 1950s, we see that their interest at that time was greater than that of voters in older age groups. Even though different persons were interviewed in the different surveys, it is clear that the tendencies among this cohort are consistent over time.[18]

The lower levels of most kinds of political involvement shown among old voters can also be attributed primarily to the effects of historical-generational experiences. Voters in this age grouping were already in their late thirties and forties at the end of the war, and presumably were somewhat less affected by major postwar social and political changes.[19] The cohort analysis just discussed lends support to this interpretation, as does the multivariate analysis. Nevertheless, trends in social disengagement and status among old voters still had their effect in some instances, even though they were not as important as the residual effects of age alone (see Table 7-9).

---

[18] In the findings of four national surveys conducted in the period 1952–56, political interest was clearly lower after the age of forty. See Allan B. Cole and Naomichi Nakanishi, *Japanese Opinion Polls with Socio-Political Significance, 1947–57* (Medford, Massachusetts: Fletcher School of Law and Diplomacy, Tufts University, and Williamstown, Massachusetts: Roper Opinion Poll Research Center, Williams College, n.d.), pp. 396, 400, 413 and 420.

It should be noted that some of the studies from the early 1960s cited here were conducted in primarily rural districts, and thus could not be used in cohort analysis. But Kōmei 1966/2, Kōmei 1966/3, and Chiba 1963 all included sizable proportions of urban respondents in their samples, permitting them to be used.

[19] It is also possible that persons who grew up before or during the war may have lost confidence in politics or in political leadership as a reaction to the defeat of Japan in the war, and that tendencies toward political disinvolvement among older persons reflect this to some degree.

It is notable, however, that in a few cases there were higher levels of involvement among old voters than among youths. Even though old voters were generally indifferent to abstract dimensions of politics they were more concerned about local elections and more aware of wanting politicians to do something for them than were youths. Either local and pragmatic orientations of this kind are more consonant with prewar political attitudes, or attitudinal change in the postwar era has occurred at different rates for old voters where comparatively more remote and more immediate and substantive frames of reference are concerned. Both interpretations are plausible, but data on the tendencies in political communications exposure of old persons specifically supports the second of these explanations.[20]

The involvement attitudes of voters in their twenties reflected the effects of their lower levels of status and social involvement on the one hand, and the effects of their comparatively recent education on the other. Many youths who were interviewed had only recently graduated from secondary school or college, where contemporary political affairs received some emphasis in social studies courses or in more advanced courses. The markedly stronger orientation toward national politics observable among young voters, as well as the comparatively superior knowledge of national institutions and processes in this group, reflects recent educational experience along with an overall high level of exposure to the mass media. At the same time, the comparatively weaker knowledge of issues and lower commitment to local politics are traceable to lower levels of social status and social involvement respectively.[21]

Evaluative Attitudes. Differences in political involvement among

---

[20] Differences between old persons and their juniors were much smaller where exposure to communications about local politics and elections were concerned than was the case for exposure to communications about national politics. These differences reflect the fact that many old voters were still active in local affairs.

[21] For the logic of this interpretation see both my earlier statements about the effect of status and the results of the multivariate analysis presented later.

Where more detailed profile findings are available, some interesting patterns in involvement attitudes can be observed among youths in the 20–24 year old category and the 25–29 group. Interest in politics was much higher among persons in their early twenties than among those in their late twenties, a tendency which can be attributed to the fact that the franchise is acquired at 20 years of age. See, for example, Aichi 1964, p. 30. (Some respondents to my survey said that the time of their life when they had been most interested in politics was the year they acquired the franchise.)

different political generations are not surprising, and could readily have been forecast by anyone familiar with recent Japanese history. It is more difficult to predict just what the differences might be with respect to evaluative attitudes. May we anticipate that persons who grew up in the prewar period would be critical of politics as a result of their political experiences, particularly their exposure to the apparent failure of earlier political formulas? Or were they socialized into unquestioning and perhaps even positive acceptance of the decisions of political leaders, a norm that might still influence their perspective even in the face of the discontinuities associated with the defeat of Japan in World War II?

The evidence from various Japanese studies in the early 1960s generally supports the second of these two possibilities. Old voters were in many cases more optimistic or positive in their evaluation of candidates and political activity than the other groupings. But high levels of "don't know" answers were a complicating factor for both description and analysis. It was thus difficult at times to determine the degree to which survey responses reflected actual assessments of political activity, or the extent to which responses within age groups were influenced by the levels of political awareness associated with that group.

Nevertheless, satisfaction with politics in general, local politics, candidates in local elections and the quality of local assemblymen was generally most common among old voters (Table 7-5). In contrast, young persons reported lower levels of satisfaction as well as being explicitly more dissatisfied (Kumamoto 1960; Ibaragi 1962; Kōmei 1967A; Aichi 1964, p. 42; Miyagi 1962, appendix p. 26; Kumamoto 1962, p. 4). Tendencies in the evaluation of elections and electoral practices were similar. Old voters were less pessimistic about the effects of holding elections, while young and middle-aged voters more commonly saw "no change" or "worse" effects (Kōmei 1962A).[22] The perception that particular elections had been conducted "honestly" or "fairly" was also favored by old voters more than by young persons (Kōmei 1967BB, p. 1; Saga 1962, p. 7).

In a similar vein, old voters least often said they felt that candi-

---

[22] According to the results of Kōmei 1962A, a national survey, older voters were only less negative, but in most of the regional studies, they were also more positive. See, for example, Kumamoto 1960, p. 98; Tōkyō 1958, p. 60; Kumamoto 1962, p. 22; Kagawa 1965, p. 26; and, Saga 1964, p. 7.

TABLE 7-5. EVALUATIVE ATTITUDES, BY AGE

	Young				Middle				Old			
	Pos (%)	Neg (%)	Don't Know (%)	Total (%)	(N)	Pos (%)	Neg (%)	Don't Know (%)	Total (%)	(N)	Pos (%)	Neg (%)	Don't Know (%)	Total (%)	(N)
Satisfaction with today's politics[a]	9	63	28	100	(104)	5	72	23	100	(109)	20	45	34	99	(88)
Feelings about today's government[b]	15	50	35	100	(134)	8	55	37	100	(158)	18	36	46	100	(127)
Quality of recent local assembly candidates[c]	23	27	49	99	(470)	32	26	43	101	(546)	32	25	44	101	(397)
Politics improves by holding elections[d]	29	36	35	100	(999)	29	35	36	100	(942)	28	22	50	100	(585)
Law violations in Representatives election[e]	32	49	19	100	(488)	36	42	23	101	(541)	40	22	38	100	(398)
Effect of people's vote and interest on national politics[f]	76	10	14	100	(71)	75	4	21	100	(75)	57	17	26	100	(47)
People's vote decides operation of politics[g]	67	11	22	100	(260)	69	10	22	101	(205)	52	9	39	100	(141)
National politicians and officials are concerned with our needs[f]	49	28	23	100	(71)	43	37	20	100	(75)	47	30	23	100	(47)
Adequacy of local politics' responsiveness to people's opinions and wants[h]	44	36	21	101	(87)	57	27	16	100	(89)	38	36	26	100	(113)
Candidate voted for will realize hopes and demands[i]	31	30	39	100	(242)	39	27	34	100	(186)	34	19	47	100	(155)

SOURCES:
[a] Kumamoto 1960, p. 35. [b] Ibaragi 1962, p. 47. [c] Kōmei 1967A, p. 134 (national). [d] Kōmei 1962A, p. 45 (national). [e] Kōmei 1967BB, p. 43 (national). [f] Richardson, 1964 postelection study. [g] Osaka 1961, p. 71. [h] Miyagi 1962, appendix, p. 6. "Old" here refers to persons 50 years and older. [i] Gumma 1963, p. 54.

For meanings of "Pos" (positive) and "Neg" (negative) see Table 3-1.

dates violated the election laws, and young people especially felt that violations were on the increase in recent years (Kōmei 1967BB; Kōmei 1964A, p. 128; Saga 1962, p. 42; Nagasaki 1964, p. 43; Tōkyō 1962, p. 29). In contrast with the general optimism of old people and cynicism of youth, the evaluative attitudes of middle-aged voters were surprisingly inconsistent. But there were still some regularities, and the outlook of people in the middle-age grouping was more like that of youths with regard to evaluations of national political performance, but more closely resembled that of old people in regard to local politics.

The patterns among old people and youths described thus far were in part reversed, however, where questions called for evaluation of ordinary people's political efficacy. Indeed, inefficacy was a constant theme in old people's replies in studies conducted throughout the country and at different times. Old persons felt less commonly than either young or middle-aged voters that "people's votes have some effect on what politicians and officials do" (Richardson 1964). Also, voters in their sixties agreed more often than young persons that ordinary people have "little effect on the machinations of politics" (Iwate 1963, appendix pp. 8–9). Similarly, old voters in urban Ōsaka prefecture felt less commonly than either of the other two age groups that the "people's vote decides the way the country is run" (Ōsaka 1961, p. 71), and in another district old voters were least often of the opinion that "politics is moved by the people's power" (Fukushima 1963, p. 176).

Substantially identical patterns were shown in responses to questions about the responsiveness of politicians. Old persons felt least optimistic in this context; however, there were some differences in the relative tendencies among young and middle-aged voters on different kinds of evaluations. On one occasion young voters felt more often than both middle-aged and old persons that national politicians and officials were responsive to the needs and interests of ordinary people (Richardson 1964). Elsewhere, middle-aged voters were more confident than others that the candidate they had supported would realize their expectations (Gumma 1963; Gumma 1962, p. 33), that the prefectural administration was paying attention to "people's voices" (Kumamoto 1960, p. 8) or that "local politics reflects our needs adequately or to some degree" (Miyagi 1962).

A multivariate analysis of responses to the questions on efficacy and politicians' responsiveness from my own survey indicates that generational differences were the most important determinant of patterns in evaluative attitudes among different age groupings. Differences in group membership and, in one or two instances, in income did have some trace effect on differential tendencies between age groupings (see Table 7-9), but the residual effect of age alone was still of primary importance. Old voters grew up in a period when questioning the actions of their governors was not encouraged, and it is certainly plausible that they are comparatively less negative even today as a result of this earlier socialization. It is also possible that old voters simply believe that criticism of leaders is detrimental to the need to maintain overt community or public harmony. Restraints of this kind would be more operative with respect to questions concerned at least implicitly with local affairs or personalities than with remote national political processes.

In contrast, young voters have grown up in different times and seem more inclined than old voters to freely express their opinions and to be more openly critical of political figures. This is certainly one of the implications of the study of national character by the Institute for Mathematical Statistics in Japan, and particularly the findings about the *legitimacy,* or value of criticism among different age groups.[23] But youths, and middle-aged persons as well, are substantially more attentive to the mass media coverage of public affairs, and may develop more negative views on the basis of their greater exposure to the media's accounts of dramatic violations of parliamentary procedural norms, corruption and election law violations. Finally, youths and middle-aged voters are more often found in the ranks of leftist parties than are old persons, and this also may be associated with tendencies toward pessimistic assessments of political activity.[24]

---

[23] See Tōkei Sūri Kenkyūjo, *Nihonjin no Kokuminsei: Dai Niji Chōsa* (Tōkyō: 1959), p. 95. The effect of age on feelings that "It's better for the public to be attentive to public issues than to depend on fine leaders" was especially dramatic, and was exceeded in scale only by that of education.

[24] Old voters are correspondingly more inclined toward conservative party support, and this may affect the nature of their evaluative attitudes. But available findings indicate that there is a weaker relationship between conservative preferences and positive assessment of political performance than exists between leftist party support and negative evaluation, possibly because the platforms of leftist parties are more conspicuously critical in content (as might be expected in the case of opposition parties).

It is also highly possible that generational differences in Japan are associated with some very special kinds of responses to democratic ideas. On the one hand, young and middle-aged voters reflect higher levels of internalization of democratic norms in positive feelings of political efficacy and positive appraisals of the responsiveness of politicians. But the feelings of dissatisfaction with political life sometimes reported by young voters might also be attributable to the same underlying source. It is safe to say that many young persons have a highly ideal picture of politics; hence their perception of reality can be especially distorted. In effect, their dissatisfaction with politics stems from higher expectations about political activity, and their consequent ambivalence where different dimensions of evaluative attitudes are concerned compares quite clearly with that of many urban residents and well-educated people.[25]

Evidence supporting this interpretation is found where questions have been asked about voters' tolerance of electoral law violations. Young voters commonly subscribe in overwhelming proportions to the idea that "it's bad for a candidate to break the laws." Middle-aged voters also support this view, although with lower ratios of agreement than youths in the case of the findings of some studies; in contrast, old voters, more than persons in the other age groupings, typically support the idea that infractions of the electoral laws are "natural" or "can't be helped." [26]

Once these contrasts in the normative orientations among persons in different age groups are fully understood, the diverging tendencies within different groupings where different kinds of evaluative attitudes are concerned can also be comprehended. Young voters and middle-aged persons, in certain circumstances, more often subscribe to statements that most literally reflect the content of democratic ideas; they also reflect their intensity of attachment to democratic concepts in critical evaluations of much of what goes on in Japanese politics, as we have

---

[25] The lower status and group involvement of youth may be important to their assessment of politics, but this would not explain the generally positive feelings of efficacy among young voters. However, status considerations and low levels of group memberships might be important where most evaluative attitudes are concerned, if it is assumed that the heightened feelings of efficacy among youths actually result from the recency of their formal schooling in democratic precepts.

[26] This is shown in the results of several of the Kōmei Senkyo Remmei's national surveys; one example is found in Kōmei 1958, p. 77.

just observed. On the other hand, old voters are less familiar with democratic ideas and respond less automatically to statements that most literally reflect the tenets of democracy, while at the same time they appraise political performance in comparatively more positive terms for the reasons I have already outlined.

Participation Attitudes. The attitudes of Japanese citizens regarding political participation clearly reflected in most instances generational differences between prewar and postwar socialization. This was true for both attitudes about the vote as an obligation and feelings about political activism. Where respondents were asked direct questions about their reasons for voting, old persons more often reported that they voted because of feelings of duty than for any other reason. By contrast, both youths and middle-aged voters tended to emphasize motivations such as the belief that the vote was "a basic right" or a "chance for expression of one's opinions" (Richardson 1964; Shizuoka 1963, p. 44; Aichi 1964, p. 48).

Indirect questions about the vote and abstention produced generally similar results (Table 7-6). Here, however, the tendency among middle-aged voters was a higher level of feelings of duty than in answers to direct questions about voting motivations. Middle-aged and old persons felt more than young people that "it's everybody's duty to go out and vote" (Richardson 1964), and the former also expressed more often than young voters the opinion that "one should vote even when there is no strongly preferred candidate" (Gifu 1963). Middle-aged and old voters also were more often of the opinion that "it's bad to abstain except in the case of absence, sickness or infirmity" (Gumma 1962; Gumma 1963, p. 63).

The fact that old voters, and occasionally those in middle age, clearly were more inclined to vote because of duty is not surprising in view of discontinuities in political socialization in Japan. There were also some notable generational differences in willingness to support or engage in more active kinds of political participation than simply voting (Table 7-7). Old voters were in most cases more passive, while youths, and sometimes middle-aged persons, preferred an active part in politics. This was evident from the tendencies of answers to a substantial variety of questions. For example, in replies to a very general kind of question about participation or direct involvement, old voters in one district felt more often than others that "it's better to leave

TABLE 7-6. ABSTENTION ATTITUDES, BY AGE

	Young				Middle				Old			
	Yes (%)	No (%)	Don't Know (%)	Total (%) (N)	Yes (%)	No (%)	Don't Know (%)	Total (%) (N)	Yes (%)	No (%)	Don't Know (%)	Total (%) (N)
It's everybody's duty to go out and vote[a]	34	39	27	100 (71)	48	32	20	100 (75)	49	32	19	100 (47)
It's better to vote for the best candidate rather than abstain, when the person you prefer isn't running[b]	45	31	23	99 (132)	59	25	17	101 (121)	58	12	30	100 (81)
It's bad to abstain from voting except under special circumstances[c]	62	28	10	100 (—)	65	30	5	100 (—)	69	24	7	100 (—)

SOURCES:

[a] Richardson 1964 postelection study.   [b] Gifu 1963, p. 66.   [c] Gumma 1962, p. 36.

TABLE 7-7. Participation Attitudes, by Age

	Young				Middle				Old			
	Yes (%)	No (%)	Don't Know (%)	Total (%)	(N)	Yes (%)	No (%)	Don't Know (%)	Total (%)	(N)	Yes (%)	No (%)	Don't Know (%)	Total (%)	(N)
Bad to leave politics alone and not get involved[a]	34	33	33	100	(114)	30	38	32	100	(112)	19	46	35	100	(90)
Would take an active role in the resolution of local problems[b]	22	60	18	100	(92)	37	60	3	100	(99)	23	57	19	99	(47)
Would cooperate with a recall movement when an assemblyman is corrupt[c]	18	71	10	99	(234)	15	72	13	100	(326)	12	64	24	100	(208)
Would stress group activity and petitions to improve our lives[d]	30	66	4	100	(199)	17	81	2	100	(207)	20	71	9	100	(111)
Bad to depend on politicians and refrain from expressing opinions[e]	47	26	27	100	(180)	39	29	31	99	(180)	22	33	44	99	(180)
Better to pay attention to politics than just to follow leaders[f]	73	10	17	100	(89)	85	6	9	100	(81)	42	22	34	98	(77)

Sources:
[a] Iwate 1962, appendix, pp. 6–7. [b] Aomori 1961, p. 25. [c] Kōmei 1967A, p. 81 (national). [d] Miyazaki 1964, p. 150. [e] Kumamoto 1962, p. 5. [f] Kōmei 1966/3, p. 62. Figures are for small city portion of sample only.

politics alone than get too involved" (Iwate 1962). Elsewhere, voters in their sixties least commonly preferred to hear more about politics or engage more often in political discussions (Aichi 1964, p. 45).

While tendencies toward passivism among old voters were relatively stable, there were somewhat contradictory trends among voters in the other age categories, reflecting largely urban-rural differences in outlook. Young voters in Tokyo were more willing to be leaders or "cooperate" in the resolution of local problems than were any of their elders, who would more often "depend on others" or do nothing because they felt apathetic about such problems (Tōkyō 1958, p. 27). But apart from the large city sample, young voters were more like old citizens in their tendency to accept passive roles, while persons in middle age were most oriented toward active participation (Aomori 1961; Saitama 1962, p. 29; Miyagi 1962, appendix, p. 7; Aomori 1962, p. 23). Elsewhere, young rural voters showed similar tendencies to those just described in agreeing, along with old voters, that it was better "to wait for the proper time" to take action about local problems; at the same time, rural middle-aged voters were again more actively oriented and felt that they would "try to help resolve problems as soon as possible" (Ōita 1964, p. 31).

These differences between urban and rural youths with regard to attitudes toward roles as active participants in local politics are quite easy to explain. Reports on the national character study by the Institute of Mathematic Statistics have shown that rural residents are more likely to respect status differences than are people in the cities. Rural residents believe slightly more than do urban residents that recognition of status differences should be preserved in the Japanese language; people living in the country hamlets also report more often than urban dwellers that they would remain silent if rebuked by a superior or that they would prefer a paternalistic supervisor.[27] It is my own belief that rural youth display a greater propensity to accept status differences than do urban young people, and, as a consequence, do not feel that active roles in community decision-making are ap-

---

[27] See Tōkei Sūri Kenkyūjo, *Kokuminsei no Kenkyū* (Tōkyō: 1959), pp. 60, 62 and 81. It should be remembered that the urban-rural differences are not typically enormous, and the relative differences in belief systems should not be seen as reflective of truly dichotomous general cultural patterns.

propriate as much as urban youth do. It is also possible that the higher education typical of many urban youths may bring greater automatic familiarity with democratic concepts and thus encourage acceptance of activist attitudes. Or the special idealism of the urban intellectual environment may encourage the acceptance of activist roles.[28]

These special rural patterns, where very specific questions about the possibility of assuming roles as leaders or activists are asked, do not reflect the general tendencies in the participation attitudes of young persons. In effect, these sectoral differences among age groupings toward active roles in local affairs were an exception to the more general rule, whereby young voters typically endorsed activism more often than other ages. Regardless of residence, young, and sometimes middle-aged, voters indicated greater preferences for collective political activity, in contrast to the generally more passive attitudes of old persons. For example, young voters were more commonly inclined to support collective expression of frustrations or articulation of interests (Kōmei 1967A; Miyazaki 1964). Similar patterns exist where questions were about more general attitudes toward participation. Young voters preferred to "state their opinions actively" regarding national political problems more often than their elders, in contrast with older persons who would more commonly "depend on a politician" (Fukushima 1962, p. 172). And, where the query was simply agreement or disagreement with the statement that "it's best to depend on a fine politician" to get things done, young voters were less inclined to prefer dependency than their elders (Kumamoto 1962). Finally, young and middle-aged citizens felt more often than old voters that one must "pay

---

[28] However, I am reluctant to push this point further, since it is well-known that school teachers in rural districts are progressive in outlook in many instances. Nevertheless, the intellectual centers are urban, and while it is also true that there are both progressive and conservative elements in the Japanese intellectual world, it seems safe to identify the educational atmosphere (to which urban youth is disproportionately exposed) as more modern and progressive in character.

The *relative* disinclination of middle-aged persons in Tokyo to exhibit activist predispositions might also reflect their perceptions of the absence there of opportunities for participation in community decisions. Many urban residents do not know their neighbors well and participate less in neighborhood activities than their rural counterparts, so that the real chances for being active in community decision-making may seem low to them. I think that many urban dwellers also simply do not want to be active in the areas of the city where they live.

attention" rather than rely on national leaders in public affairs (Kōmei 1966/3).

Generational differences seem especially great in these findings on participation attitudes. Looking first at attitudes toward the vote, both our understanding of historical socialization processes and multivariate analysis (Table 7-9) point more than any other factor to the importance of generational experience. It is true that the franchise was popularly considered a right both before and after the war; it is equally true that the vote has been considered a matter of obligation in both periods. This sentiment was presumably an extension of more general ideas about elite social obligation in the early stages of the development of the franchise, when the right to vote was limited to comparatively affluent citizens. The special emphasis on citizen duties prevalent in certain periods before the war probably influenced attitudes toward the vote as well. It seems safe to say that exercise of the franchise has always been bound to values of social obligation in Japan, despite occasional instrumental connotations of some influence.

Yet there are important qualitative differences in socialization between the prewar and postwar periods. It is a well-known fact that school curricula were revised after the war; the affirmation of citizen obligation to the state and other prewar political norms was replaced by a self-conscious articulation of democratic ideas. These changes, especially the newer emphasis on participation based on self-interest, are reflected in the age differences reported here.[29] It is also apparent that the postwar mood of individualism and egalitarianism provides a reinforcement to reforms in the curricula — changes in attitudes toward voting should certainly be viewed in relationship to more general cultural themes in postwar Japanese attitudes.

However, in a few instances generational differences in feelings that the vote is a duty were not very great — this was particularly true in responses to some indirect questions about abstention attitudes. Clearly, feelings of duty are not unknown to youths. Even though educational experiences have differed in emphasis over time, both formal and in-

---

[29] This interpretation of the tendencies in older voters' attitudes toward the vote is supported by evidence that there are lower levels of appreciation of the political potential of the franchise among old voters. See Kumamoto 1960, p. 93; Kumamoto 1962, p. 24; and, Ōsaka 1961, pp. 72–73.

formal socialization processes have maintained the ideal of dutiful citizenship.[30]

Historical differences in socialization also have an effect on tendencies in attitudes toward the legitimacy or desirability of collective political action or activist political roles. While status was factoral — at least in the samples from country hamlets — generally speaking, earlier values are clearly reflected in the attitudes of old persons, while more recent values are reflected in the attitudes of particularly very young respondents. The latter is also true in several instances for middle-age voters.

Voting Attitudes. In contrast with participation attitudes, tendencies in voting attitudes among different ages in Japan cannot be clearly foreseen on the basis of either ideas about the effects of normal aging or of historical-generational experiences. If findings on American voter attitudes were applicable here, we could anticipate that political parties have a special importance for middle-aged and old persons. But the Japanese political system has been less stable over time than the American and the same patterns of stable and increasing party loyalty may not be present among persons in the middle-aged and old categories. Moreover, it is plausible that the kinds of attitudes toward candidates in Japan have some connection with earlier value systems,

---

[30] It must be noted that postwar textbooks do contain the idea that the vote is a duty. This practice helps keep this norm alive, as do appeals by election officials to vote. Still, the shifts in both general social and political values in the postwar era favor a more instrumental view of the vote than prevailed before the war.

With the exception of my own study, all findings reported here on attitudes toward the vote were from studies conducted in rural areas. It is possible that tendencies among urban inhabitants might be somewhat different, and that urban youths in particular might be less duty-oriented than rural youths. This was indeed the case in Yokohama, according to my findings.

The attitudes of middle-aged voters toward voting have not been discussed in detail because the tendencies are somewhat less systematic than for youths and old persons. Tendencies in the middle age grouping resemble those of youth in replies to direct questions about the importance of various motivations, reflecting of course the influence of postwar socialization. But in responses to indirect questions on abstention the tendencies were more like those of old people. This can best be explained by the fact that an attitude of duty is still more widespread among the population than any other norm about the vote, that persons in middle age are typically more involved than youths in politics, and that they therefore internalize general norms more than persons less involved. They are also older, and despite their experience in the postwar era they may constitute a transitional generation where some kinds of political attitudes are concerned.

and that even where partisan loyalties have been formed, "candidate" may still have more importance than "party" among old voters.

The evidence shows some differences in voting attitudes among persons in different age groupings. But it is important to note that these differences were often overwhelmed by trends throughout the general population (Table 7-8). For example, more Japanese voters considered "candidate" rather than "party" to be the more important basis for voting-choice, and this was true for persons in all age categories. Still, young voters reported a greater emphasis on "party" than did their elders; moreover, concern for "candidate" was slightly more common among old people (Kōmei 1964B). Tendencies in replies to questions about party support show roughly similar patterns. Of the three ages, old persons were least inclined to support a party, while middle-aged persons were more inclined than youths to support a party. Thus, the tendency in party support in Japan was curvilinear, in contrast to the linear tendency among different age groups in the United States.[31]

These tendencies in attitudes toward political parties are a matter of some importance in view of the fact that recent Japanese political history is substantially different from the United States. In effect, discontinuities in party labels and organization in parts of the postwar period, and between the prewar and postwar periods, might have had some effect on generational tendencies in the consideration of "party" in voting-choice or on tendencies in partisan support. Young voters in the early 1960s conceivably could have formed more stable party attachments than middle-aged or old persons.[32] Young voters became politically mature at a time when partisan alternatives were comparatively more stable, with the exception of the defection in 1959 of the Democratic Socialists from the Japan Socialist Party and the emergence of the Komeito. This may have been conducive in many cases

---

[31] For the relevant evidence from American studies, see Crittenden, p. 326; and Angus Campbell, et al., *The American Voter*, pp. 161–162.

[32] Recent research affords some support for these observations about young voters. They are seen as receptive to the same parental transfer of loyalties found in the United States; it is doubtful if this would occur during periods of frequent change in party labels. See Robert E. Ward and Akira Kubota, "Family Influence and Political Socialization in Japan: Some Preliminary Findings in Comparative Perspective," *Comparative Political Studies* 3 (July 1970), pp. 140–175.

TABLE 7-8. VOTING ATTITUDES, BY AGE

		Young (%)	Middle (%)	Old (%)
Party or candidate in national election:[a]				
Party		36	23	23
Candidate		52	51	55
Don't know		14	26	23
	Total	102	100	101
	(N)	(437)	(445)	(339)
Support a political party:[b]				
Yes		80	86	77
No		5	3	1
Don't know		15	13	22
	Total	100	102	100
	(N)	(121)	(138)	(81)
Reasons for voting choice in national election:[c]				
Fine character/honest		14	28	21
Strong politician		6	15	13
Party affiliation		24	10	6
Represents local area		27	26	31
Represents workers		13	7	4
Endorsements/requests		6	3	4
Other/don't know		9	10	19
	Total	99	99	98
	(N)	(78)	(96)	(67)
Reasons for voting choice in national election:[d]				
Agreement on principles		47	35	24
Candidate's experience		5	6	21
Respect the candidate		15	16	12
Candidate from around here		4	7	12
Represents our occupation		21	32	21
Other		7	4	10
	Total	99	100	100
	(N)	(127)	(100)	(58)

SOURCES:
[a] Kōmei 1964B, p. 49 (national).   [b] Fukushima 1962, p. 140.   [c] Kumamoto 1960, pp. 130–33.   [d] Niigata 1963, pp. 9–10.

to political partisanship. By contrast, middle-aged and old voters might have felt some confusion or alienation regarding partisan attachments because of their exposure to the complex and frequent alignments in earlier periods.

In some of the studies I reviewed young voters did in fact place more emphasis on "party" in their voting-choice than did either middle-aged or old persons. Still, middle-aged voters in other studies reported levels of concern for "party" comparable to, or higher than those of youths, and we have already seen that they support parties in higher frequencies than youths. Some explanation other than differences in historical-generational experiences is necessary here. It is possible, for example, that political involvement is a particularly important factor where attitudes toward political parties are concerned. Outside Japan, political involvement and party support have been shown to be highly correlated, and there is some evidence to indicate that this is the case in Japan, although here the links may be more complex than in other political systems.

In my opinion, it is the *national* focus of political involvement (which characterizes the outlooks of many young and middle-aged voters) that provides the critical link in an explanation of the tendencies in attitudes toward parties among different age groupings. Political parties are more active in national than local politics, and interest in national politics favors a greater awareness of parties.[33] According to this view, the higher levels of exposure among young and middle-aged voters to mass media coverage of politics affords greater familiarity with parties and leads to higher levels of concern for parties in voting-choice. Correspondingly, the greater concern for "candidate" reported by old voters may reflect the fact that they are less attentive to mass media and less interested in national affairs. Old voters, however, are more involved than at least youths in local politics, and this implies more extensive contacts with influentials and politicians. While these relationships may be more prominent in the rural sector, wherever they are present they obviously contribute to greater familiarity with the reputations and qualities of particular candidates.[34]

---

[33] Feelings that *national* elections were more interesting than local contests have been positively related to support for some political party (Fukushima 1964, pp. 160–61).

[34] There is some evidence to support this interpretation. Persons sixty and over

It is also important to remember that emphasis on "candidate" was seen earlier as an outgrowth of the prevailing concern for personal contacts in Japanese society. Since this practice is related in turn to the residual importance of earlier social practices, it is quite possible that old persons have a greater concern for personalities than do other age groupings. This seems especially reasonable, in view of the supportive evidence on social practices and norms among persons in different age groupings in the national character survey.[35]

Age differences in voting attitudes were also evident where questions included expanded alternatives pertaining to partisanship, candidate qualities and instrumental expectations. In this case, young voters showed higher levels of partisanship, while tendencies among old voters remained consistent with earlier trends in an emphasis on candidate character and experience, or on the fact that he came from the local area (Kumamoto 1960; Niigata 1963). Young voters also emphasized instrumental expectations and concern for "principles" more than did old people, although the latter showed somewhat greater concern for the importance of representation of local interests than did youths.[36] At first glance this might seem to be a contradiction. But

---

reported greater confidence than did youths that before the period of the election campaign they had known something about the candidate they voted for in prefectural elections. See Kōmei 1967A, p. 63.

Old persons reported lower levels of participation in political discussions than did voters in other age groups, however, so that it must be assumed that their greater familiarity with candidates is the result of informal, less memorable communications — particularly since informal communication seem to be most responsible for information about candidates.

The comparatively high levels of participation in political discussions reported for middle-aged voters also presumably affords them considerable familiarity with candidates. (This is indeed the case in reality, according to the results of Kōmei 1967A.) But their reported greater familiarity with parties — the result of high levels of exposure to mass media — is more important in voting-choice, presumably because of the additional effects of their greater involvement in national politics.

[35] See Tōkei Sūri Kenkyūjo, *Nihonjin no Kokuminsei*, p. 55. Old persons were obviously more serious about obligations stemming from personal ties than were youths or middle-aged persons. Nevertheless, there is some ambiguity in replies to questions about dependency on paternal figures; youths, reflecting a comparative insecurity, preferred a "protector" more than did old persons (*ibid.*, p. 62).

[36] Middle-aged voters showed somewhat inconsistent tendencies; they were more inclined to be concerned with candidate qualities in some contexts, and "principles" elsewhere. As with participation attitudes, we must infer that this reflects both their special status as a transitional generation and the fact that they are highly exposed to not only media communications that carry messages about the cosmopolitan world of political parties and policies, but also informal discussions that convey information about individual candidates (see Table 7-1).

it will be remembered that old voters were somewhat more aware of wanting local politicians to do something on behalf of their self-interests than were youths (Richardson 1964). Hence, it can be assumed that a concern for both representation of self-interests in local affairs and local representation in more extended political arenas is a strong factor in the emphasis on candidate qualities or experience in the voting attitudes of old persons.[37]

Generational Differences and Political Culture. At the beginning of this chapter two main hypotheses about the relationship between age and political attitudes were set forth. Differences in political socialization and experiences between persons who came to maturity before and after the war were presumed to contribute to distinctive political attitudes. It was also suggested that the effects of exposure to the political climate of the immediate postwar period resulted in a special generational pattern among persons who either came to political maturity or were in their youth at that time.

However, we saw that life cycle differences in status and social involvement might also have important implications for tendencies in political attitudes. In the discussion so far I have endeavored to establish the importance of historical-generational experiences as well as the impact of different stages in the biological life cycle. In a few cases we have also looked at the effects of communications exposure. At this point I shall review and consolidate all the explanations advanced, as well as give special attention to some qualifications which have so far been considered only briefly.

Looking first at old voters, it will be recalled that they reported comparatively lower levels of most kinds of political involvement, political efficacy and preferences for active forms of political participation. They also reported higher levels of feelings of obligation about the vote and showed somewhat higher levels of satisfaction with, or optimism about political performance (or at least lower levels of negative evaluation). These tendencies were attributable in most cases to

---

[37] Shizuoka 1963 (p. 31) shows that old voters are actually more concerned about representation of their interests in voting-choices in replies to questions where alternative considerations are absent. In addition to supporting the judgment about the underlying relationship between "candidate" emphasis and concern for representation of self-interests among older persons, these findings also provide a basis for believing that the political involvement of many youths is somewhat superficial.

the influences of generational experiences. Exposure to authoritarian political styles and socialization norms in which "subject" orientations toward the state were emphasized thus seems an obvious factor in attitudes typically found among old voters.

The persuasiveness of the generational interpretation was enhanced by comparing some of the above tendencies of old voters with those of voters in the same cohort in the 1950s. Multivariate analysis also supports a generational explanation of the tendencies among old voters, despite some qualifications. Table 7-9 shows the results of an analysis in which the effect of age difference was examined with separate controls for education, income, group membership and sex, respectively. If we confine our examination at this point to the effects of social status (income) and social involvement (group membership), we see at once that the residual effects of age are only modestly reduced by controlling separately for the effects of each of these variables.[38] There are instances where effect parameters are lowered below the level of statistical significance, but the remaining index is still much larger than the reduction resulting from variable control. From this we can infer that a modest status decline (measured by income) has little to do with the differences in political involvement and evaluation between middle-aged and old voters. However, the fact remains there is some small effect attributable to status decline, and it is interesting that this is reflected principally in attitudes toward national politics.

Controls for group membership resulted in comparably modest reductions in the residual effect of age where local politics was concerned. This seems intuitively correct since group involvement and social engagement (or disengagement) presumably have a greater impact at the local level in Japan. The meaning of the modest effects of income declines on attitudes toward national politics is less clear. But it is certainly possible that they reflect the results of retirement more than anything else.

An analysis of the differences in political attitudes between old voters and persons in the young and middle age categories, with sex controlled, also lends support to a generational interpretation. Although I have not dealt extensively with the possibility that the effects

---

[38] Since Coleman multivariate analysis was used here, both the earlier general discussion of this technique and the explanation of its use in this study are again relevant.

TABLE 7-9. AGE AND POLITICAL ATTITUDES, MULTIVARIATE RELATIONSHIPS

	Youth-Middle					Middle-Old				
	Age	(Sex)	(Education)	(Income)	(Group Memberships)	Age	(Sex)	(Education)	(Income)	(Group Memberships)
Interest — N	.022	.022	.037	.023	.016	.151	.153	–.135	–.127	–.129
Concern — N	.019	.019	.043	.017	.017	–.063	–.065	–.048	–.026	–.060
Responsiveness — N	.019	.019	.033	.019	.033	–.019	–.021	–.006	–.013	–.008
Efficacy — N	.048	.048	.070	.048	.029	–.105	–.108	–.089	–.096	–.094
Relevance — N	.057	.057	.087	.058	.079	–.102	–.105	–.070	–.068	–.098
Civic Duty	.038	.038	.031	.037	.014	.032	.032	.041	.034	.045
Wants	.155	.155	.145	.153	.098	–.070	–.071	–.091	–.073	–.032
Interest — L	.113	.113	.104	.113	.064	–.104	–.105	–.109	–.082	–.062
Concern — L	.144	.144	.149	.143	.119	–.106	–.107	–.107	–.100	–.094
Responsiveness — L	.078	.078	.083	.076	.077	–.159	–.161	–.162	–.161	.130
Efficacy — L	.003	.003	.010	–.004	–.034	–.078	–.080	–.055	–.063	–.060
Relevance — L	.016	.016	.029	.018	.011	–.009	–.012	–.009	–.014	.000

These are effect-indexes for differences between youth and middle age, and between middle age and older age, respectively. Age is categorized in three groups: 20–34, 35–49 and 50 years and over.

The indexes listed under "age" headings are the pure bivariate indexes of effect. Under the other headings in parentheses, each index indicates the residual effects of age after controls for the other variables were introduced. No change in the index indicates that the effects of age were in no way related to the underlying effects of the other relevant variable. A diminution of the effect of age in the direction of or beyond zero, when other effects are controlled, indicates that the other variable was contributing to effects previously assigned to age alone. When the effect indexes increase, the effect of age is actually greater once the confounding influences of variables otherwise associated with age are removed.

of age could be traced in part to differences between the sexes in experiences, there are some obvious reasons for considering this possibility. As is well-known, women in Japan received the franchise only after World War II. For this reason women might have been much less aware of political matters before the war, and old women may still be influenced by these earlier experiences. It is also possible that prewar and postwar differences in attitudes towards women's roles also have something to do with the political perspectives of women in different age groupings. In effect, old women might be markedly less involved in politics than are old males, as a result both of disenfranchisement during their formative years and the fact that women's status was apparently considerably lower in the prewar period than more recently.[39]

In view of this, some interesting conclusions can be drawn from a comparison of the trends among men and women, respectively, in different age groupings. In the first place, there are markedly lower levels of involvement among old women, in comparison with the attitudes of both middle-aged and young women (Richardson 1964; Iwate 1963, appendix p. 4).[40] At first glance, this might be assumed to be an effect of special experiences among old women. Nevertheless, attitude tendencies were fairly similar between both men and women in old age, according to both the studies cited above and other representative investigations, although it is true that the levels of involvement after age 60 were sometimes closer for men more than for women to those of middle-aged persons. This leads me to conclude, as before, that generational effects attributable to the general differences in prewar and postwar political climate were at work.

The Coleman multivariate analysis shows much the same results, particularly with regard to differences between middle-aged and old persons (Table 7-9). Sex differences have no meaningful effect on the

---

[39] These special experiences of women obviously constitute a kind of generational experience. However, I have refrained from using the term in the text for the simple reason that it makes it difficult to separate these comments about specialized experiences of women from discussion of the more general prewar and postwar differences in political experiences.

[40] In the Iwate study the question was "thinking about the candidates and issues" in a national election, while my findings were based on interest in "national politics." Largely similar differences are shown in attitudes toward taking active roles in local political decisions. See Aomori 1962, p. 23.

relationship between age and involvement or evaluative attitudes in this case.[41] The involvement levels of women in every age grouping clearly reflected differences in political roles between the sexes. But there was no special visible effect attributable to comparatively late enfranchisement among persons who might be expected to be most directly affected.[42] From this two things are clear: the main generational interpretation about differences between the effects of socialization before and after the war still stands; women in the old age category (in studies from the early 1960s) were not as severely affected by earlier social experiences as might be anticipated. Presumably, women were more exposed to political information in earlier periods than is generally supposed. Or, more plausibly, postwar changes in women's self-concept, favoring more progressive definitions of their social status, have been sufficiently great to overcome the effects of earlier social experiences in the case of those age groups which might otherwise show their effects. In the final analysis, although women are substantially less involved than men, tendencies between the sexes across age groupings are remarkably similar.

Both generational and life cycle (status-involvement) interpretations seem intuitively applicable with respect to the analysis of the high levels of involvement and participation attitudes found among most middle-aged voters. A cohort analysis of tendencies in interest in politics did permit the inference that the comparatively higher involvement of middle-aged voters in the 1960s, in comparison with other age groups, does indeed reflect continuity from an earlier period, presumably the early postwar years. Nevertheless, this cohort analysis was based on a very limited number of studies, and it is necessary to look to the results of my multivariate analysis for confirmation. The multi-

---

[41] It should be remembered that the Coleman effect-indexes measure *differences* between groups resulting from the presence of any independent variable(s). For this reason, statements of the kind I have just made are based on the fact that the difference between middle-aged and old voters does not change when controls for sex are introduced. It is particularly important to remember that it is the differences which we are looking at, even though for sake of economy the inferences are stated in terms of comments about particular age groupings.

[42] Role differences are evidenced by the lower involvement of women across age groupings. Even though at times there are varying differentials between men and women in the different age categories (reflecting the modest effect, particularly on young women, of postwar increases in women's social status), a clear delineation of political roles according to sex is generally the case.

variate analysis favors a generational interpretation (Table 7-9), at least where attitudes toward national politics are concerned. Status differences seem to have no effect on the differences in involvement and evaluative attitudes between youth and middle-aged persons, even though earlier analysis showed that status appeared to be important in participation attitude tendencies, at least in the rural sector. However, some of the differences between youths and middle-aged respondents were attributable to differences in levels of group memberships. Group membership as a factor thus contributes roughly half the differential otherwise attributable to age where interest in *local* political affairs is concerned. It also noticeably contributes to the differential in levels of instrumental awareness (feelings that representation is wanted) and concern about local election outcomes. But generational differences in social involvement (measured by group membership levels) still have little effect on most attitudes toward national politics, and social involvement is not related in any important or consistent way to some of the more abstract dimensions of political involvement at the local level.

Somewhat more specialized interpretations of the political attitudes of youths seem necessary. The multivariate analysis showed that in most instances neither status nor group membership are important in affecting youths' attitudes (Table 7-9). More than anything else, young people reflect recent education under the postwar school system in high levels of idealism and formal knowledge. It is important to note, however, that young people in the 1960s do not necessarily constitute a special historical generation, in the same sense that older generations are historically unique. Even though they appeared different in some respects from middle-aged and old voters and very plausibly form part of a postoccupation generation, there is no reason to believe that the youth in the studies cited here are markedly different from future youth, who will come to political maturity under the same postwar and post occupation influences.[43]

---

[43] In other words, persons who came of age after 1952 were not exposed to the special reformist enthusiasms of the early postwar era. While they share with persons now in middle age exposure to the postwar curricula on social studies and politics, their attitudes can still be expected to differ from persons in the group who came of age at the height of interest in new political formulas.

In addition to looking at the effects of other control variables, I also examined the tendencies among age groups with education controlled. There are substantial

In earlier chapters I included some cross-national comparisons in an effort to contribute further meaning to the Japanese patterns. In some cases, however, such cross-national observations had to be qualified, largely because of problems with equivalence in measures. Still, comparison of attitude variations among age groupings in different countries is obviously desirable, given the probable uniqueness of Japanese political experience. Furthermore, tendencies among age groupings, like those between other subgroups of populations, are generally somewhat easier to compare cross-nationally than the simple tendencies among simple proportions in whole national populations.[44]

Looking first at research conducted in the United States, it is seen that political involvement increases systematically with age once the effects of sex and education are controlled.[45] Despite the fact that curvilinear tendencies have occasionally been seen in voter turnout in the United States, involvement attitudes at least seem to reflect the effects of a long-term political stability in their linearity, which contrasts sharply with the findings on Japan here.[46] This lends further support for the generational hypothesis emphasized here.

But in the case of the Federal Republic of Germany tendencies quite like those reported for Japan are once again evident. Moreover, the year groups in which old age is associated with political disengagement are comparable in both the Japanese and German findings.[47] The comparabilities in the tendencies among old people in Germany and Japan lend further support to the generational interpretation of the Japanese data, given the partial similarities between German and Japanese political history in the periods relevant to our analysis.

---

differences in the levels of educational attainment among different age groupings in the Japanese population — young people are much better-educated than their elders — and these might have contributed to the tendencies I have attributed to age. This was not the case according to the results of my multivariate analysis, and I concluded again that generational effects were the most important influence on the political attitudes of persons in different age groups.

[44] In other words, where the categories of the independent variable are comparable (as they are in the case of age), it is possible to compare youths with old people and others across nations without worrying much about minor differences in wording of questions. This is simply because in this case we are comparing *tendencies* rather than precise proportions. In contrast, even minor differences in questions may affect the simple proportions among whole populations.

[45] The data are reported in Glenn and Grimes (n. 2), especially p. 571; and, Angus Campbell, *et al.*, *The American Voter*.

[46] For turnout information see Crittenden (n. 2, above).

[47] See, for example, DIVO Institut, *Pressendienst*, November I–II 1964, p. 4.

Perhaps most important in an examination of Japanese political attitudes is the inescapable recognition that so-called "popular" political attitudes are remarkably predominant in most age groupings. Thus, majorities in most age groupings—both those for which I have supplied data as well as the intervening groups left out for the sake of simplicity — are usually more involved in politics than apathetic, while only those in the old grouping show markedly lower involvement. Although it is difficult to ascertain just which is significant, whether the proportion of involved or apathetic voters, it is clear that levels of at least political involvement attitudes among Japanese are not drastically different from those in other industrial societies, with the exception of the United States. Furthermore, it is important to note that even elderly voters in Japan report attitudes that suggest they have responded considerably to the potentialities of democracy. It is doubtful this would have occurred without the opportunities presented by postwar political changes in Japan.

8

MAN AND POLITICS IN POSTWAR JAPAN

The character of political life in postwar Japan displays many of the anticipated consequences of long-term political and social modernization, as well as the impact of some discontinuities in political experience and unexpected effects with regard to urbanization. Japan obviously ranks as one of the most developed nations in the world in industrialization, popular educational attainment and development of the mass media.[1] Modern Japan is also highly integrated politically, the result of events and policies covering several centuries. Nevertheless, *widespread* diffusion of the concepts of political democracy, along with related changes in political institutions, has come only comparatively recently. In addition, social life is less integrative in Japan's large cities than in the small hamlets of the surviving rural sector. Both

---

[1] I think it is much more important to examine Japanese popular attitudes toward politics as being representative of phenomena in modern industrial societies than as somehow conforming to general patterns in non-Western societies. Although some aspects of contemporary Japanese society certainly reflect the effects of recent emergence from a generally agrarian background, too many of the influences conditioning contemporary political attitudes reflect a degree of urbanization, industrialization and communications development not found outside of the most modern societies in the world today.

Data permitting assessments of the levels of modernization in Japan in a comparative frame of reference can be found at various points in Arthur S. Banks and Robert B. Textor, *A Cross-Political Survey* (Cambridge: M.I.T. Press, 1963); and, Bruce Russet *et al., World Handbook of Political and Social Indicators* (New Haven: Yale University Press, 1964), as well as in the Japanese statistical sources cited in Ch. 1.

Japan's high levels of modernization and her somewhat unique tendencies in experience and adaptation should be kept in mind as we examine the political attitudes of contemporary Japanese citizens, whether the focus is general attitude patterns or the tendencies within specific subgroups of the population.

Several central themes can be identified in the political attitudes of contemporary Japanese voters. In the first place, there is a clear hierarchy in the levels of popular political attitudes between responses indicating more abstract dimensions of political involvement and those suggesting predispositions to active engagement in politics beyond the act of voting. In response to a variety of questions substantial majorities of the Japanese electorate report that they feel politics is relevant, and it is clear that the typical voter is integrated into the world of politics in at least this way. Many contemporary Japanese also report that they find elections and politics a subject of personal interest. By contrast, only small minorities of the electorate are inclined to assume active roles in public affairs or would participate in collective activities in order to articulate demands and influence politicians' decisions. Most people would depend on leaders or simply rely on their vote in elections. In addition to large gaps between the levels of inclination to participate in politics beyond the vote and those of feelings that politics is relevant or interesting, there are also some substantial differences between the frequencies of feelings of relevance and interest — significant differences in levels of involvement are evident in even these comparatively abstract feelings. These comparative tendencies in involvement and participation attitudes among the Japanese population have been called *formalism*. By using this term I am focusing attention on the fact of the difference between people's inclination to report involvement in politics in response to fairly abstract questions and their comparative unwillingness to engage in politics in some active way. It is felt that these tendencies are especially significant in modern Japan, and reflect in part Japan's special political experience.[2]

Tendencies toward formalism reflect more than anything else disparities between learned and experiential components of political

---

[2] For a reasonably comparable use of the concept of formalism see Sidney Verba, "Germany: The Remaking of Political Culture," in Lucian W. Pye and Sidney Verba, *Political Culture and Political Development* (Princeton: Princeton University Press, 1969), pp. 147–152.

attitudes. Democratic ideas are quite new in Japan at the mass level, particularly outside of the major urban centers. Some attitudes which are considered corollaries of democratic political concepts are substantially evident, and this reflects the ease with which most Japanese have learned new political roles in a short period of time. The fact that Japan is highly integrated both politically and in its communications is presumably important here, since somewhat slower rates of adaptation might be anticipated were conditions otherwise.

But the national experience with democratic institutions and processes is still very short, and it is certainly plausible that contemporary formalism reflects the residual effects of earlier political attitudes and experiences in Japan. For one thing, we can see that the implication of duty in the vote is strong in postwar Japan, despite changes in the content of political socialization between the prewar period and the present. This testifies to the strength and continuity of some kinds of attitudes toward politics, and it is possible that the prevalence of "subject" or dependency attitudes toward politics (presumably characteristic of the prewar period) has some residual influence today. The fact that quite a few people would "depend on a politician" is direct evidence, of course, of some continuity in attitudes, and it is assumed that there is also considerable connection between feelings of this kind and replies to survey questions that referred directly to predispositions toward political activism. Although formalism is found in other countries in varying degrees, the influence of prewar political styles is still of considerable importance in modern Japan and may result in a greater disconnection between abstract political involvement and activism than is the case in some other advanced nations.[3]

A second central theme in Japanese voters' political attitudes is that of *ambivalence*. On the one hand, majorities of voters in the early 1960s reported they believed in the effectiveness of ordinary people's vote or that interest in politics acts as a restraint on the conduct of political affairs. Indeed, popular feelings about political efficacy in

---

[3] As pointed out earlier, one can clearly see narrower gaps between somewhat comparable attitudes in both the United States and Great Britain. Moreover, the fact that formalism is even more pronounced in the cities than in the rural districts in Japan means that the tendencies are especially important in Japan compared to other countries.

Japan compare quite favorably with tendencies in other industrialized nations. On the other hand, Japanese voters were generally much less optimistic where other kinds of assessments of politics were concerned. Majorities of respondents showed either little satisfaction or outright dissatisfaction with the way politics is conducted. Similarly, feelings were very common that elections contribute little to the improvement of politics, and many voters were of the opinion that politicians do not keep promises or are not responsive to people's wants. Finally, most voters felt that they were personally incapable of understanding what goes on in politics.[4]

An ambivalent appraisal of politics and the way in which it is conducted undoubtedly reflects in part different tendencies between learned and experiential components of attitudes. If we use the term "learning" here to specifically designate the development of an awareness of democratic concepts and symbols through formal educational experiences or exposure to the mass media, we can see how it is possible for majorities of the electorate in a highly developed country like Japan to acquire a familiarity with some democratic ideas in a fairly short period of time. In contrast with the comparative ease of internalization of democratic attitudes — such as abstract feelings about people's political efficacy — other kinds of positive evaluative feelings, more dependent on the nature of one's personal experience with politics, may develop more slowly. Many Japanese lack experience as active participants in politics, and this presumably is of some importance in their evaluation of political performance. Participation, in contrast with mere awareness, might lead to greater feelings of confidence. Of even more importance is the fact that in Japan there is no tradition of popular participation in politics such as that which persists in the United States, at least folkloristically (even in the face of massive urbanization and associated declines in actual opportunities for effective participation).

But we should look further for the roots of negativism and

---

[4] Somewhat comparable patterns exist in other industrial countries, with the exception of the United States. But I feel that the tendencies in Japan are especially significant, in view of the fact that ambivalence is most prevalent among urban and well-educated persons—both types are expected by most social scientists to play special roles in political modernization and the development of democracy. As a case in point, see John J. Johnson, *Political Change in Latin America: The Emergence of the Middle Sectors* (Stanford: Stanford University Press, 1958).

ambivalence in popular political attitudes in Japan, since tendencies within subgroups of the population may be of special significance above and beyond the kinds of influences found among the population as a whole. The prevalence in Japan of pessimism toward political activity has conspicuous roots in some kinds of voters' reactions to past and present norms as well as contemporary political reality. Negative feelings are especially common among better-educated and more informed voters, a fact which reflects their more frequent attention to media criticism of contemporary politicians' behavior. The more politically aware voter also has a highly idealistic conception of the kind of behavior that should be found among democratic leaders, which is then a normative basis for negative assessments in many cases. Moreover, highly demanding criteria in the evaluation of official conduct reflects the peculiar intensity born of the newness of democratic ideas, as well as the influence of more traditional assumptions about the desirability of selfless motives in political leaders. Many aware and better-educated persons are also deeply suspicious of a potential for reversion to the authoritarianism of earlier periods, although this suspicion may be associated as much as anything else simply with support for political parties which oppose the majoritarian Liberal-Democrats (a conservative group). Finally, these same persons are also extremely self-conscious about whether Japanese politics conforms to their own concepts of modernity and traditionalism, and in many cases they condemn politicians' behavior on the basis of the fact that political elites frequently adhere to older social customs in seeking support (through demonstrations of largesse and close contacts with local influentials).

But many Japanese also feel that they lack close connections with politics or politicians, and so feel pessimistic or distrustful. Although politics is often remote from the daily lives of ordinary people in other industrialized societies, it is important to remember that Japanese evaluative attitudes are particularly sensitive to the impact of social distance, in view of the fundamental importance of personal connections in Japanese life. The effects of social isolation are especially visible in the urban sector, but feelings of this kind may also be found in certain rural districts.[5] Moreover, hierarchical social structures are

---

[5] The critical kind of isolation, in my view, is that of separation from contacts with local influentials and politicians in a society where personalism still prevails as a general cultural value. Although it would be easy to refer to more general claims

still important in Japanese life, even in the face of egalitarian influences in both the prewar and postwar periods. Feelings of social distance related to acceptance of status differences may also contribute to feelings of remoteness from political affairs and thus contribute to attitudes of pessimism at times.

A third major theme in contemporary Japanese political attitudes is *localism*. Most respondents indicated that they are most interested in local politics or find local politics most relevant to their lives, where questions directly compared the importance of national and local affairs. More voters reported that local politics is easy to understand than felt the same about national politics. The same is true of evaluations of ordinary people's efficacy and estimates of the responsiveness of politicians in either local or national affairs. That this is the case in both urban and rural districts is even more striking, given the urban tendency toward greater involvement in national affairs. Finally, concern for satisfaction of local interests is a major component of both general feelings about wants from politics and voting attitudes, although sentiments of this kind are much more important in the rural areas than in large cities.

The prevalence of localist concerns of one kind or another is especially important in that modern Japan is a highly integrated political system, and regional differences are much less important than in France or Italy, for example. Sentiments of this kind have two basic origins. On the one hand, integration into local community life is very high in the rural sector, and this is associated both with high levels of interest and involvement in local affairs and with feelings of community exclusivism and competition, particularly with respect to instrumental concerns. But localist feelings are also prevalent in small cities in Japan. Although community life in small cities does not necessarily have the same intensity of involvement or the same levels of

---

about the alienative effects of urban society in general, I am consciously trying to avoid this. In the first place, there are various social networks of an integrative kind outside of the neighborhood in contemporary cities, as commentaries on urban life in Japan quite clearly show. Secondly, we have no real evidence about the basic and unchanging needs of people for intimate ties with society, even though some theorists feel such a need exists, and social alienation may be more a matter of individual psychology than it is an inevitable concomitant of urban life. But the fact remains that Japanese politics is above all a politics of local "connections," and individuals who lack "contacts" appear to feel somewhat differently from those who do, other things being equal.

feelings of exclusivism and competition that exist in the more compact and isolated rural hamlets, it is evident that neighborhood life in provincial urban centers has some similarities to rural life. These similarities are in fact reflected in tendencies in political attitudes.[6]

The prevalence of localist sentiments in Japan also reflects the distance between ordinary people's lives and especially national politics that characterizes life in both the urban and the rural sectors of Japan today. Personal connections are especially important in Japan, and people's feelings of familiarity are often limited by the scope of their own personal interactions.

The fourth theme in Japanese political attitudes is *personalism*. Rural voters reported a greater concern for "candidate" than for "party" at all election levels. Parties are typically more important to voters in the cities, but even here candidates are given more consideration than parties in local contests, even though parties are comparatively active in urban local elections. The importance of personalism in Japanese voting attitudes reflects again the importance of personal connections in daily life.[7] It is also associated with traditional tendencies toward dependence of paternalistic leaders for representation of interests, especially since there seems to be some interconnection between instrumental concerns and emphasis on "candidate" in particularly local elections. Finally, the centrality of candidates to voting-choice may be the result of the prevalence of negative images and distrust of political parties. It is also possible that the weak consideration given to parties (in contrast to the emphasis on candidate) reflects a disinclination to identify strongly with comparatively remote secondary groupings.[8]

Regarding urban-rural and generational variations in political attudes, I tested a number of hypotheses about the effects of group membership (an indicator for social involvement) and education (one of the important variables in modernization theory). At this time I will

---

[6] For the sake of simplicity, I have not included the data which support this observation in the various tables on urban-rural differences. For evidence the reader is referred to any of the Kōmei Senkyo Remmei national studies cited previously.

[7] Personalism in political choice also reflects the characteristic modes of mobilizing voter support in Japan. See Ch. 5.

[8] Obviously, this suggests some especially interesting possibilities for future research and contributions to comparative understanding of the role of secondary groups in people's political behavior.

review some of these interpretations and present summary hypotheses about the effects of certain factors critical to attitude formation, even though there are some inevitable oversimplifications in an analysis that depends on only two variables. Tendencies in group membership and education are two of the most important threads in my interpretation, and I wish to indicate their contribution to political attitudes here while still recognizing the importance of other considerations discussed in previous chapters.

It will be remembered that there were substantial differences in levels of social involvement between urban and rural voters and among different ages. Higher levels of membership in groups were reported by rural residents than by urban residents, which reflects, of course, major differences in social structure. Middle-aged voters were more involved in group activities than both young and old persons, although old voters were more commonly members of groups than were youths. In the case of both rural residents and middle-aged voters, and sometimes old persons, it was hypothesized that a comparatively higher level of social involvement was related to the tendency to be involved in local politics, to manifest an inclination to participate in local political affairs and to feel optimistic toward politics.

With some qualifications, multivariate analysis showed this to be the case. Social involvement is thus one of the core variables in Japanese political attitudes, even though its effect is greatest on attitudes toward local politics. It is especially important that we keep this local focus of its effect in mind in view of the fact that social involvement may have different implications in distinctive political cultural settings — at least this is the suggestion of my own review of the literature on organizational membership in different countries. Variation in group membership in Japan is most closely associated with tendencies in integration into local community life, with membership in specifically locally oriented groups (in contrast with groups having strong external ties) being especially common. This may not always be the case in other countries, even though social involvement seems to be generally important to attitude formation, or actual participation, in many countries.[9]

Earlier, the consequences of modernization was associated with sectoral tendencies in educational attainment and mass media exposure. In so doing, however, I was careful to avoid the impression of attempting to evaluate processes of change by examining only contemporary evidence. At the same time, I felt there was some legitimacy in juxtaposing models of individual attitude formation posited in modernization theory with the hard data of the effects of urbanization (and other correlatives of modernization) on attitudes in Japan. Thus, we might see whether political culture at the sectoral level in modern Japan conformed to expectations of modernization theory about individual level attitudes.

By and large, this part of my analysis showed two kinds of results. The sectoral distribution of educational attainment, and probably mass media exposure in some cases, actually underlay many of the urban-rural differences in attitudes toward national affairs. In other words, residence was of little importance for attitudes toward national politics in most instances, once the effects of education were controlled. This tendency markedly contrasted with the contrary effects of residence and social involvement on urban-rural attitudes toward local politics, and identification of these countervailing trends constitutes a path-breaking development in the study of attitude formation in Japan.

Secondly, and of equal importance, was the fact that educational achievement and urban residence were associated with especially pronounced patterns of ambivalence in evaluative attitudes. Since modernization in Japan can be identified with these phenomena, it is possible to conclude that modern life in Japan has become politically both alienative and integrative at the same time. This has especially important implications for theories of social modernization and political behavior.

In the past, one of the limitations of political culture analysis has been the a priori assumption that political attitudes have specific behavioral consequences, without any attempt to demonstrate that this is the case in reality. In order to obviate this shortcoming in the presen-

---

[9] The importance of social involvement (or organizational membership) as a major factor directly influencing patterns of political participation has recently been established in cross-national research, and is reported in Norman H. Nie, G. Bingham Powell, Jr., and Kenneth Prewitt, "Social Structure and Political Participation: Developmental Relationships," *American Political Science Review* 63 (June and September 1969), pp. 361–378 and 808–832.

tation here, I subjected the findings of my own 1964 survey to some additional bivariate and multivariate statistical analyses, with the purpose of establishing the links between different kinds of political attitudes and actual participation. Since the nature and sources of political participation form a separate major inquiry — in regard to which my data also had some limitations — only a brief analysis of a few relationships was attempted.[10] In particular, the aim was to see if any of the categories of attitudes discussed here had any import for behavior, either as independent influences or in terms of the residual effects of each with controls for all other attitudes. I also pursued the question of whether the sectoral distribution of attitudes had anything to do with the rural predominance in actual participation observed in Japan. Since most of the kinds of participation were measured with dichotomized questions, I again employed the Coleman effect parameter analysis.

Following the practice established in recent studies of political participation, behavior was viewed as differentiated.[11] Five kinds of participation were analyzed — voting in national and local elections, paying attention to political campaigns, discussing politics at election time, asking officials or political leaders to take care of some demand, and solicitation of the votes of others — with the following results (Table 8-1):

1. Attitudes reflecting psychological involvement and optimism were more important to the more active forms of participation, such as paying attention to campaigns (including attending speeches) or discussing politics, than to voting. By contrast, going out to vote depended more on motivations based on feelings of duty about the vote itself, the perception that neighbors were going out to vote or, to some degree, interest in political matters.[12]

---

[10] The fact that the sample was local was one of the limitations, although it should be noted that the results reported hereafter by and large conform to Jōji Watanuki's path analysis of the relation between attitudes and participation for Japan. See Watanuki, "Social Structure and Political Participation in Japan," Report No. 32 of the Laboratory for Political Research, University of Iowa, May 1970.

[11] See Sidney Verba, Norman H. Nie and Jae-on Kim, "The Modes of Democratic Participation: A Cross-National Comparison," *Comparative Politics Series* 2 (1971), Report 01-013, especially pp. 9–19.

[12] The measure of perceptions of voting habits of their neighbors was included in my survey in order to verify the often-emphasized role of social conformism in Japanese voter turnout. Obviously, this conventional wisdom about Japanese behavior is quite correct.

TABLE 8-1. POLITICAL CULTURE AND POLITICAL PARTICIPATION, MULTIVARIATE RELATIONSHIPS

	Residence	Interest	Concern	Responsiveness	Efficacy	Relevance	Comprehension	Wants	Civic Duty	Neighbor's Vote
National I										
Turnout	−.144	−.139	−.145	−.141	−.144	−.144	−.148	−.128	−.151	−.117
Campaign Attention	−.149	−.135	−.156	−.144	−.151	−.172	−.165	−.092		
Discussion	.011	.022	.006	.018	.011	.009	−.010	.014		
Articulation	−.104	−.116	−.121	−.105	−.108	−.123	−.114	−.095		
Solicitation	−.103	−.099	−.105	−.103	−.103	−.107	−.106	−.076		
Local I										
Turnout	−.128	−.112	−.125	−.119	−.128	−.127	−.120	−**.081**	−.123	−.033
Campaign Attention	−.236	−.172	−.222	−.188	−.237	−.236	−.200	−.161		
Discussion	−.167	−.136	−.161	−.145	−.168	−.167	−.151	−.129		
Articulation	−.104	−.085	−.111	−.120	−.112	−.092	−.092	−.095		
Solicitation	−.097	−.088	−.097	−.105	−.098	−.097	−.088	−**.080**		
National II										
Turnout	−.128	.084	−.010	.030	—	−.068	—	.024	.142	.077
Campaign Attention	−.136	.217	.151	.058	.107	**.041**	.011	.017		
Discussion	.017	.148	.214	.097	.100	.100	*.752*	.098		
Articulation	−.154	.176	.223	.023	.057	.079	.013	.096		
Solicitation	−.094	.713	.099	−.013	−.066	−.002	.005	.080		
Local II										
Turnout	−.016	−.042	.112	−.005	—	.006	—	.042	.152	.188
Campaign Attention	−.157	.221	**.063**	.057	.116	.076	.002	.054		
Discussion	−.104	*.705*	*.719*	−.020	.060	.073	.013	−.004		
Articulation	−.084	.012	.082	.063	−.005	.222	*.127*	.068		
Solicitation	−.103	−.007	.009	−.124	.082	.077	.045	.049		

Based on a Coleman multivariate analysis. Figures under National I and Local I are the effects of residence, or residence with controls, for various attitudes. Comparison of the bivariate relationship between residence and participation, and the effect-index of residence when attitude levels are controlled, provides a basis for determining whether sectoral patterns in political culture are important as a linking factor between residence and participation.

National II and Local II present multivariate effect-indexes where all variables are simultaneously controlled, and show the overall importance of each attitude and of residence.

(For an explanation of bold and italic figures, see notes in Table 6-11.)

2. Being psychologically involved in politics — especially being interested in politics — contributed more to participation than optimistic evaluative attitudes. (Evaluative attitudes may be extremely important for some participants, and the pessimism prevailing in Japan could be the basis for political extremism when other unidentifiable conditions are present. Alternatively, evaluative attitudes may be especially important at times of crisis. But evaluative attitudes do not affect ordinary people's participation at ordinary times as much as involvement attitudes.)

3. Urban-rural patterns in attitudes contributed little in the way of reducing the effect of residence on participation, at least where participation in national elections or participation directed toward the national political sphere was concerned. However, the urban-rural attitude patterns did influence participation at the local level. The fact that rural voters were more involved and more optimistic about local political life was, in fact, the basis for their greater participation in local politics in contrast with persons living in the cities.

What this means is simply that many rural people participated in national elections without being motivated by feelings that politics was interesting or that their vote would influence what goes on in politics. The fact that rural people were more duteous had a slight effect, and their concern for having their interests represented (designated as "wants" in Table 8–1) was also instrumental in voting turnout. Still, the prevailing idea among observers of Japanese politics that the vote is influenced heavily by the efforts of local influentials and others to get a high turnout is probably largely valid for national elections. But this is not the case with respect to local politics, where participation is typically attributable to identifiable attitude structures.

These results, while cursory in nature, tell us something about the importance of political culture for political behavior in Japan. We can see clearly that political culture attitudes, which have been the subject of this book, are in fact relevant for participation in politics. Secondly, it is clear that some kind of political attitudes may have more direct and visible effects on behavior than others. At least this is the implication of my findings, which indicate that political involvement attitudes are more commonly associated with becoming active participants in politics than evaluative attitudes. Finally, it is clear that political culture attitudes may affect participation of some kinds more than others

— participation beyond the act of voting in national politics is an example here. It is important to keep each of these observations in mind in reviewing the importance of the configurations of attitudes I have described.

In my introductory statements I said that I would give special attention to the question of the visible impact on political attitudes of postwar democratic reforms in Japan. Although I wish to avoid unnecessary repetition of details discussed earlier, it is advantageous here to recapitulate some observations.

The postwar epoch in Japan witnessed an emphasis on democratization in both school curricula and political institutions that was unprecedented in the political development of Japan. To be sure, there was substantial interest in popular government in Japan at various times between the Meiji Restoration and World War II. But in the prewar period concern for democratic reform was more fragmentary than that of more recent years, in addition to being confined to a comparatively narrow sector of the population — mainly some elites and better informed people. Some exponents of democracy in prewar Japan also were more interested in advancing their own group or regional interests through the device of a pluralistic parliamentary polity than they were in pervasive egalitarian reforms. Thus, democracy as a major theme in political rhetoric and as an explicit goal of reform policies which were widespread in scope is a conspicuously *postwar* phenomenon. Even though the long process of social and political change accompanying modernization in Japan undoubtedly created an especially receptive climate for the catalytic reforms of the postwar period, the postwar period is itself a major epoch in Japan's century of change, and can be seen as encompassing a separate set of causal influences where the attitudes of contemporary voters are concerned.

Three central tendencies can be seen in the attitudes of contemporary Japanese which reflect the effect of postwar democratization in Japan. First, levels of political involvement among Japanese voters in the early 1960s are often comparable with those in other highly industrial nations. The scope of contemporary involvement in Japan reflects in no small way the fact that earlier prewar policies, as well as the war itself, created a widespread awareness of national affairs and politics among most voters. Also significant in the fact that both the levels of educational attainment and the development of modern communications in Japan are comparable to conditions in the most advanced industrial nations. This is important, of course, inasmuch as educational attainment generally has been shown to be of special importance in the development of political knowledge and involvement attitudes. A similar causal nexus can be assumed between mass media development and stimulation of political awareness at the aggregate or societal level.

The second notable contribution of postwar democratization in Japan is the development of high levels of instrumental expectation regarding politics in the rural sector. This tendency is sustained by the special character of rural community life and leadership. Indeed, some kinds of instrumental attitudes were to be found there before the war, but it is quite clear that rural political pragmatism reflects at least in part the favorable effects of postwar changes in the political climate. The consistently high incidence of instrumentalism evident in rural districts today could only be nurtured in an environment where democratic representation is a part of popular conceptions of the political process, and explicit in the rhetoric and action of political figures.

Finally, postwar democratization has had a somewhat contradictory effect on the attitudes of urban resident and many youths. Formal learning of democratic concepts in the postwar era has been associated with a comparatively high incidence of both some kinds of psychological involvement (including knowledge of politics) and critical evaluations of the conduct of political affairs among particularly young voters and those residing in the cities. Comparatively high levels of education and exposure to the mass media seem to be closely associated with these tendencies among youths and urban residents in the early 1960s, in ways I have specified earlier.[13] Diffusion of democratic concepts obviously can have alienative effects under certain conditions — it remains to be seen how long these manifestations of transition will be characteristic of the outlooks of important social groups in Japan's population.

Here it would be appropriate to conclude with a general assessment of the prospects of popular democracy in Japan, although it must

---

[13] These comments are made on the basis of relationships between levels of involvement and pessimism and education and media communications exposure among different subgroups of the sampled populations, and should be tested in the future at the individual level.

be recognized that any such assessment is inevitably highly speculative. To begin, we might conclude that Japan is only partially democratized at present, and that in many ways the electorate in Japan today manifests the symptoms of political transition; tendencies toward formalism and ambivalence are reflections of this transition, and indicate in many instances the newness of democratic concepts to the Japanese voter. However, it is possible that formalism and ambivalence will remain as major characteristics of Japanese political attitudes, given the fact that these tendencies are more pronounced in the urban sector than in the country, and urbanization can be expected to continue for the foreseeable future (even if in the form of the development of regional cities, which the Japanese government prefers).

Although we obviously need more precise measures to tell how much involvement is desirable for the successful working of a democratic system, it would seem that if the electorate is to play the role of guardian of its own interests, the Japanese electorate is somewhat more passive in attitude than is optimally desirable. This condition, too, may continue in the foreseeable future. However, high levels of pragmatism in rural Japan, where a strong sense of local self-interest seems to have developed, may sharpen the sensitivity of political leaders to the importance of representation in at least that sector.[14]

It is equally important to speculate about the future stability of democratic politics in Japan. In this case the rather high level of cynicism in at least the urban sector does not bode well for the future, since feelings of this kind could in some circumstances result in support for antidemocratic movements.[15] Indeed, the fact that the major support for the Kōmeito has so far come from the urban sector may be a reflection of the isolation from politics and associated negativism found in the urban population, although it would not be correct to

---

[14] Many observers of Japanese politics feel that this has already occurred, and some critics even feel that there is already too much representation of rural interests at the expense of others.

[15] The cynicism found among Japanese youths is important here, and obviously may be a correlative of participation in radical student movements. Unfortunately the materials used here did not lend themselves to further investigation of these important matters. It is a well-known fact that the number of student activists appearing in general population samples is substantially below the frequencies actually necessary for satisfactory statistical analysis. (Student activists, moreover, are not identified as such.)

say that this group is specifically antidemocratic in attitude.[16] But we lack information about the stability over time of individuals' partisan inclinations in Japan, and this would certainly be important in any assessment of future trends in partisan support. In other words, we need to know the limits to which new groups may be able to find supporters free from other attachments.

The fact that involvement among urban residents is somewhat formalistic and low in intensity might mean the chances for urban support of antidemocratic movements are low in the future, simply because people who are only superficially involved would not become attached to any kinds of movements. (But many scholars feel that mass movements mobilize support from people who are normally apathetic.) By contrast, attitudes in the rural areas in some ways seem more favorable to stability, given higher levels of optimism toward the political process and widespread instrumentalist attitudes. Finally, we cannot yet tell whether a drastic change in the future economic condition of Japan might not have an unstabilizing effect. Obviously, precise prediction of the future is impossible without knowledge of the large number of conditions that cannot at present be identified.

Given the comparatively short history of democratic processes and ideas in Japan, the overall picture may be quite salutary. Perhaps the most important conclusion to be drawn is that some democratic concepts can be internalized at the mass level in a relatively short period of time.[17] But, as in the case of other countries with a longer history of

---

[16] Support for the Kōmeito, as distinct from support for the Soka Gakkai religion, presumably is the result of widespread proselytizing in election campaigns as well as of the presence of cynicism or other political attitudes. As a case in point, the *only* campaign workers who had attempted to mobilize the vote in a white collar *danchi* I studied in Yokohama were from the Kōmeito; their efforts were obviously directed at a larger public than the membership of the Sōka Gakkai. It should also be noted that the Kōmeito places special stress on "clean government" and "pure motivations" in its electoral appeals, and while this accords with the religious perspective of the Sōka Gakkai, the potentially wider appeal of such policies is obvious.

[17] I have found that a similarly favorable assessment can be made of the Federal Republic of Germany, on the basis of time-series data that permit examination of adaptational processes over most of the postwar period. Unfortunately, the sanguine outlook afforded by my evidence on these two countries still is somewhat separated from reality in at least one sense. We lack evidence on the depth and stability of cultural attitudes in any country, and "de-democratization" could conceivably occur as fast as democratization. Indeed, the emergent cynicism evidenced by recent research in the United States is a case in point in support of this pessimistic possibility.

democratic institutions, speculation about future tendencies in the behavior of mass electorates must remain highly qualified. The study of political culture reported here should contribute to an improvement in the knowledge of mass attitudes in Japan. At a future date, when other studies are completed, speculation about the long-term tendencies of mass publics will be better-informed than it is today.

APPENDIX: POLITICAL BEHAVIOR RESEARCH IN JAPAN

Since the end of World War II public opinion research has flourished in Japan as it has in many other modern industrialized nations. Research on political behavior by professional polling groups, newspapers and individual scholars has developed dramatically since the early postwar era, and a large number of polls in each year either include political questions or are specifically focused on political behavior. Indeed, it is possible to say that in a certain sense political behavior has been better researched in postwar Japan than in most other countries. In the following paragraphs the general patterns of this research in recent years are outlined and, using my own survey experience as an example, some special considerations in the conduct of individual field research within Japanese culture will be discussed.

One of the major sponsors of political survey research in the postwar period has been the Japanese newspaper industry. The major national newspapers — *Asahi, Mainichi* and *Yomiuri* — have conducted polls at election time on political attitudes and voting intentions and have included political questions in more general public opinion surveys or in studies of topics other than politics. The three major national newspapers have been joined in these efforts by other newspapers or newspaper related groups, such as the *Jiji* interests, Chūbu Nihon Shimbun, the Shimbun Yoron Chōsa Remmei and Kyōdō Tsūshin.

Surveys conducted by the Japanese newspapers provide a special kind of research source of value to the social scientist. In addition to special studies conducted at election times, newspapers have afforded time-series data on such topics as party support and evaluation of governments and cabinets. While limited in scope to a fairly narrow range of questions, the evolution of Japanese public opinion in the postwar era can be traced at least in regard to this narrow range. However, with the exception of results included in the comprehensive anthologies cited below, the published findings of newspaper polls are unfortunately limited. To be sure, marginals are often published in the newspaper sponsoring the survey, and in some cases results are broken down by socioeconomic categories. But in many cases these highly desirable socioeconomic breakdowns are not published, and the researcher's only recourse is to seek access to private files in the research offices of various newspaper companies. Furthermore, results of newspaper polls are not widely available for secondary computer analysis (the Roper archive does have some data sets from polls from the 1960s). Nevertheless, findings from newspaper polls do provide an important time-series data base which could be analyzed by scholars interested in the narrow range of topics normally covered. In particular, they would be especially useful for cross-national analyses of the effects of various events and policies on popular evaluation of governments and parties, since time-series information on directly comparable topics has been collected by major American polling groups, British Gallup and National Opinion Polls, the Institut Francaise d'Opinion Publique, and German groups such as EMNID, Demoskopie or DIVO.

A second kind of political survey in postwar Japan has been sponsored by the Kōmei Senkyo Remmei (Fair Election League). The Kōmei Senkyo Remmei has by now conducted over five hundred studies at the national, prefectural or local level. The findings of these studies are normally issued in privately circulated reports, with local studies emanating under the authorship of the various Senkyo Kanri Iinkai (Election Administration Committees), whose activities are closely linked with those of the Remmei. The Remmei and Senkyo Kanri Iinkai reports have the special advantage of including a fairly wide range of cultural and behavioral information of a political nature; the results are generally from replicative studies and are broken down by socioeconomic groupings. These are the main source of data for my aggregate analysis in this book, and while limited by the fact that in most instances secondary computer analysis cannot be conducted, these surveys still form the largest body of replicative survey findings on political culture in the world today. While it is certainly true that scholarly research on political behavior is substantially more developed in the United States than in Japan, still the Remmei findings afford a level of descriptive generalization rarely afforded by either scholarly or nonscholarly efforts in other nations.

Thirdly, the Japanese Prime Minister's Office and various individual ministries have conducted periodic polls on national political topics, as well as more specialized questions such as local autonomy and regional development. These polls have often been conducted by the Chūō Chōsasha, and in several cases include question items which duplicate those used by the Kōmei Senkyo Remmei. This reflects in part the close cooperation between the Remmei and various agencies of the government, particularly the Autonomy Ministry. But some replication may also reflect the fact that the Chūō Chōsasha, a major commercial polling group, conducts the national surveys for the Kōmei Senkyo Remmei. Data sets from several surveys conducted by the Chūō Chōsasha for the government or for the Remmei are now available from the Roper Public Opinion Archive in Williamstown, Massachusetts. Since the sample frames used by the Chūō Chōsasha are carefully selected, these materials should be of special interest to the American scholar interested in conducting secondary computer research on some aspects of Japanese political culture or political behavior.

A fourth source of political research in postwar Japan is the variety of projects by individual scholars and research groups, within both universities and private research institutes. The latter category includes the Tōkei Sūri Kenkyūjo of Tōkyō, which has been associated with the ongoing time-series study of Japanese national character. Various reports from this research have been cited earlier; information from this project can be found in these and other reports available from the Kenkyūjo, or in various published books and articles by Chikio Hayashi and Shigeki Nishihira, among others.

Various surveys have emanated from the sociology faculties and social science institutes of Tōkyō and Kyōto universities. Following the pioneering activities of Masamichi Royama, researchers have included Hajime Ikeuchi and Jōji Watanuki among many others. The *Shimbun Kenkyūjo Kiyō* of the Institute of Journalism, Tōkyō University, contains the results of some of these surveys, but the reader should refer to the sources below in order to find specific items from the growing scholarly literature on political behavior in Japan.

The research project conducted in Uji, in the environs of Kyōto, by a team of social scientists from the University of Kyōto merits special attention. By singling out this project I do not mean to imply that there are not many other worthwhile scholarly efforts, but there are reasons for commenting on this project in particular. Led by Ichirō Miyaki, Tomio Kinoshita and Toshichi Aiba, this research incorporated the panel technique and various elements of the social psychological model of the Michigan Survey Research Center into a study wherein a large complex of attitudes — focusing alternatively on local, prefectural and national politics — are compared.

Finally, it should be noted that much scholarly research on political behavior has been conducted by scholars in the regional universities of Japan. Prominent in this area are Masao Sōma of Chiba, Tadao Sakuma of Tōhoku, Takeshi Shibuya of Niigata, Kanji Naitō of Kyūshū, and Seiji Yamada and Eiichi Yamaoka of Shimane. Many of the research efforts originated by these scholars have been reported by the Kōmei Senkyo Remmei, both in their local reports issued under the auspices of the various Senkyo Kanri Iinkai and in the 1966 and 1967 coordinated research series reports issued by the Remmei's Tōkyō office.

There are several sources of information on the content or location of Japanese research findings on topics of political culture and behavior. Allan B. Cole and Naomichi Nakanishi have assembled a large number of findings from various newspaper and other polls in *Japanese Public Opinion Polls with Socio-Political Significance, 1947–57*. Also important as a source of selected poll findings on political topics from the period of the early 1950s onward is the series *Zenkoku Yoron Chōsa no Genkyō*, issued annually by the Secretariat of the Prime Minister's Office. In addition to reporting various results in the form of marginals, this series lists all known public opinion surveys conducted in each of the years since this coverage began. Finally, of major importance to Western scholars is the bibliography on Japanese political culture and political behavior research currently being compiled by Douglas Johnson of American University. This work will include major studies conducted outside the academic community.

In the early postwar period concern was expressed in various circles about possible problems in conducting surveys on political matters among the Japanese. In particular, observers of Japanese society were concerned that either the assumed unfamiliarity of the Japanese masses with politics or special rural sensitivities toward revealing community voting practices might make the conduct of accurate surveys particularly difficult. To be sure, there may be other problems of interviewer or response bias in Japanese surveys, but the converging nature of the findings reported here as well as those in the Cole and Nakanishi work and the *Zenkoku Yoron Chōsa no Genkyō* serve to disprove pessimistic expectations to a considerable degree.

The conduct of large scale national research efforts by Ward and Kubota and the Verba-Ikeuchi group — whose findings are still largely in the stage of analysis — also witness to the viability of survey research in Japan. Large numbers of surveys have in fact been competently and scientifically conducted. It would be inappropriate to say therefore that special characteristics of Japanese society are somehow uncongenial to political behavior research.

Nevertheless, the foreign scholar may encounter some special difficulties in conducting field research in Japan, particularly if he endeavors to conduct interviews himself or with his own interviewing staff. To be sure, these problems are often only variants of those typically discussed in books on methodology based on American research experience. Nevertheless, the scholar who conducts his own field inquiries will probably meet certain difficult situations resulting either from his being foreign or from concentrating his effort, if he chooses, within a limited geographical area. Some of those problems are broached in the following paragraphs on the basis of my own field experience. The discussion will also serve to indicate the various assumptions and motivations underlying my study.

One of the main objectives of my own research was to indicate the character of political culture in different known types of community situations in postwar Japan. Accordingly, nine different localities were chosen for investigation. These included four districts in the city of Yokohama and five hamlets located in two rural locations. In the city of Yokohama samples were drawn from among the white-collar class residents of a new apartment block, from two *"shitamachi,"* or "downtown" areas, where small shops and industries abound, and from among the members of a shipyard labor union and their wives. Two rural environments were chosen for comparison with Yokohama. A rapidly industrializing flatland farm village, located some fifty minutes by train west of Tōkyō and Yokohama, was selected as representative of both flatland farm areas and industrializing rural communities. Within this community three hamlets with varying degrees of proximity to industrializing influences and train lines were chosen for special investigation. In Shimane prefecture, five hundred miles southwest of Tōkyō, where there has been practically no industrialization since the war (and where prewar industrial development was very scanty), I chose an upland farm village in an area noted for its traditional and "feudal" characteristics. Two hamlets, one a small commercial center, the other an isolated, pure agricultural community, were chosen. Within each of these areas a random sample was selected from the election registers.

As in any research design, strategic decisions had to be made regarding choices of emphasis and method. It was decided to ask large number of open questions, which was expected to have several advantages. More topics could be covered by using many questions, and it would be relatively easier to carry out what might be termed an "anthropological" examination of various factors in social context and political behavior. Secondly, voter attitudes and behavior could be examined from enough aspects to be able to detect formalistic answers — this was in part a reaction to the formalistic replies I had seen in other studies. A total of 166 questions and follow-up probes were asked.

I also felt that background information on local political and social contexts would be useful in later analysis of survey replies. Hence, my explanation of the findings is based in part on interviews with local politicians, community (hamlet and neighborhood association) leaders and group or union officials, from whom information on local tradition, patterns of political support and organization, and cetera, was sought.

Attitudinal measures corresponding to those found elsewhere as well as voluntary comments which showed the range of content of particular opinions were sought in the general survey. Given the rapid social and economic change of recent years, as well as the possible tenacity of certain traditional feelings in some areas, it was felt that

APPENDIX 253

formal questions about what are believed to be traditional or democratic values would not be reliable indicators of actual attitudes in many instances. In other words, considerable knowledge about the dimensions and varying contents of different attitudes had to be gathered. Consequently, it was felt that the immediate task was as much one of identification as of measurement, and questions were chosen so as to conform with this assumption. (Findings from open-ended questions of the kind indicated have been reported throughout this book, particularly with respect to the content of interest in politics.)

As is the case in many research projects, there were special problems inherent in both the nature of the subject and the location of research. Politics is probably less central to people's lives in Japan than, for example, in the United States. (This is not meant to be a value judgment, since it is my impression that much of the political interest among American voters is spectator motivated, and as such may have less system impact than the instrumentalism found in some sectors in Japan.) Japanese attitudes towards politics or self-assessments of personal motivations may therefore be more casual or superficial than among people who are, in certain senses, more "politicized." Also, because of dependence upon group consensus in the place of individual decisions, the Japanese may in many cases be unable to discuss their motivations concretely. One has the impression that many respondents were taken by surprise by the content of some of the questions, in that they had been asked questions they had never really thought about. This seemed to be the case more in the city than in the country regarding voting attitudes, while the reverse appeared to be the case regarding involvement attitudes at the national level. Urban respondents had great difficulty in recalling the person for whom they voted in an election held only two months prior to the survey. By contrast, rural respondents could in most cases identify the person they had supported, although in some cases this could have been more an indication of loyalties to a local politician than accurate recall of voting choices in the past election. Whatever the case, there may be greater error in describing what people really feel than would be the case where politics is viewed more intensely, whatever the motivation. Central trends are probably not distorted greatly, but there were certainly instances in my survey where people simply said whatever came into their mind at the moment rather than reporting firm opinions.

There is also much self-consciousness among respondents about what "should" be answered. There is a considerable attempt to please the other party in face-to-face encounters in Japan, and this is expressed by a desire to conform to the expectations of the person who is asking the questions. This obviously leads to questions of validity, especially when the interviewer or identified sponsor is American — and thus identified with "democracy" — or is introduced by a political figure. My emphasis on open-ended replies was partly motivated by a desire to obviate possible distortions in replies owing to respondents' knowing the sponsor's origin, as well as to avoid solely normative answers. Great care was also taken in obtaining introductions to local leaders in order that the survey not be identified with a particular political group or with the government.

Rural communities have traditionally been "closed," in many senses, to outsiders; rural people are believed to be somewhat reluctant to discuss their activities and opinions with investigators from outside the community. I did not find this to be a particularly serious problem, although some people were reluctant to answer questions. But this may have been as much a problem of embarrassment due to low confidence as of reluctance to talk for other reasons. Generally, there were greater problems of access in Nita, the upland village in Shimane, and this is reflected to some extent in the higher proportion of "don't know" answers from respondents there. But it was also evident that some people there were simply more poorly informed and politically unaware.

In my own interviews with informants and politicians I found considerable differences in willingness to talk — to some extent willingness depends upon the ease of the interviewer — but certain "types" of respondents could be identified. Some rural people were very reluctant to talk for fear of saying anything which would reflect upon their actions or the actions of others in the community, which might in any way be related to election violations. Others, as we have already suggested, were not articulate or were ignorant about some of the subjects which we studied. Others replied with a naive openness, which at first seemed incredible if greater reluctance or evasion was anticipated. Still others were delighted to have a chance to express their opinions, possibly because there was no apparent threat to their reputations.

Experience with interviewers was varied. In the beginning every attempt was made to use interviewers who had previous experience in surveys conducted by Japanese scholars. A few untrained interviewers were also used, and in some cases they were better in "open question" interviews than the experienced interviewers — the latter tended to record only an abbreviated version of answers to open questions, as their earlier experience had consisted of interviews generally using closed questions.

On the whole, I was pleased with the high degree of cooperation received from both local leaders and ordinary people. Indeed, in a few instances it was necessary to refuse voluntary interviews in order to maintain the integrity of the random preselected sample. While problems of validity were clearly present, as they inevitably are in survey situations, the checks built into the survey instrument and the methods used in pretest and application ensured only minimal errors.

SELECTED BIBLIOGRAPHY

The following bibliographical items constitute the basic survey materials used in this study. The entries include an abbreviated reference in parentheses, which is used throughout the text. All of the entries in this list are unpublished reports circulated within the Kōmei Senkyo Remmei and governmental channels.

Aichi ken Senkyo Kanri Iinkai, "Kōmei Senkyo no Jittai" (Aichi 1961)
———, "Senkyo Ishiki to Tōhyō Kōdō no Henyō" (Aichi 1963)
———, "Senkyo Ishiki to Kōmei Senkyo Undō" (Aichi 1964)
———, "Shimin Ishiki to Tōhyō Kōdō" (Aichi 1967)
Akita ken Senkyo Kanri Iinkai, "Kōmei Senkyo no Jittai" (Akita 1963)
Aomori ken Senkyo Kanri Iinkai, "Kōmei Senkyo Yoron Chōsa Kekka" (Aomori 1961)
———, "Kenmin to Seiji Ishiki" (Aomori 1962)
———, "Shūgiin Giin Sōsenkyo to Seron" (Aomori 1964)
Chiba ken Senkyo Kanri Iinkai, "Seiji Ishiki no Jittai Chōsa" (Chiba 1962)
———, "Senkyo Kōdō no Jittai Chōsa" (Chiba 1963)
Chūō Chōsasha, "Chōsa Hōkokusho, Sangiin Giin Senkyo ni tsuite no Seron Chōsa" (Chūō 1965)
Ehime ken Senkyo Kanri Iinkai, "Kōmei Senkyo Seron Chōsa no Kekka ni tsuite" (Ehime 1960)
———, "Kōmei Senkyo Seron Chōsa no Kekka ni tsuite" (Ehime 1961)
———, "Kōmei Senkyo Seron Chōsa no Kekka ni tsuite" (Ehime 1962)
Fukuoka ken Senkyo Kanri Iinkai, "Kōmei Senkyo Undō no Kōka Sokutei" (Fukuoka 1960A)
———, "Kiken no Jittai" (Fukuoka 1960B)
———, "Kiken no Jittai" (Sokuhō) (Fukuoka 1961)

―――, "Kōmei Senkyo no Machi ni okeru Seiji Ishiki" (Fukuoka 1964A)
―――, "Chikuhō Chiiki Jūmin no Seiji Ishiki" (Fukuoka 1964B)
―――, "Santanchi Jūmin no Seiji Ishiki" (Fukuoka 1964C)
―――, "Santan Chiiki Jūmin no Seiji Ishiki" (Fukuoka 1964D)
―――, "Moderu Chiku ni okeru Seiji Ishiki" (Fukuoka 1964E)
―――, "Toshi Fujin no Seiji Ishiki" (Fukuoka 1965)
Fukushima ken Senkyo Kanri Iinkai, "Kōmei Senkyo Yoron Chōsa no Kekka" (Fukushima 1961)
―――, "Fukushima ken ni okeru Seiji Ishiki ni kan suru Seron Chōsa Kekka" (Fukushima 1962)
―――, "Kōmei Senkyo Seron Chōsa Kekka — Chihō Senkyo no Jittai" (Fukushima 1963)
Gifu ken Senkyo Kanri Iinkai, "Senkyo to Kenmin no Seiji Ishiki" (Gifu 1963)
Gumma ken Senkyo Kanri Iinkai, "Gumma Kenmin no Seiji Ishiki to Tōhyō Kōdō" (Gumma 1962)
―――, "Kenmin no Seiji — Senkyo Ishiki" (Gumma 1963)
Hiroshima ken Senkyo Kanri Iinkai, "Senkyo Ishiki ni kan suru Yūkensha no Jittai" (Hiroshima 1965A)
―――, "Senkyo Ishiki ni kan suru Yūkensha no Jittai" (Hiroshima 1965B)
Ibaragi ken Senkyo Kanri Iinkai, "Kōmei Senkyo Undō no Kōka Sokutei" (Ibaragi 1960)
―――, "Ibaragi Kenmin no Seiji Ishiki ni kan suru Chōsa Hōkoku" (Ibaragi 1962)
Iwate ken Senkyo Kanri Iinkai, "Kōmei Senkyo Undō wo meguru Iwate no Jittai" (Iwate 1959)
―――, "Iwate no Jittai" (Iwate 1961)
―――, "Seiji Ishiki to Kōmei Senkyo Undō no Hōto" (Iwate 1963)
―――, "Iwate no Jittai" (Iwate 1965)
Jichichō Senkyokyoku, "Sōsenkyo no Jittai — Seron Chōsa Kekka no Gaiyō" (Jichi 1958)
Jichishō Senkyokyoku, "Dai 7 Kai Sangiin Giin Tsūjō Senkyo no Jittai — Seron Chōsa Kekka" (Jichi 1966)
Kagawa ken Senkyo Kanri Iinkai, "Kōmei Senkyo no Jittai — Seron Chōsa Kekka no Gaiyō" (Kagawa 1965)
Kōchi ken Senkyo Kanri Iinkai, "Kōchi ken ni okeru Seijiteki Kanshin to Kōmei Senkyo ni kan suru Jittai Chōsa" (Kōchi 1963)
Kōmei Senkyo Remmei, "Kōmei Senkyo no Jittai" (Kōmei 1958)
―――, "Sōsenkyo no Jittai — Seron Chōsa Kekka no Gaiyō" (Kōmei 1961)
―――, "Kōmei Senkyo no Jittai — Seron Chōsa Kekka no Gaiyō" (Kōmei 1962A)

SELECTED BIBLIOGRAPHY 259

———, "Sangiin Giin Tsūjō Senkyo no Jittai" (Kōmei 1962B)
———, "Tōitsu Chihō Senkyo no Jittai — Seron Chōsa Kekka no Gaiyō" (Kōmei 1964A)
———, "Dai 30 Kai Sōsenkyo no Jittai — Seron Chōsa Kekka no Gaiyō" (Kōmei 1964B)
———, "Seiji Ishiki to Senkyo Kōdō no Jittai — Nishinomiya shi Shōtengai no Jirei" (Kōmei 1966/1)
———, "Seiji Ishiki to Senkyo Kōdō no Jittai — Fukuoka Kenmin no Seiji Ishiki" (Kōmei 1966/2)
———, "Seiji Ishiki to Senkyo Kōdō no Jittai — Yamanashi ken Toshi to Nōson" (Kōmei 1966/3)
———, "Seiji Ishiki to Senkyo Kōdō no Jittai — Tōhoku 3 ken ni okeru Jitsurei" (Kōmei 1966/4)
———, "Seiji Ishiki to Senkyo Kōdō no Jittai — Gifu ken nai 6 chiten no Chōsa" (Kōmei 1966/5)
———, "Seiji Ishiki to Senkyo Kōdō no Jittai — Shimane ken Nōsonbu no Baai" (Kōmei 1966/6)
———, "Dai 6 Kai Tōitsu Chihō Senkyo to Yūkensha" (Kōmei 1967A)
———, "Sōsenkyo no Jittai" (Kōmei 1967B)
———, "Shūgiin Giin Sōsenkyo no Jittai" (Kōmei 1967BB)
———, "Seiji Ishiki to Senkyo Kōdō no Jittai" (Kōmei 1967C)
Kumamoto ken Senkyo Kanri Iinkai, "Senkyo no Jittai" (Kumamoto 1960)
———, "Seiji Ishiki to Senkyo Ishiki Chōsa Shūkei Kekka" (Kumamoto 1962)
Kyōto shi Senkyo Kanri Iinkai, "Senkyo ni kan suru Seron Chōsa no Gaiyō" (Kyōto 1962)
Mie ken Senkyo Kanri Iinkai, "Kōmei Senkyo Seron Chōsa no Kekka" (Mie 1962)
———, "Mie ken ni okeru Senkyo no Jittai to sono Chōsa Kekka no Bunseki" (Mie 1964)
Miyagi ken Senkyo Kanri Iinkai, "Kōmei Senkyo Jittai Chōsa — Kenmin no Senkyo Ishiki to Kōmei Senkyo Undō no Kōka" (Miyagi 1962)
Miyazaki ken Senkyo Kanri Iinkai, "Dai 2 Kai Kōmei Senkyo Seron Chōsa no Kekka" (Miyazaki 1962)
———, "Dai 3 Kai Kōmei Senkyo Seron Chōsa no Kekka — Seiji Ishiki no Jittai" (Miyazaki 1962B)
———, "Dai 5 Kai Kōmei Senkyo Seron Chōsa no Kekka — Seiji Ishiki no Jittai" (Miyazaki 1964)
Nagano ken Senkyo Kanri Iinkai, "Kōmei Senkyo no Mondai ten" (Nagano 1961)
———, "Kōmei Senkyo Undō no Jittai" (Nagano 1963)
———, "Kōmei Senkyo Undō no Jittai" (Nagano 1965)

Nagasaki ken Senkyo Kanri Iinkai, "Nagasaki ken no Senkyo no Jittai" (Nagasaki 1962)

Nagoya shi Senkyo Kanri Iinkai, "Daitoshi ni okeru Senkyo to Shimin no Seiji Ishiki — Nagoya shi no Chūkansō ni kan suru Chōsa Hōkoku" (Nagoya 1959)

Nara ken Kōmei Senkyo Suishin Remmei, "Sōsenkyo ni okeru Kikensha no Jittai" (Nara 1960)

―――, "Shin Yūkensha to Senkyo" (Nara 1962A)

―――, "Minna wa kō Kagaeteiru — Kōmei Senkyo no Seron Chōsa Kekka no Gaiyō" (Nara 1962B)

Niigata ken Senkyo Kanri Iinkai, "Kōmei Senkyo Undō no Jittai" (Niigata 1962)

―――, "Kōmei Senkyo Undō no Jittai" (Niigata 1963)

―――, "Senkyo Ishiki no Jittai" (Niigata 1964)

―――, "Senkyo Ishiki to Kōmei Senkyo Undō no Jittai" (Niigata 1965)

Ōita ken Senkyo Kanri Iinkai, "Senkyo no Jittai — Seron Chōsa no Kekka Gaiyō" (Ōita 1962)

―――, "Sangiin Giin Tsūjō Senkyo no Jittai — Seron Chōsa Kekka no Gaiyō" (Ōita 1963)

―――, "Moderu Chiku ni okeru Kōmei Senkyo Undō no Jittai" (Ōita 1964)

―――, "Tōitsu Chihō Senkyo no Jittai" (Ōita 1964B)

―――, "Moderu Chiku ni okeru Kōmei Senkyo no Jittai" (Ōita 1965)

―――, "Seiji Ishiki to Senkyo Undō no Jittai Chōsa" (Ōita 1968)

Okayama ken Senkyo Kanri Iinkai, "Kōmei Senkyo Seron Chōsa Kekka" (Okayama 1962)

Ōsaka fu Senkyo Kanri Iinkai, "Kōmei Senkyo Undō no Kōka Sokutei — Ōsaka fu Yūkensha no Seiji Ishiki to Tōhyō Kōdō" (Ōsaka 1961)

Saga ken Senkyo Kanri Iinkai, "Kōmei Senkyo Seron Chōsa no Kekka" (Saga 1963)

―――, "Sōsenkyo no Jittai Seron Chōsa no Kekka" (Saga 1962)

―――, "Senkyo ni kan suru Seron Chōsa Kekka" (Saga 1963)

―――, "Senkyo ni kan suru Seron Chōsa Kekka" (Saga 1964)

Saitama ken Senkyo Kanri Iinkai, "Kōmei Senkyo Undō no Kōka Sokutei" (Saitama 1962)

Shiga ken Senkyo Kanri Iinkai, "Shojo hyō no Mita Senkyo — Shin Yūkensha ni tai suru Seron Chōsa no Hōkoku" (Shiga 1959)

―――, "Hikone shi oyobi Kōhoku machi ni okeru Senkyo ni kan suru Jittai Chōsa" (Shiga 1962)

―――, "Hikone — Nagahama ryōshi ni okeru Senkyo no Jittai Chōsa" (Shiga 1964)

Shimane ken Senkyo Kanri Iinkai, "Shimane ken ni okeru Seiji Ishiki to Tōhyō Kōdō" (Shimane 1960)
——, "Shimane ken ni okeru Seiji Ishiki to Tōhyō Kōdō" (Shimane 1961)
——, "Seiji Ishiki to Chihō Senkyo no Mondai ten" (Shimane 1963)
——, "Shimane ken ni okeru Nōsonbu Jūmin no Tōhyō Kōdō" (Shimane 1965)
Shizuoka ken Senkyo Kanri Iinkai, "Kōmei Senkyo Undō no Kōka Sokutei Hōkokusho" (Shizuoka 1963)
Tochigi ken Senkyo Kanri Iinkai, "Kōmei Senkyo Seron Chōsa no Kekka" (Tochigi 1959)
——, "Kōmei Senkyo Seron Chōsa no Kekka ni tsuite" (Tochigi 1960)
——, "Kōmei Senkyo Seron Chōsa no Aramashi" (Tochigi 1962)
Tokushima ken Senkyo Kanri Iinkai, "Toshi ni okeru Senkyo no Seitai" (Tokushima 1958)
——, "Moderu Chiku ni okeru Kōmei Senkyo Undō no Jittai" (Tokushima 1961)
——, "Nōsangyoson ni okeru Senkyo no Seitai" (Tokushima 1962)
Tōkyō to Senkyo Kanri Iinkai, "Kōmei Senkyo Seron Chōsa no Gaiyō" (Tōkyō 1958)
——, "Kōmei Senkyo Seron Chōsa" (Tōkyō 1962)
——, Senkyo ni kan suru Seron Chōsa" (Tōkyō 1965)
Tottori ken Senkyo Kanri Iinkai, "Kōmei Senkyo Seron Chōsa no Kekka (3)" (Tottori 1963)
Toyama ken Senkyo Kanri Iinkai, "Toyama ken ni okeru Senkyo no Jittai" (Toyama 1961)
——, "Senkyo Ishiki ni kan suru Jittai Chōsa" (Toyama 1963)
Wakayama ken Senkyo Kanri Iinkai, "Kōmei Senkyo Seron Chōsa no Kekka (1)" (Wakayama 1962)
Yamagata ken Senkyo Kanri Iinkai, "Kōmei Senkyo Undō no Jittai" (Yamagata 1962)
Yamaguchi ken Senkyo Kanri Iinkai, "Senkyo no Jittai" (Yamaguchi 1964)

INDEX

age, 189–228
  categories, defined, 193n
  and community leadership, 192
  cross-national comparison, 227
  effects of historical-generational experiences, 203
  and evaluative attitudes, 204–210
  and exposure to communications, 193–195
  interest in politics strong among middle-aged persons, 202–203
  and involvement attitudes, 196–204
  old voters more optimistic, 205–207
  and participation attitudes, 210–216
  and political culture, 189–228
  and political efficacy, 207–208
  retirement, 191n
  social status increases with, 191
  tendencies toward passivism among old voters, 213
  and voting attitudes, 216–221
  and voting motivations, 210
  young persons ambivalent, 209
Almond, Gabriel, 187
ambivalence, 64, 67–70, 97, 243
  cross-national comparison, 75–78
  and education, 237
  about responsiveness of politicians, 71–75
  summary, 231–233
  in voter attitudes, 68–70, 81–82
  among youth, 209
American Voter, The, Angus Campbell et al., 189

Atsugi City, 146n
attitudes
  defined, 4, 22–23
  dependency, 99, 99n
  differentiation, factor analysis, 62
  evaluative, *see* evaluative attitudes
  formation processes, 3
  instrumental, *see* instrumental attitudes; instrumentalism
  involvement, *see* involvement attitudes
  measures of, 30
  negative, 79
  participation, *see* participation attitudes
  political, *see* political attitudes
  about speaking critically, 164–165
  structures, 61
  voting, *see* voting attitudes
  see also ambivalence; authoritarianism; collectivism; efficacy; formalism; passivism; paternalism; personalism; pessimism; pragmatism
authoritarianism, 66–67, 233
  and old voters, 221–222
  prewar, 13, 46, 79
  see also prewar period

behavior
  attitudinal effects on, 11
  democratic, 13–14
  political participation, 237–240
bloc voting, 13, 13n, 184

candidates
　behavior and voting choice, 105
　character and voting choice, 114–116
　Confucian images of, 111
　importance of percepitons in voting choice, 106–112
　low levels of voter affect, 117–118
　perception of, defined, 106
　voter choice based on perceptions of, rather than party, 125
　see also politicians; voting choice
center-periphery approach, 20
　and political attitudes, 185–186
　politics has many centers, 186
center-periphery relationships
　and evaluative attitudes, 157
　models, 129–130
　in political involvement, 150–151
Civic Culture, Gabriel Almond and Sidney Verba, 84
class in Japan, defined, 107n
cohort analysis, 14, 189n
　of middle-aged voters, 225–226
Coleman, James, 27. *See also* effect parameter analysis; multivariate statistical analysis
collectivism
　in Japanese society, 3
　preference for among young and some middle-aged voters, 214
　rural tradition of, 173, 173n
　see also community cooperation
communications, see mass media
Communist Party, see Japan Communist Party
community cooperation
　cross-national comparison, 100
　norms exist favoring, 98, 98n
community ethnocentrism, 137
community leadership varies with age, 192
community life, 135
　in cities, 137–138. *See also* **urban sector**
　effects of, 6
　and group membership, 145. *See also* group membership
　intercommunity rivalry, 153
　localism in, 234–235. *See also* localism
　rural, develops positive attitudes, 163–165. *See also* rural sector
　strong rural obligation to participate, 170. *See also* rural sector
　urban-rural contrasts, 140, 154–155, 162. *See also* urban-rural variations

community structure important in election turnout, 85
community ties, primacy of, in Japan, 125
commuting to work
　in cities, 139
　from rural areas, 134n, 137
competition, distaste for, 80
Confucian images of candidates, 111
consensus
　in hamlet life, 137
　as major goal, 3, 98, 98n, 99
corruption, political, 6, 78–80, 208
　urban-rural attitudes, 161–162
cross-national comparison, 2–3
　age, 227
　ambivalence, 75–78
　community cooperation, 100
　evaluative attitudes, 75–78
　personalism, 116n
　political efficacy, 231–232
　political interest, 56, 62–64
　political participation, 96
　political parties, 118
　political relevance, 33
　urban-rural variations, 101n
　variations in political attitude, urban-rural, 186–187
culture and subculture, defined, 5–6. *See also* subcultures

democratic concepts, diffusion of, can have alienating effects, 242
Democratic Socialist Party, 217
democratization, 7, 241–243
　visible impact of postwar reforms, 241
　see also postwar period
Deutsch, Karl, 130, 130n, 131, 184, 185
Diet, 41, 51, 54, 58, 115, 149, 174, 198
　rural over-representation, 133
downtown, defined, 139n

education
　and attitudes of efficacy, 165–166
　factor in mass media exposure, 155
　and group membership, 235–237
　Japan one of most developed nations, 229
　major factor in national political involvement, 153, 155
　and modernization theory, 130
　overlap with leftist party support, 164n
　overlap with party support, 179

postwar changes in requirements, 193n
and residence, 163
urban-rural differences main factor in national political involvement, 186
urban-rural variation, 145, 180–182
effect parameter analysis, 27, 145, 153n, 181, 238. See also multivariate statistical analysis
efficacy, political, 71–75, 77
and age, multivariate analysis, 207–208
cross-national comparison, 231–232
and feelings of satisfaction, 97n
urban-rural variations, 165–166, 182
Election Law, 149
elections
evaluations, 68–71
participation, importance of feelings of duty, 85–87
urban-rural variations, 85, 159–160
see also political participation; voting; voting attitudes
Election System Deliberation Council, 41
empirical theory, Japanese political culture, 6–21. See also political culture
evaluative attitudes, 22, 65–82
and age, 204–210
cross-national comparison, 75–78
as determinants of participation, 66
essentially negative, 81
favorable to experientially proximate politics, 75
link to viability of governments, 75
and political system, 75–82
sensitive in Japan to impact of social distance, 233
urban-rural variations, 156–167
see also ambivalence

factor analysis, 73–75
defined, 74
of attitude differentiation, 62
Fair Election League, see Japanese Fair Election League
formalism, 46, 73, 93, 243
and low levels of affect for parties and candidates, 117, 117n
summary, 230–231

generational differences, 221–228. See also age
generations as subcultures, 190

group membership
and age, 193, 208
and age difference, 222
and community life, 145
and education, 235–237
major factor in Japanese society, 3
rural, 154. See also rural sector
urban, 139n
urban-rural variation, 131, 145, 156, 180–182
and youth, 209n
see also collectivism

hamlets, 135–137. See also rural sector
harmony
as dominant cultural goal, 98n, 99
in hamlet life, 137
and old voters, 208
see also consensus
House of Councillors, 57, 86, 110, 112n, 113, 113n, 120n, 149, 159, 200
House of Representatives, 42, 57, 110, 112n, 113, 113n, 151, 198, 200

Ike, Nobutaka, 131
income doubling plan, 41, 49, 198
industrialization
Japan one of most developed nations, 229
in rural sector, 134n
Institute for Mathematical Statistics, 208, 213
institutional reform, 100n
instrumental attitudes, 59–61. See also instrumentalism
instrumentalism, 235, 242
and age, 196–198
and candidate perceptions, 110–112
and modernization theory, 130
in political attitudes, 46
in political culture, 112–127
in rural sector, 147
and urban-rural voting choice, 177
intellectualization of urban middle class, 80
involvement attitudes, 22, 29–64, 146–156
and age, 196–204
cross-national comparison, 186–187
education major factor in national politics, 153
and higher economic status, 192–193
more commonly associated with active political participation than evaluative attitudes, 240

involvement attitudes (*continued*)
  national focus and attitudes toward parties, 219
  patterns show consistency in age groupings, 198–199
  peaks among persons in fifties and sixties, 190–191
  summary, 61–64
  urban-rural differences in education main factor, 186
  of voters in their twenties, 204

Japan Communist Party, 120n
Japan Socialist Party, 107n, 120n, 217
Japanese Fair Election League (Kōmei Senkyo Remmei), 23–26, 95
Japanese political attitudes, tendencies toward formalism, pragmatism, and instrumentalism, 46. *See also* formalism; instrumentalism; political attitudes; pragmatism
Japanese political system, transitional, 29
Japanese society, group oriented, consensualistic and paternalistic, 3. *See also* consensus; group membership; paternalism

Kōmei Senkyo Remmei, see Japanese Fair Election League
Kōmeitō, 120n, 217, 243, 244
Kyōgoku, Jun'ichi, 131

labor
  organized, economic protest activity, 99n
  unions, 124, 140n, 144
labor force statistics, rural, 132n–133n
land reform, 100n, 121n, 134
  differences of interest between landlords and tenants eliminated by, 185
leftist political parties
  became viable force, 121n
  more negative, 164
  support and education overlap, 164n
  urban support, 154
  youth and middle-aged support more than old, 208
  See also Democratic Socialist Party; Japan Communist Party; Japan Socialist Party
Lerner, Daniel, 130, 131n
Liberal Democratic Party, 10, 49, 107n, 114, 149, 164
  corruption in, 78
  rural areas support, 144
localism
  cross-national comparison, 44
  summary, 234–235
  in voter concern, 57

Mannheim, Karl, 189
mass media
  attention to politics, 43
  criticism of politicians, 233
  exposure, *see* mass media exposure
  Japan one of most developed nations, 229
  political news, 37
  reports of political corruption, 78–80
mass media exposure
  and age, 193–195
  could be alienating, 185
  and education, 237
  higher among young and middle-aged, 219
  important to formation of negative attitudes, 79, 80–81
  interest in political coverage highest among youths, 200
  and involvement attitudes, 155–156
  and modernization theory, 130
  penetrates rural areas, 184
  urban-rural variations, 141–143, 155, 177–178, 186
media, *see* mass media
Michigan Survey Research Center, 90. *See also* University of Michigan Survey Research Center
Milbrath, Lester, 129–130
modernization, Japanese levels of, 229n
modernization theory, 20, 129–131, 149, 184–185, 235–236
  defined, 130
  and urban-rural political involvement, 146, 183
multivariate statistical analysis, 26–27
  age difference, 222–226
  education, residence and feelings of efficacy, 165–166
  effect of education, 153
  evaluative attitudes, 161, 163
  participation attitudes and age, 215
  political efficacy and age, 207–208
  supports generational explanation of tendencies of old voters, 222
  of youth, 226
  see also effect parameter analysis

INDEX 267

Mutual Security Treaty of 1960, 51n, 200. *See also* United States—Japan Security Treaty

Nie, Norman H., 183

participation, defined, 85n
participation attitudes, 22, 83–101
  and age, 210–216
  close to actual behavior, 83
  parallel turnout trends, 167–170
  urban-rural variations, 167–174
  voting and political participation roles, 84
  young persons endorsed activism more often, 214
  see also voter turnout
partisan preferences, stability of, 10. *See also* political parties
passivism, 91–94, 95
  among old voters, 213
  does not originate in feelings of contentment, 97
paternalism, 3, 12, 99n, 115n, 124, 213, 235
  corporate, 139n
  rural, 165
personalism, 112, 115–116, 125, 133, 183, 233n
  cross-national comparison, 116n
  summary, 235
  urban-rural differences, 126n
pessimism, 79–82, 233
  more common in urban sector, 80–81
  due to anticipation of authoritarianism, 79–80
  and frequent media exposure, 79, 80–81
  negative evaluations of politicians, 55
  in nonaffective candidate perceptions, 117
  and social isolation, 117
Police Duties Bill, 51n
political attitudes
  and actual participation, 238–240
  research, *see* political attitude research
  visible impact of postwar democratic reforms, 241
  see also attitudes; evaluative attitudes; instrumental attitudes; instrumentalism; involvement attitudes; participation attitudes; voting attitudes

political attitude research
  conceptual categories, 21–22
  cultural approach, 1–6
political campaigns candidate oriented, 113
political candidates, *see* candidates; politicians
political corruption, *see* corruption
political culture
  and age, 189–228
  analysis and voting-choice research, 102–103. *See also* voting choice
  approach, *see* political culture approach
  attitudes relevant for political participation, 248
  center-periphery approach, 20, 185–186
  effects of cultural traits, 12
  effects of discontinuities, 13
  empirical theory, 6–21
  and generational differences, 221–228
  inductive perspective, 7–8
  participant culture approach, 7
  personalism, partisanship and instrumentalism, 112–127
  postwar and prewar, 13. *See also* postwar period; prewar period
  prewar, largely subject oriented, 124. *See also* prewar period
  and subculture, 5–6. *See also* subcultures
  urban-rural differences, 132. *See also* urban-rural variations
  see also political attitudes
political culture approach, 1–6
  and idea of political generations, 190
  methodology and organization, 21–28
political efficacy, *see* efficacy
political evaluation, *see* evaluative attitudes
political generations, concept of, 189–190
political interest
  cross-national comparison, 56
  local and national, 57
political instrumentalism, *see* instrumentalism
political involvement attitudes, *see* involvement attitudes
political participation
  active, attitudes about, 91–95, 100
  appropriate forms of, 94–95
  and beliefs about effectiveness, 99
  central to democratic theory, 83

political participation (*continued*)
  cross-national comparison, 96
  dependence, 99–100
  effects of postwar changes, 100. *See also* postwar period
  effect of urbanization, 96. *See also* urbanization
  urban and rural, 15, 18, *See also* urban-rural variations
  see also participation attitudes
political parties
  American, voter loyalty to, 103
  chosen by urban voters, 174–175
  compared to U.S., 122
  considered more important by young voters, 217, 219
  cross-national comparison, 118
  deemphasized, 118
  discontinuities in party labels in postwar period, 217
  and education in voting choice, 177–178
  identification with, 118–124
  ideological appeals of, 119–120
  incidence of intergenerational conformity, 122n
  leftist, *see* leftist political parties
  more important in urban sector, 120n
  orientation toward, defined, 107
  urban-rural variation, 118n, 144, 177
  voter choice based on perceptions of candidate rather than, 125–126
  voters have negative images of, 122
  and voting attitudes, 106–112
  voting choice based on, 154
  see also Democratic Socialist Party; Japan Communist Party; Japan Socialist Party; Kōmeito; Liberal Democratic Party
political passivism, *see* passivism
political pessimism, *see* pessimism
political reforms, postwar, 14n. *See also* postwar period
political relevance, *see* relevance
political representation, variances in expectations, 124–125
political scandals, 6. *See also* corruption
political socialization processes, 3
  effect of cultural traits on, 12
  and generational differences, 221–228
  prewar period, 190, 196. *See also* prewar period
political subcultures, generations as, 190. *See also* urban-rural variations

political support mobilization, *see* support mobilization
political understanding and awareness, 36–47
  compared to feelings of relevance, 37–39
  cross-national variations, 42–45
politicians
  age of, urban-rural variations, 192n
  awareness of, urban-rural variations, 178, 182
  contacts, urban-rural variations, 144
  evaluations, urban-rural variations, 160
  negative evaluations, 55
  self-assertiveness undesirable, 98
  see also candidates
politics
  degree of satisfaction with, 68–71
  has many centers, 186
  interest in, 47–59
  negative evaluations of, 55, 97
  prewar, 66–67, 79. *See also* prewar period
population distribution, 133n
postwar period
  affluence, 185
  changes in education requirements, 193n
  changes in school curricula and articulation of democratic ideas, 215
  conservative dominance, 133
  democracy a major theme of political rhetoric, 241–243
  discontinuities in party labels, 217
  effect of changes on political participation, 100
  high levels of instrumental expectation in rural sector, 242
  identities of political parties changed, 121
  improved opportunities for active leadership by younger persons, 192
  land reform, 100n, 121n, 134
  leftist parties became viable force, 121
  mood of individualism and egalitarianism, 215
  political climate produced special generational pattern, 221
  and political generations, 190
  politics in, 229–245
  pre-1955 and post-1955 phases, 121
  urban growth in, 15, 17, 19
  urbanization, 134
  viable Socialist movement, 121

Powell, G. Bingham, Jr., 183
pragmatism, 243
  dominant theme of Japanese voting attitudes, 125
  in political attitudes, 46
  result of diffusion of democratic ideas, 124
primordial, defined, 115n
Prewitt, Kenneth, 183

relevance, 31–35, 230
  and age, 196–198
  compared to feelings of understanding, 37–39
  cross-national comparison, 33
  urban-rural variation, 147–148, 182
residence, see urban-rural variations
rural sector
  activist tendencies greater, 171–173
  community cooperation in, 98, 98n, 99
  community life develops positive attitudes, 163–165
  conservatism, 133
  dependence on collective action, 173, 173n
  depend more on politicians, 165. See also paternalism
  and development of democratic sentiments, 101
  effect of age, 192n
  farm income, 134n
  feelings of obligation about voting, 167
  higher group membership, 154
  high levels of instrumental expectation, 242. See also instrumentalism
  increase in instrumental awareness, 135
  involvement in local and national politics, 147–149, 151
  labor force statistics, 132n
  modern influences, 134
  most people live in hamlets, 135
  over-representation in Diet, 133
  political attitudes, 15–17
  recent affluence, 17–20
  stronger obligation to participate in community activities, 170
  traditionalism, 133n
  vote on basis of candidate reputation, 174–175
  voters more positive, 157, 162
  voters more aware of interests, 124
  voter turnout, 132, 149n, 167
  see also urban-rural variations

social change, 135, 183
social disengagement and aging, 193
social isolation
  political effects, 117
  in urban sector, 81
social modernization concepts, 20
social modernization theory, see modernization theory
Socialism movement, 121
Socialist Party, see Japan Socialist Party
Sōka Gakkai, 120n, 244n
subcultures
  defined, 5–6
  generations as, 190
  see also urban-rural variations
subject, defined, 13n
support mobilization, 112–114, 120–121, 123, 125–126, 167, 235n
  rural, 159
  urban, 143n

Tarrow, Sidney, 186–187

United States-Japan Security Treaty, 49. See also Mutual Security Treaty
University of Michigan Survey Research Center, 84
urbanization, 243
  and empirical theory, 128
  and evaluative attitudes, 157
  and modernization theory, 131, 183. See also modernization theory
  and participation attitudes, 167
  penetrated rural areas, 184
  and political violence, 157n
urban middle class, intellectualization of 80
urban-rural variations, 6, 128–188
  activist tendencies, 171–173
  affect for political parties and candidates, 118n
  age of politicians, 192n
  analytical methodology, 145–146
  attitude structures, 132
  attitudes toward leadership, 174
  attitudes about political corruption, 161–162
  attitudes about speaking critically, 164–165
  awareness of politicians, 178
  community life, 140, 154–155, 162
  contacts with politicians, 144
  contradiction between theory and observed reality, 132
  cross-national comparison, 101n

urban-rural variations *(continued)*
  derivations from earlier findings, 131
  differences in personalism, 126n. *See also* personalism
  education, 145, 163
  education and sensitivity to democratic norms, 166–167
  election participation, 85
  elections, 159–160
  and empirical political theory, 180–188
  Europe, 96n
  evaluative attitudes, 156–157
  group membership, 131, 145, 154
  instrumentalism, 177–179
  interest in national politics, an exception, 182–183
  local and national politics, 147–149
  many rural persons in cities, 146
  mass media communications, 141–143, 155
  monetary income, 140
  multivariate analysis, 156
  participation attitudes, 167–174
  political attitudes, 15–20
  political attitudes, cross-national comparison, 186–187
  political involvement, 146–150
  political parties, 144
  recreational activities, 140
  relevance, 147–148
  residence as variable, 128
  rural voters more aware of interests, 124
  social differences, 135–144
  women's social participation, 138n
urban sector
  downtown, defined, 139n
  educated more sensitive to democratic norms, 166–167, 170
  effect of patterns originally rural, 133
  involvement in local and national politics, 147–149, 151
  leftist party support, 154
  neighborhood differences, 138, 138n
  political pessimism more common, 80–81. *See also* pessimism
  postwar growth, 15, 17, 19
  social isolation in, 81
  support mobilization, 143n
  vote on basis of party labels and national issues, 174–175
  voter turnout, 149n
  see also labor unions; urban-rural variations

Verba, Sidney, 187
voters
  behavior and American party loyalty, 103
  content of interest, 53
  efficacy, attitudes toward, 165–166
  participation, 8–10
  rural more positive, 157
  as spectators, loyalists or instrumentalists, 52–54
  turnout, *see* voter turnout
voter turnout
  attitude tendencies, 167–170
  in general elections, 149
  high rural, 132, 149n, 167
  and residence, 128n
voting
  abstention disfavored, 87, 91
  age and motivations, 210
  attitudes, *see* voting attitudes
  bloc, 13, 13n, 184
  choice, *see* voting choice
  cultural dimension of motivation, 103n
  feelings of duty strong, 231
  generational differences, 215
  motivation, 83, 91
  as obligation, 35
  and residence, 128n
  residual effects of prewar political socialization, 89. *See also* prewar period
  tendencies, 46–47
  see also participation attitudes
voting attitudes, 22, 102–127, 174–180
  and age, 216–221
  and candidate behavior, 105–106
  candidate perceptions, 106–112
  defined, 104
  instrumental expectations, 106, 110–112
  partisanship, 112–127
  party orientations, 106–112, 123
  personalism, 112–127
  significance of patterns for comparison of levels of politicization, 126–127
  studies have focussed on ideal solutions, 91
  toward turnout and abstention, 85–91. *See also* voter turnout
  see also ambivalence
voting choice, 11
  and attitude formation, 103
  based on party, 154

importance of candidate character, 103, 114–116
influenced by rational appeals, 126
made by majority on basis of candidate perceptions, 125
research and political culture analysis, 102–103

Ward, Robert E., 131
women
　and generational effects, 190n
　prewar and postwar differences in attitude, 223–225
　social participation, 138n